INSIDE THE
ROLLS-ROYCE & BENTLEY
STYLING DEPARTMENT
1971 to 2001

VELOCE

Graham Hull

Also from Veloce –

Bentley Continental, Corniche & Azure 1951-2002 (Bennett)
Rolls-Royce Silver Shadow & Bentley T-Series – The Essential Buyer's Guide (Bobbitt)
Rolls-Royce Silver Shadow/Bentley T Series Corniche & Camargue – Revised & Enlarged Edition (Bobbitt)
Rolls-Royce Silver Spirit, Silver Spur & Bentley Mulsanne 2nd Edition (Bobbitt)

Veloce's other imprints:

WWW.VELOCE.CO.UK

First published in February 2014, this Veloce Classic Reprint published June 2019 by Veloce Publishing Limited, Veloce House, Parkway Farm Business Park, Middle Farm Way, Poundbury, Dorchester, Dorset, DT1 3AR, England. Fax 01305 250479/Tel 01305 260068/e-mail info@veloce.co.uk/web www.veloce.co.uk or www.velocebooks.com.
ISBN: 978-1-787115-47-7 UPC: 6-36847-01547-3
Readers with ideas for automotive books, or books on other transport or related hobby subjects, are invited to write to the editorial director of Veloce Publishing at the above address.
British Library Cataloguing in Publication Data – A catalogue record for this book is available from the British Library.
Typesetting, design and page make-up all by Veloce Publishing Ltd on Apple Mac. Printed and bound by CPI Group (UK) Ltd, Croydon, CR0 4YY.

CONTENTS

GLOSSARY

1990s project codes (not in order of allocation

P7	Rolls-Royce Phantom V11 Thailand
P8	Rolls- Royce Phantom V111 Ambassador
P9	Rolls-Royce Phantom V111 Public Edition
P10	P2000/3000 Armoured Level A
P15	P2000/3000 Armoured
P20	P3000 + 500mm stretch
P22	SZ 2-Door Coupé
P25	Quarter-Scale Models
P30	Bentley Continental R GT (+ 125mm stretch)
P40	P3000 + 1000mm stretch
P50	Bentley Continental Gold 50
P59	Park Ward Rolls-Royce Touring Saloon (Seraph + 250mm stretch)
P70	Rolls-Royce Silver Spur Park Ward (division +14 inch stretch)
P80	Park Ward Touring Limousine (Silver Spur+24 inch stretch)
P80A	P80 Armoured – Kensington
P90	Park Ward Limousine (48 inch stretch) – Thailand
P91	Park Ward Limousine (48 inch stretch) – Morocco
P92	Rolls-Royce Convertible – (Azure based) – Borrego
P95	Park Ward Limousine (48 inch stretch)
P100	Bentley Azure
P103	Rolls-Royce Corniche replacement
P104	Bentley Spectre (convertible)
P105	Bentley Phoenix (convertible)
P110	Bentley Continental R Superfast
P113	Bentley Continental R – Pebble Beach Show Special
P114	Bentley Continental R – Jack Barclay Limited Edition
P115	Bentley Camelot
P116	Bentley Continental R – Talamo
P117	Bentley Continental T
P118	Bentley Turbo Estate
P120	Bentley (sports car – proposal)
P125	Bentley (sports car – proposal)
P130	Bentley Continental R Estate
P130A	Armoured P130
P140	Bentley Continental R 4-door – Sedan
P144	Bentley Continental R 4-door – Sedan LWB
P144A	Armoured P144
P150	Bentley Silverstone (retractable hard-top)
P153	Park Ward Limousine – Chester – (armoured 10 inch stretch)
P155	Bentley Continental R (retractable roof)
P190	Bentley '190mph' (sports car 'Grand Prix' became P250)
P200	Rolls-Royce Phantom Royale
P200F	Rolls-Royce Phantom Royale – follow-on
P210	Rolls-Royce Phantom Majestic
P215	Radical Limousine (proposal on P200 package)
P220	Bentley Java Concept
P230	4-Door replacement (SXB4)
P240	Rolls-Royce Cloudesque
P250	Bentley Grand Prix (4WD)
P255	Bentley Rapier
P260	Bentley Grand Tourer – Monte Carlo
P270	Bentley Grand Tourer – Imperial
P280	Bentley Continental R Limousine
P290	Rolls-Royce Phantom V James Young (replica)
P300	High performance L410 V8 engine
P305	High performance L410 V8 engine
P310	98MY engine strategy
P311	Continued powertrain engineering
P330	L410 V8 engine for Limousines
P340	High performance L410 V8 engine
P350	Supercharged V8
P360	Unique V8
P400	Limited slip differential
P410	Four-wheel-drive

P420	Rear axle
P425	Rolls-Royce Armoured Sedan
P430	Traction control
P450	Rolls-Royce Phantom Statesman
P460	Bentley Mid-Engine (proposal)
P480	Rolls-Royce Touring Limousine
P500	2000MY legislation
P550	Bentley Buccaneer
P560	Bentley Highlander
P570	Bentley Typhoon (proposal)
P600	98MY Four-Door Replacement
P650	Bentley Pegasus Coupé
P655	Bentley Pegasus Convertible
P660	Bentley Pegasus Estate
P700	Bentley Java Convertible
P705	Bentley Java Coupé
P710	Bentley Java Estate
P800	Bentley Dominator (4X4)
P900	Special exercise
P950	97MY SZ
P960	2-Door face-lift
P961	98MY Evaporative Emission Requirement
P965	Bentley Continental R Retractable Hard-top (mock-up)
P966	Bentley Continental SC – Targa
P980	2-Door Bentley quality improvements
P1000	Bentley Java (BMW)
P2000	Bentley 98MY 4-Door replacement – Arnage
P3000	Rolls-Royce 98MY 4-Door replacement – Silver Seraph
P4000	Medium-Sized Bentley (MSB)
BY713	(BY614) Bentley Continental GT
BY711	(BY611) Bentley Flying Spur
BY811	Bentley Arnage post-VW (L410 engine, etc)

Non-numerical 1990s codes (not exhaustive)

SZ	4-Door replacement for SY – Rolls-Royce Silver Shadow
RTL	Rolls-Royce Touring Limousine
BTL	Bentley Touring Limousine
Nepal	Pre-launch Bentley Continental R
SXB	Early P600
P'M'	BMW 8 Series with 'Bentley' interior
Contan	Pre-launch Bentley Azure
Sufacon	Bentley Continental R Superfast
Springfield	H R Owen Limited Edition Rolls-Royce Silver Spur
Bali	Bentley 2-Door Coupé
MSB	Medium-Sized Bentley
Siam	P3000-based P92
Endeavour	Rolls-Royce 4-Door – Alias Computer Exercise (post-P3000)
China	Rolls-Royce Phantom – (2D exercise post-P3000)
Hawaii	Rolls-Royce 4-Door Convertible – (2D exercise post-P3000)

Company acronyms

ADC	Advanced Design Concepts
ASC	American Sunroof Company
BL	British Leyland
BMW	Bayerische Motoren Werke AG
DRA	Design Research Associates
DZN	The Design Group – Los Angeles. Cal
GMD	Geoff Mathews Design
IAD	International Automotive Design
MGA	Mike Gibbs Associates
MIRA	Motor Industry Research Association
MPW	Mulliner Park Ward
MSB	Medium-Sized Bentley
PPL	Product Policy Letter
PSF	Press Steel Fisher
PSK	Produkt Strategie Komitee (VW equivalent of Crewe's Product Policy Committee)
R-RMC	Rolls-Royce Motor Cars
SRV	Styling Research Vehicle (Vauxhall)
TWR	Tom Walkinshaw Racing
VW	Volkswagen (People's Car)

Styling terminology

Alias Computer Part of Silicon Graphics International. In the mid-1990s, Alias was a revolutionary, computer-based graphics system which enabled, for the first time, a styling shape to be created on the computer screen. In its simplest form, a wire-frame model could be increasingly developed into a photographic-quality car image, which could be rotated through any angle, with different backgrounds reflected on to its surface (it could be animated, for example, to show it driving through different scenery). Crewe exploited this system to study possible future styles. The interior images were just as useful as it was possible to 'sit' behind the wheel and check the view through the glass.

A post, BC post, D post The structure at the side of the windscreen is the A post. The structure at the trailing edge of the front door aperture and front of the rear door aperture is the BC post, and the structure at the rear of the rear door aperture is the D post.

Body-in-white (BIW) The unpainted bodyshell, including all 'closures,' ie doors/bonnet lid/boot lid.

Bonnet catwalks These are the two styling feature lines which feed back the shape of the radiator 'header tank' onto the bonnet, splaying as they reach towards the windscreen, especially found on Rolls-Royce and Bentley motor cars. On the Continental GT they extend up the A posts: a popular modern trend that avoids the difficult A post to front wing intersection.

Brown paper exercise A very simple process employed at the start of a project to encourage often newly-formed teams to identify required activity, leading to swift identification and understanding of the critical path. It can be applied generically, but very often is literally a large sheet of brown paper stuck on a wall to which post-it notes are attached.

Buck A seating mock-up of a car's interior. As well as seats, it will include dashboard/facia, front and rear bulkheads, doors, side panels, door and windscreen apertures. Used initially to model the interior in clay, purely for appearance, it is then upgraded to fully-trimmed seats, etc, that can be sat on. Often on castors and split into two for easier working.

Builds Styling/Design projects are a series of aesthetic or practical development steps: there is never an immediate 'solution.' Whether in two dimension or three, input from the stylist, chief stylist and directors changes through an agreed work list, which can be a modified radius to a comprehensive list of many items. The list is recorded.

CAD (Computer Aided Design) The universal method of various computer modelling techniques supporting the styling and engineering design process, largely replacing traditional draughting.

Cantrail The structural box section running along the roof sides above the door apertures. It will often incorporate a water management feature, and usually an adjacent joint line to the roof (though not on Rolls-Royce or Bentley).

Car Bond Finished cars are secured in this area to await delivery/ collection.

Cd (coefficient of drag) The aerodynamic performance of a vehicle is measured in the wind-tunnel, and the most commonly quoted figure is Cd: the disturbance caused by air flow on the vehicle's frontal area. Air management is very complicated, with variables such as air intake, attitude, yaw angle, and so on.

CHMSL (Central High Mounted Stop Lamp) A relatively late addition to the display of rear lamps, brought about as a result of legislation introduced due to the increase in motorway traffic, whereby early warning of braking is critical. Awkward to design with light bulbs but LEDs (Light Emitting Diodes) allow a neat strip of light in the rear glass.

Copy milled The highly sophisticated technique of running a probe over a – usually – scale model. Digitized measurements are then taken to full size, and a robotic milling cutter machines a full-size clay. (Mecoff is a well-known trade name of the sort of machine used.)

Cut-through doors Classic cars tend to have a simple, metal section, upper door frame round the glass (as Silver Shadow and Silver Spirit). To reduce wind noise, this structure needs to be stiff and stable. The best approach is to make the door out of pressings – like Continental R and Silver Seraph – which won't flex but are thicker; hence 'cutting' into the roof and A post.

Design brief The written requirements of any new vehicle project. Anything that will affect the technical or visual elements is set out: marketing and all principle Company functions are involved, and sign up to this document.

DLO (Daylight Opening) The area of glass you can see through, as distinct from the glass area. The exterior glass on a car never lines up with the interior trim; hence the large areas of dark obscuration bands, especially on the windscreen and back-light.

This mismatch isn't a mistake, it's just that the stylist tries to make the glass look as good as possible from the outside.

Dynoc A plastic film on a paper backing which is sprayed with paint. The paper is then soaked in water to remove it, leaving a sheet of paint like a transfer, which can be stretched over the clay mock-up, giving a shiny surface. Apart from helping to create the illusion of a real car, the surface reflections can be checked for the all-important 'highlights.' The dynoc can then be stripped off and the clay re-worked.

Dynoc tank A large, shallow tank of water in which to soak off the dynoc's backing paper.

Dynoced clay Once a clay has been locally dynoced to check the surfaces, it can be completely covered and 'dressed' for a major viewing.

Data Control Model Accurate measurement is fundamental to engineering. There comes a point in a car programme where the approved clay is digitized by measuring millions of points from the surface. These 'clouds' of measurements are smoothed in a computer, checking for any slight irregularity, and in turn used to machine another clay. Once the data has been checked in this manner, it becomes the Data Control Model for tooling.

Engine turning A simple but attractive process of machining small, overlapping, decorative circles on aluminum. Traditionally, Bugatti was a devotee of this technique.

Epowood A two-part plastic wood which, once set, is worked by conventional woodworking tools to an accurate surface. Re-works and modifications are laborious due to the need to apply the material in thick patches and wait for the material to 'go off.' Pininfarina used it for Camargue and Crewe for Silver Spirit. Clay is far more suitable for styling/design.

Flip-tones Different paints such as metallics, micas and pearlescent contain flakes of various materials designed to reflect light in different ways. In extreme cases the colour can 'flip' and change hue: eg silver changing to green areas in direct sunlight.

Gang-boss (Chief Modeller) Slang term for a very important position. A full-size clay exterior and interior can easily involve ten clay modellers. A studio can be working on several clays in various stages. Each clay probably has a lead modeller who often acts as the interface between stylist and modellers. Above a lead modeller is the Chief Modeller who is managing the whole modelling operation, from arranging clay stocks to organising a heated van to transport a clay across Europe (cold clay can crack). This individual needs to have good 'hands-on' experience and managerial skills. Lead modellers and Chief Modellers are often like sergeants advising less experienced officers (stylists).

Hard modelling/soft modelling Replicas will use fibreglass, metal, perspex, etc, which is hard modelling. Clay is soft modelling.

Hard points The elements of the platform/underbody that cannot be moved – engine, occupants, and wheel envelopes, etc – around which the style is formed.

Hologram The technique of projecting a car image from pure data to create the illusion of a three-dimensional object.

HOSCAR Rolls-Royce Motors-speak for Head of State Car, usually for royalty, presidents, etc. Often 'one-offs' or very limited production, or highly bespoke, stretched production cars.

Hygiene Refers to upgrades to an existing production car – legislation 'fine print' or ongoing engineering development – which do not qualify as Model Year changes.

Lead loading Many classic cars have lead 'loaded' body joints. Hot lead is hand applied by paddle or spatula, whilst kept hot by a flame, and worked until smooth. Once hardened, the lead can be filed and sanded. Highly toxic, operators had to wear 'spacesuits' with air lines when handling the lead. Heath and Safety has pretty much outlawed its use, and blistering under paint was not unknown. Plastic fillers can now do the same job: smoothed-off braising was used on Silver Spirit. Any filling technique requires great skill and many man-hours. Styling was tasked with avoiding metal-to-metal joints, and plastic front and rear ends help in this respect; also, large lamp areas often replace awkward-to-press corners.

Model Year (MY) An in-house term regarding a package of changes to a car already in production. This was preferred to drip-fed changes, which Marketing couldn't really promote.

0 Datum Drawings of a vehicle are covered by a measuring grid, usually of 250mm (10 inch) squares. These are based round two '0 Datum lines:' one horizontal at sill height and the other vertical through the front bulkhead (the plan view has a centre line). These datums stay with the vehicle, whether in two- or three-dimensional form.

Package drawing A comprehensive side/front/rear/plan set of vehicle drawings, comprehensively showing the components and general outline. As well as mechanicals, the outline of manikins sitting within their 'comfort angles' (head/torso/knee/ankle) are also shown. The manikin is arranged around an H-point (pelvic area); importantly, the 'eye-elipse' (range of percentile eye positions) is shown, which is critical for fields of vision outside the vehicle and mirrors. A specified suitcase stack is shown in the luggage area. The information is available on CAD, but full-size drawings allow stylists to experiment with tape lines around the package.

Platform Today's equivalent of a chassis, the lower understructure/floor pan of a vehicle, comprising engine/gearbox, suspension, steering, fuel tanks, front bulkhead/air conditioning, etc, and elements of front and rear crumple zones. Because this represents much of a vehicle's cost it's used under as many bodyshells as possible – and even by different manufacturers!

Ramp angle The clearance under the nose and tail (and sills of an 'off-roader'). Most cars have deep front aprons for aerodynamics, with a flexible bottom part to prevent damage by kerbs and ramps.

This can be a problem with softly-sprung cars, because braking on approach to a ramp drops the nose, exacerbating the risk of grounding.

Replica A fibreglass body taken off the styling clay. The painted exterior is completely representative of the proposed car, down to the smallest detail, and often has fully-trimmed interiors and opening doors. Most Motor Show concept cars are styling replicas.

Sill A complex structural assembly of box sections, especially critical for convertibles, which often require further reinforcement, this is the area at the bottom of the door aperture that is stepped over on entry.

Scale factor Scale models are a useful early styling aid, but when taken to full size they rarely look quite right and require adjustment.

Surface plate A large, heavy and dimensionally stable steel table, usually flush with the floor, which a vehicle mock-up or clay can be located on for accurate measuring.

Styling frozen Styling work on a car until 'sign-off' approval by the Board of Directors, after which no styling changes are permitted (although engineering changes after this point are not unknown).

Tape layouts Sticky tape of various widths and colours which are used to 'draw' full-size shapes over a package drawing. Lines can be measured and transferred to a clay, and tapes used directly on the clay.

'Tear-up' Slang term for a complete re-think/re-work of large areas of a styling project, as a result of a change of mind by Styling, or feasibility issues or vehicle specification changes, usually when well into a project. Best avoided.

The clay The shape of the proposed new car modelled from a special wax-based clay which can be refined to an extraordinarily smooth surface, and is capable of limitless re-working and modification. It is heated in a low temperature oven and can be comfortably applied by hand. The skilled and talented modellers use a bewildering array of, often personalised, tools.

Tooling stacks Directly related to the Data Control Model, this approach has been used since the advent of pressed steel bodies. The styling clay is measured, any surface anomalies eliminated, and the data used to machine or hand-work the body shape in blocks of hardwood. These blocks are then stacked together on an armature, thus creating the car shape. Usually finished in gloss black or painted dynoc to check surface reflections (highlights). Accuracy is vital as production press tools can be machined from these blocks, resin copies cast off areas such as lamp apertures for suppliers, and checking fixtures taken off door apertures, etc, for production aids. Thanks to sophisticated computers, production tooling can now be machined directly from digital information, although some three-dimensional data 'prove-out' has to exist before tooling is cut.

PREFACE & INTRODUCTION

PREFACE

This book is written from the personal perspective of the author, and the views expressed are not those of Bentley Motors Limited or its predecessors, or any of its subsidiary or affiliated companies. It is not an official record or description of the products or personnel of those companies, and is not supported or endorsed by them.

Certain photographs and images reproduced in this book are the property of Bentley Motors Limited, and are reproduced with its permission; those which are not are identified individually. If any other copyrighted material has been included this was in error; for which I apologise.

INTRODUCTION

Apologies and explanations

The following chapters are an account of my time working in the Rolls-Royce and Bentley Styling Department from November 1971 to March 2001.

Motor car design is not straightforward. Considering the impact that automobiles have had in shaping the modern world, how they came about is not common knowledge as the media concentrates, quite reasonably, on what a new car is like and not how it came to be. When a manufacturer chooses to lift the curtain to show what went on behind the scenes, it is unveiling a stage set: the commercial stakes too high and the creative process too complicated for anything other than a Public Relations approach. In addition, the real action will have happened some four years previous to a launch; those involved will already be preoccupied with something new, or will have moved on, so can hardly be praised if now working for a rival manufacturer.

It is a rather confused area: someone once said that of all the thousands of people watching a game of football, only those on the pitch know what is really going on. For a profit-making organization to completely lower its guard, and accurately describe the workings of the creative process that leads to the product it is selling, is not easy or lightly done. Hopefully, the following chapters lift the veil slightly in this respect on one particular, unique institution.

The background

1971-2001 saw great changes in both society and the motor industry. In 1971 Rolls-Royce went bankrupt due to development costs of the RB211 aero engine; in 1973 Rolls-Royce Motors was floated. By 2001, Rolls-Royce Motors and Bentley Motors had been individually bought by BMW and VW. Whilst there are those able to research and record this eventful period, I appear to be the only one who experienced all of the issues affecting styling design.

Having spent three years studying archaeology part-time at Keele University, I know how important archives are. Therefore, for better or for worse, it seems necessary to attempt to record some kind of reference, however imperfect. As memory can be selective or play tricks, I am happy to say that I kept desk diaries: not, I should add, in the interests of preserving information for posterity, but rather for posterior protection. Once it became known that you jotted down key developments or decisions, you had the upper hand in 'who said what' sessions. There are some fine people out there, but mendacity is not unknown.

Due to the complexity of everyday events, it has been generally necessary to isolate and describe separate projects as if they were the only things going on, which, obviously, was not the case, especially in the 1990s. I've tried to include the names of some key players but apologise for missing out the huge number of people involved; neither is it possible to include blow-by-blow accounts of all the activities involved. In addition, some attempt has been made to gloss over as many as possible of my failures and blind alleys.

A quandary of this account – and indicative of tensions surrounding the aesthetic in engineering – is what to call the 'styling' activity. Any design activity should have a prefix such as dress design or bridge design. In the car world styling design is the correct term, as is chassis design or body design. For years this terminology has caused trouble, as many styling designers are overly sensitive to the cosmetic connotation of the word 'styling.' This word has never bothered me, and simply calling styling 'design' strikes me as a bit precious: apologies if this gives offence.

To avoid repetition, I won't always refer to the full name of the car company dealt with here. Apart from anything else, the name has changed over the years: I originally knew it as Rolls-Royce Limited (1971), then Rolls-Royce Motors Limited. On a Bentley brochure of 1978 it's known as Rolls-Royce Motors (Car Division), and in a 1994 company brochure Rolls-Royce Motor Cars. By 1999 company notepaper was headed Rolls-Royce Motor Cars & Bentley Motor Cars, with appropriate logos, and at the bottom Rolls-Royce Motor Cars Limited. Finally, at Crewe, it was Bentley Motors Limited, and at Goodwood, Rolls-Royce Motor Cars. The abbreviation R-RMC was also generally recognized, and locals always called the factory Royce's (now just Bentley). During later years I think of the Crewe car factory as Rolls-Royce and Bentley, and in the text it's often easier to simply refer to Crewe. Of course, the town of Crewe is known for its railway station and works, but hopefully I'll be forgiven for using 'Crewe' as shorthand for the car factory.

H J Mulliner, Park Ward, always called MPW, of Willesden, London, was an institution as unique in its way as Crewe. I worked for, or with, several people from MPW, as previous to going to the Royal College of Art (RCA), I was offered a job there. The company was absorbed into Crewe during the period that this book is concerned with,

and warrants a book in its own right, really. Conscious of not really doing the London factory justice, all I can stress is that it was capable of craftsmanship the equal of any in the world.

A motor car is a product of engineering. Whilst styling and marketing tend to create the immediate persona of a car, ultimately, the test is what the ownership experience is, day in, day out, as owner satisfaction leagues testify. Although ease of use and reliability are taken as a given, it is the engineer who shoulders most of the responsibility for these factors. Imagine being a chief engineer, worrying whether a product recall may become necessary due to the remote possibility of a component failing, or the irritation when the managing director storms into your office complaining that "All the locks were frozen up again this morning!" Your concern might be about new airbag deployment during a side impact test, whilst the styling and marketing departments debate typefaces on said airbag warning label.

Engineers have been completely undervalued in the UK, as indeed has manufacturing in general. All car design is a compromise, and a balance has to be struck between styling and engineering. If you occasionally detect a degree of animosity toward the latter discipline, the simple truth is nothing I ever worked on could have gone into production without the support of engineers.

Completing several personality profile questionnaires on various management courses, my strengths and weaknesses were predictable. Undoubtedly, the most annoying trait for anyone working with me was the implication that nothing they did was ever quite good enough, and my only defence in this regard is the fact that I applied the same criteria to myself. Excellence really is the bottom line in business: sorry, but there you are.

The final and perhaps most important rider that must preface my recollections concerns the general workforce at Crewe. With Rolls-Royce or Bentley the cars are the stars; the men and women making these exceptional vehicles are somewhat overlooked, so perhaps by mentioning Peter Ollerhead's *Making Cars at Crewe*, some compensation is possible. This book is an interesting reference source for anyone studying manufacturing and industrial relations as 20th century Britain developed, and, as always, if the product is interesting, the people involved are usually even more so.

Graham Hull M Des, RCA

ARRIVAL
TURN LEFT OFF THE M6

On a dark, wet and windy Sunday night in November 1971, I drove slowly past the iron gates and into the courtyard of the Rolls-Royce Apprentice Hostel in Minshull New Road in Crewe: the next day to begin what turned out to be a thirty-year career working on Rolls-Royce and Bentley Motor Cars.

Driving up to Crewe, Cheshire, from London in an Austrian Steyr-Puch, I was going to work for an Austrian and, over a quarter of a century later, an Austrian would buy the company. I was so daunted by how to survive in this new job I didn't even fully appreciate that the company was in the hands of the Receiver!

Since leaving school I had tried to get a job designing motor cars, but in late 1960s England it was a Catch 22 situation: to get a job you needed experience but to get experience you needed a job. Ironically, although finally landing a job with such a prestigious company, Rolls-Royce was definitely not my first choice, and I delayed accepting its job offer because British Leyland had also shown interest. In fact, given that Chrysler UK had provided sponsorship for the new Royal College of Art (RCA) Automotive Design Course, I'd assumed I would be going there, but, as it turned out, in 1971 Chrysler was firing, not hiring ...

At age 24 it was difficult to relate to Rolls-Royce on virtually any level. Young motoring enthusiasts are mainly interested in fun or sports cars: a very large, perpendicular saloon with a stainless steel model of a Greek temple on the front was hardly rock-and-roll or groovy. Also, my Methodist upbringing had scarcely prepared me for a close

association with this establishment icon of great wealth, but, having said that, a Bentley it was that changed my schoolboy allegiance from aircraft to cars.

We lived in North Harrow, a quiet corner of Metro-land, north west London. One midday in the 1960s, the traffic was snarled up on Pinner Road outside the quaint old ABC cinema. Suddenly, there was a discordant roar as a four-and-a-half litre Bentley in British Racing Green broke ranks and charged up the wrong side of the traffic islands. Bellowing like a bull elephant it bypassed the traffic jam and stormed off up the road towards Pinner. The open tourer towering above the Ford Populars and Hillman Minxes seemed full of excited bright young things, the antithesis of the mundane. The image, once seen, was never forgotten, and reminiscent of Bentley derring-do in the film *Reach for the Sky*. The sound and sight was totally brilliant; nothing else on earth comes close to the drumbeat exhaust and screaming gears of a Cricklewood Bentley. The A410 to Pinner is not the road to Damascus but the conversion nevertheless occurred, and from that day on my fascination with cars took hold. Of course, by 1971, Bentley's glory days were long forgotten; the marque barely had a pulse in the new car market.

My initial reaction on seeing the Rolls-Royce car factory at Crewe was surprise at its size. Knowing it had been the home of the Merlin aero engine, I'd guessed it was not some backyard operation behind a country house, but the reality still impressed. This was a large site on the north west edge of Crewe with the classic sawtooth skyline

A 1970 exercise at Chrysler UK's Advanced Styling Studios, Coventry (later Jaguar): a two-door sports estate exploiting the compact dimensions of a multi-lobe Wankel engine. The large-scale, split model was photographed against a mirror (later Photoshopped). This probably helped the interview at R-RMC with Fritz Feller as he had led the clever 'Cottage Loaf' Wankel diesel engine programme. (Author collection)

of large uniform buildings and a water tower. The frontage was pure 1930s utility: the dull, featureless brickwork and metal window frames evident all over industrial Britain.

Chief Stylist Fritz Feller interviewed me on my original visit. His office was on the first floor near the main entrance, with a view of Pyms Lane car park and cows in the adjacent field. Fritz was middle-aged and short in stature, his remaining hair brushed sleekly back. Ignoring my CV, he asked whether I had any children I was aware of! Wrong-footed and assuming there was little prospect of a job, I mechanically went through the presentation of my portfolio. Although not recalling much of the interview I remember showing him my best rendering, and him suggesting that he had seen something like that design previously. His parting words were, "It helps in this job if you can present your work well." Had I? Nothing was explained about the department's facilities or, indeed, what the job might entail. It seemed a fair guess that it would be different to Chrysler UK's Advanced Styling Studio at Coventry that I'd worked in, but just *how* different, it was impossible to predict.

Crewe seemed a foreign land, a railway town in the middle of the Cheshire Plains. On arrival at Crewe Station the thought occurred that the description by comedian Les Dawson of grinning sandwiches in the station buffet was spot-on. A taxi ride through railway worker's terraced cottages did little to dispel the 'It's grim up-north' theme. Although desperate for a job, if Chrysler wouldn't have me British Leyland or Jaguar would have been at least as attractive. In 1971, the Midlands were still very much the heart of the British Motor Industry, and the M1 put it within easy reach of London, allowing me to get 'home.' Rolls-Royce was barely on my radar.

The offer

It came as something of a surprise when, a few days later, Fritz Feller offered me a job. As British Leyland's Doug Thorpe had also shown interest, I stalled the Rolls-Royce Personnel Department for a couple of weeks, hoping a letter would come from BL. It wasn't just the apprehension of trying to design a product I didn't have much of a feel for that caused me to hesitate, but also the fact that I would be so far from my family, which did not do much for my comfort zone. However, my father – always a source of worldly wisdom – encouraged me to step off into space and accept the offer.

On the first Monday morning, after reporting for work, Personnel formally showed me to Fritz's office, and

his first words of greeting were, "So, you've decided to join us, then." There was an edge to his voice; I'd obviously got off on the wrong foot by apparently playing hard to get with the most famous name in the motoring world.

Fritz led me through to the adjacent 'Studio,' essentially a well-lit, smallish office on the corner of the front block, where I was introduced to three people who were obviously waiting to find out who the new boy was. It took me some months to appreciate just how exceptional these three individuals – Bill Allen, Martin Bourne and Ron Maddocks – actually were.

The team

Bill Allen was a comfortably built, white-haired gentleman. With a background in coachbuilding, styling and design, he was expert in laying down body lines that could be converted into three-dimensional tooling stacks. Bill appears to have been directly responsible for the exterior style of the Mulliner Park Ward (MPW) two-door; latterly named the Corniche.

Martin Bourne was a youngish, but very experienced, Stylist/Draughtsman, often referred to as 'Biggles' due to his Flying Officer style of moustache. A keen private pilot, he played piano or electric organ in a dance band, and had a deep knowledge of Grand Prix racing.

These two had worked with John Blatchley, highly regarded stylist of the Rolls-Royce Silver Cloud and Silver Shadow, amongst others. The third person, Ron Maddocks, seemed about the same age as Martin and had responsibility for making scale models. Fritz had somehow conjured up Ron from the shopfloor, where he had been working in road test. He had seen a lot of the world and could make virtually anything involving engineering or electronics, and, as things turned out, I probably wouldn't have survived the early years without his skills.

The reality

Leaving the London suburbs to move up north was a shock to my system. After years of trying to gain access to the motor industry I was now in the inner sanctum of Rolls-Royce Motor Cars, and Cheshire Council's road signs were a constant reminder that this was the 'Home of the Best Car in the World.'

Another reason for hesitating to join Rolls-Royce was that I couldn't imagine what its styling setup would be. Vacation placement at Chrysler UK, my RCA sponsor, had been a privileged insight into how Detroit styled cars, using 'anything-money-can-buy' facilities to succeed in a

Personal projects –
A Messerschmitt Kabinenroller mated to two Mini front sub-frames, it was built at my father's school and entered into a BP 'Build a Car' competition. Enthusiastically tested by *Motor* magazine on March 24, 1973, it's pictured at Harrow Driving Centre (above). (Author collection)

1380cc, 450kg, Mini-powered three-wheeler has a Kevlar/foam body.

Morgan replica intended to use a Weslake 1000cc V-twin. Ron Maddocks, Styling's model maker, is on the right. Ron grins because he knows what sort of sound those exhaust pipes will make – and the author doesn't. (Author collection) hugely competitive market fed by flow-line production. Rolls-Royce in the 1970s had no competitor, and cars were built by calendar, not stopwatch. New designs were generations apart.

John Blatchley's small, unchanged styling studio of the 1950/60s was where the Silver Cloud and Silver Shadow (SY) were crafted using quarter-scale models, which were enlarged to full size by coachbuilder's drawings, and made into full-sized, wooden mock-ups. This was still state-of-the-art for Crewe in 1971, with no intention to change this approach for the Company's pending replacement of SY.

One could never escape the 'presence' of the marque's famous founders, Sir Henry Royce and the Honourable Charles Stewart Rolls, the most famous names in the motoring world. Maintaining and developing this almost mystical reputation was a source of pride to those involved, but also, often, a stifling burden. (Bentley, at this time, was barely a sideshow, and mainly for UK enthusiasts.)

So, I found myself a long way from home, in a foreign country, virtually, and expected to contribute to the design of a product whose reputation completely overawed me and which I had little feel for. The Studio's facilities, complete with ex-Air Ministry furniture and drawing boards, was like part of an industrial heritage site. Bentley, my one possible source of inspiration, wasn't even on the agenda.

Not a great start.

The author and Ron Maddocks consider manikin comfort angles in the first viewing studio of the 1970s. This inner sanctum of the Experimental Garage featured in the *1977 Company Report and Results* brochure. The seat is from a Camargue.

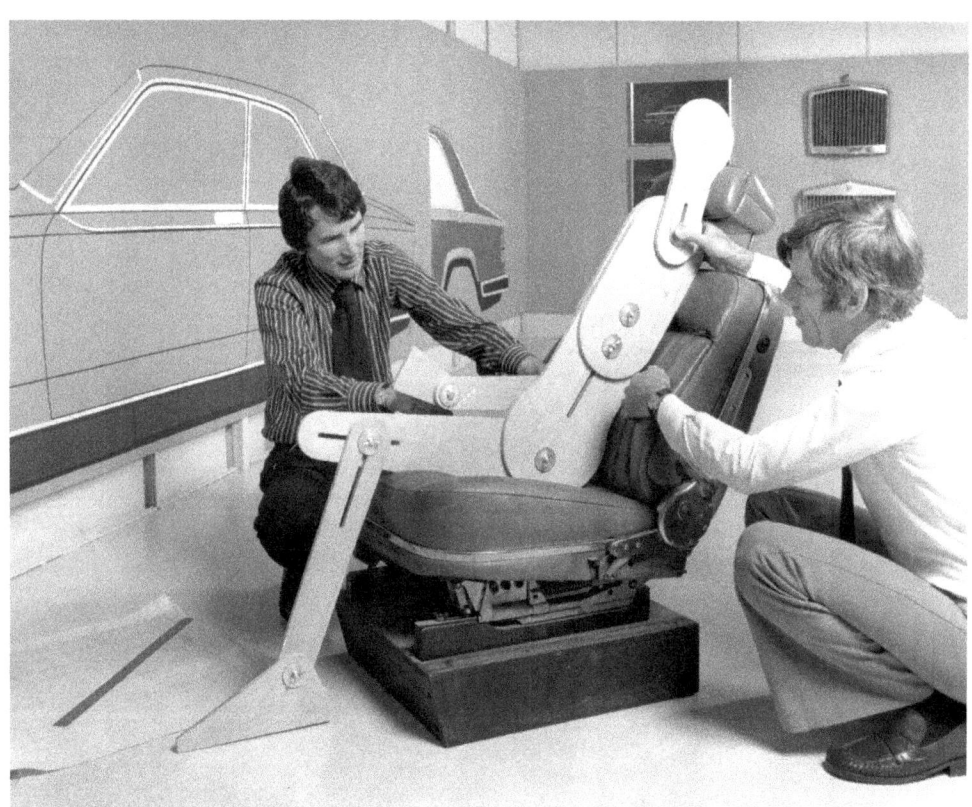

Before my time at the RCA, I'd acquired a pre-diploma at the wonderful old Harrow Art School; then a diploma at the Central School of Art and Design. Central's engineering facility was run by an ex-member of Sir Alec Issigonis' team. Another tutor, Peter Cambridge, had been head-hunted from Ford by Colin Chapman to create the interior of the original Lotus Elite. Peter, later working for Bell Helicopters, taught me that industrial design can benefit from a little styling magic, and it was following his advice that got my final project into Design Magazine.

RCA's Sir Misha Black told us, "Having good ideas isn't difficult, getting them into production is." How true.

THE STYLING DEPARTMENT
MORE THAN MET THE EYE

Background – financial reality of styling at Crewe

The Rolls-Royce Silver Shadow (SY) was in production for 15 years, and the Silver Spirit (SZ) for 18, which may give the impression that the styling and engineering design side of the Company didn't have much to do. The Crewe factory could have functioned with a handful of engineers for day-to-day product support, but R-RMC would eventually have had little credibility as a standard-bearer for design engineering excellence and progress.

The moderately-sized plant in Cheshire, with several thousand employees, was virtually a stand-alone unit. Ever-accelerating technical demands in all fields – and especially electronics – called for a strong team to simply keep abreast of developments, let alone come up with any innovation. Increasingly, suppliers had to be relied on for updates and input, although the kudos of supplying Rolls-Royce was evaporating by the 1970s in the face of orders from huge conglomerates: factors that demanded continuous efforts from a large, in-house engineering team to keep the product viable.

Vulnerable to all economic and social upheavals, Rolls-Royce needed a stable home market, and yet stability had hardly been the nation's watchword. Commerce is a battlefield; to win battles you must choose where to fight and to have unfair advantage. Rolls-Royce couldn't be complacent: technical superiority such as power-assisted controls, superb quality and comfort could be emulated by others, and the marque's extraordinary status depended on it being different to the mass-market. There is little point in winning if you can't then hold the ground.

Profitability is a big question mark hanging over car production of any kind. If you don't build many units, each one has to carry a large burden of overhead. Even a Rolls-Royce has a price ceiling; therefore, working backwards, a minimum production target is easily ascertained. As the factory is a fixed overhead, the key variable left after materials is payroll, which is why, like most manufacturers, R-RMC had painful redundancy periods as sales ebbed and flowed.

There were many initiatives to streamline and cut waste. For instance, in May 1983, 'zero budgeting' was implemented as a way of establishing a department's minimum size. Peter Ward famously said in his early days as Managing Director, "You can't charge Rolls-Royce prices for a metal bracket with holes drilled in it." All departments subsequently became profit centres, selling its product to the next department that required it. At the heart of all such initiatives was the message that there was no innate right for any one part, or indeed the Company itself, to survive.

Realistically, there were never enough funds at R-RMC; every spare cent was soaked up by the magnificent but demanding motor cars. Coupled with continuous striving for product perfection, no avenue was left unexplored in an effort to save money. One issue that caused Styling a headache was the general ban on outside recruitment, and rumour had it that Chief Engineer Mike

Dunn had to persuade Peter Ward not to close us down altogether! Peter did suggest the possibility of sacking me on a couple of occasions, but that was over Colour Committee issues rather than due to economics.

The MD and his board were caught in crossfire: on one hand pretending to be a compact, up-market version of General Motors, and on the other running an under-invested factory. The firm's image was potent but, to the people responsible, akin to having a tiger by the tail. It was this image that tended to protect Styling, as Engineering realized it needed everyday aesthetic input, and Marketing knew it wasn't possible to be a serious player without a Styling Department.

Styling Department – the 1970s

Fritz Feller, an engine designer who dabbled in painting, had assembled a small but perfectly formed team, which comprised –

Fritz Feller – Chief Stylist
Bill Allen – Stylist/Design Draughtsman
Martin Bourne – Stylist/Design Draughtsman
Ron Maddocks – Model-Maker
Norman Webster – Design Engineer
Graham Hull – Stylist (replacing Chris Johnston)

– and was charged with replacing SY. Bill and Martin were the only experienced stylists, both having worked with John Blatchley on 1950s and 1960s classics. Their processes and techniques were based on quarter-scale models enlarged to full-size wooden replicas.

Bill and Martin did all the day-to-day 'survival' work. Bill, for instance, had the depressing task of putting the energy-absorbing federal bumpers on Shadow 2, whilst Martin generally covered interior requirements. Their work went straight down the production line to the marketplace. Continuing the John Blatchley tradition (obviously holding him in high regard), the pair produced top quality technical drawings, logged in a Dickensian tome called the SG book. The rest of us mainly pursued the four-door replacement SZ, the early lines of which were established by my predecessor, Chris Johnston, and Ron Maddocks.

When Bill Allen retired, Fritz employed another RCA graduate called David Chammings, a good chap who didn't stay long (declaring it a job for stoics). He was eventually replaced by Ryan Lewis, an RCA furniture design graduate. The Engineering Department's general opinion of ex-RCA graduates seemed to be that we were black belts in flower arranging, which, needless to say, I found grossly unfair, having already been involved with building one 'special' at home and considering another.

My early career at Crewe was a unique time. The product was extraordinary – as, too, was the workforce and factory. Chief Executive David Plastow (DP), had star quality, and Fritz Feller remains one of the most exceptional people I've ever met. A refugee from 1930s Austria, Fritz was better at spoken and written English than most of the natives, and from a difficult start achieved the highest levels in UK engineering.

At Rolls-Royce, the pursuit of engineering perfection was a type of religion. However, the old order was changing, and marketing and image were on the ascendancy. The pace of life was increasing, and the world was hungry for excitement and rapid change. When SZ was completed Fritz felt he'd given the Company the Rolls-Royce it needed for the next couple of decades – and he almost had – but suddenly Bentley woke from its slumber and there was also the need to consider a smaller, lighter vehicle.

Styling Department – show time: the Viewing Area

David Plastow giving Fritz Feller a Styling Viewing Area in the 1970s was a breakthrough for the department. Having a permanent, reasonably impressive inner sanctum for the factory was a win-win arrangement: we had somewhere to work on and view mock-ups and drawings, and the powers-that-be had a little treat for VIP visits; crucially, the MD and board enjoyed monthly 'happy hour' viewings of the future product.

I worked hard to ensure that this area was always as presentable as possible, and the Company's PR benefited over the years for minimum expenditure (it was a struggle to get money for paint, display boards, and cleaners, etc, but, having said that, for a visit from the Princess Royal a new door was cut through a wall at just 24 hours' notice. This was to avoid said personage getting wet on the Grand Tour, which, naturally, included Styling).

This presentation facility was soon taken for granted. David Plastow put his head round the office door one day to say he was taking a VIP there, but, unfortunately, we'd just piled everything on to the area's large surface plate whilst we had the floor repainted. Good job DP checked otherwise two very expensive pairs of shoes would have been ruined, glued into the resin paint! Howard Mosher, my one-time American boss, blasted me once for some

Astutely combining aesthetic and social statement, the Silver Cloud was, by the 1990s, regarded by Styling as the epitome of a Rolls-Royce motor car. Often chauffeured, the owner's rear compartment offers great privacy. It was an extremely curvaceous shape to carry the stainless-steel model of a Greek temple. The antithesis of 'air-flow management,' its form is more akin to that of a yacht.

cardboard boxes lying around the floor, so I pointed out that I was sweeping the floor as there was no provision for a cleaner. Some years later, a younger team member became responsible for this area, and was blasted in the same way when Graham Morris, an MD from Liverpool, arrived in the Viewing Area at the end of a messy clay-modelling session. Graham exploded angrily, stating that, "Some council houses can look like palaces." The unfortunate recipient went around for days doing a fair impersonation of this statement in a scouse accent, but the incident underlined the perceived value to the Company of this inner sanctum.

Styling Department – the 1980s

The old guard began to change in 1983 with the arrival of new MD Dick Perry; new Chief Engineer Mike Dunn; new Marketing Director Peter Ward, and John Stephenson, Crewe's first Product Planning Director. At the same time, Fritz Feller's health began to fail.

Despite these radical changes at the top, styling

resources to meet the aspirations of these new brooms were inadequate and even shrinking. I had pioneered the use of full-size clays to replace wood or plastic wood for mock-ups, introducing this industry norm for down-sized saloon exercise SX. Sadly, the involvement of Ron Maddocks – our talented model-maker – was vetoed by a union demarcation issue: the personnel that Ron would need to involve from the Experimental Woodshop were hourly-paid trade union members, whilst Ron was non-union salaried staff. For fellow employees to deny the Company Ron's expertise reflected the fundamental relations issues that the UK was experiencing, and, understandably, Ron took voluntary redundancy at the earliest opportunity as a result. Norman Webster wanted to return to the saner environment of Engineering Design, so when I formally took over from Fritz on February 6, 1984, the roll-call comprised –

Graham Hull – Acting Chief Stylist
Martin Bourne – Stylist/Draughtsman

Whilst lacking virtually all of Silver Cloud's visual charisma, the Silver Shadow was a commercial success, and a bold step for the Company, technically. The tasteful, perpendicular, three-box shape perfectly conveyed the slightly reserved nature of a Rolls-Royce, and, like Silver Cloud, rear occupants had privacy. Federal bumper design demonstrates how regulations can encroach on styling freedom.

Ryan Lewis – Stylist
Brian Hassall – Model-Maker

John Stephenson, who had worked in Wayne Cherry's superb Vauxhall styling facilities at Luton, must have been amazed we could function at all. Aware of Crewe site union restrictions, he used the outside consultancy route for the 1985 Bentley show car, Project 90. Dick Perry, in a rare moment of weakness, must have taken pity because in 1985 I was allowed to recruit Steven Everitt, a young graduate from Coventry University's Transport Design course.

In-house we accommodated production of alloy wheels, a new front apron for the Bentley Turbo, and interior requirements for both marques. Items such as airbag steering wheels took an inordinate amount of time to produce as they used new technology.

I worked with Peter Horbury at MGA (Mike Gibbs Associates) Coventry on the late 1980s Bentley Turbo R exterior, although the all-new seats, etc, were done at Crewe. Again, although working off-site with consultants for the Bentley Continental R, all interior work, alloy wheels, and some exterior details were done on-site.

Due to the ongoing frustration of not being able to work on full-size clays at Crewe, we lost our second modeller, Brian Hassall, to another department, having to then get an important desk-top model made by Experimental Woodshop. This Rolls-Royce concept was shown in a press article being admired by Sir David Plastow and Sir Colin Chandler of Vickers, and was the first hint that the Company could be up for sale.

Styling Department – the 1990s

During 1990 we managed to employ ace clay modeller Jim Dimbleby. We still couldn't beat the system at Crewe, but Jim was able to work full-size at MGA on the saloon replacement programme. In September 1991 we lost our third modeller when Jim resigned, although between us we had figured out the sweeping side section that Silver Seraph was to use. We lost Ryan Lewis in the same year, but were joined in October 1991 by Simon Loasby. Mike

Dunn, who knew his father (Mike Loasby had been a key engineer on the De Lorean Sports car project), had agreed to partially sponsor Simon at the RCA for two years. At least R-RMC had given something back to the college.

Stephen Everett moved on to another department in 1991, leaving three people to meet the challenges of the decade before the new millennium –

Graham Hull – Chief Stylist
Martin Bourne – Stylist
Simon Loasby – Stylist

Due to extraordinary pressure to reduce the head count at Crewe, Martin Bourne took voluntary redundancy and left the Company on October 30, 1992, thus severing the last link with John Blatchley's era. Martin had played an important part in maintaining the credibility of the Styling Department, particularly in world-class interiors. However, as he then became freelance locally, happily, we continued to work together.

Increasingly, I was supervising work at consultancies. Styling of alloy wheels, etc, remained in-house, as did all interior work. Our Viewing Area continued to be a prime Company asset, and when Styling became part of Marketing, rendered schemes for individual customer orders added significantly to the workload, enabling me to recruit Darren Day, a Coventry University graduate with a keen interest in computer-aided design, on October 17, 1994. Prior to this, Richard Stevens left R-RMC for the Coventry Transport course, with hopes of joining us on completion.

April 1994 was a landmark date for aesthetics at Crewe as we finally managed to get a professional team of clay modellers working in the Styling Studio/Viewing Area in Third Avenue. After successful exercises off-site we now had to create the definitive replacement for SZ, and the only way we could achieve this as well as other projects – including involvement with BMW – was to bring in an established team: the advantage being that I could stay close by and the in-house team could see the techniques involved.

We hastily upgraded our modelling facilities and Richard Hamblin's Omni Design people set up camp. For a while, Jim Dimbleby, our old clay modeller, re-joined us, such was his enthusiasm for the project.

By late August 1995, Robin Page had joined us, also from Coventry University, and the department now comprised –

Graham Hull – Chief Stylist
Simon Loasby – Senior Stylist
Darren Day – Stylist
Robin Page – Stylist
Caroline Walley – Secretary

– a team which made up the core of Styling pretty much until 2000. Although Simon, Darren and Robin were straight from college, they had the advantage of seeing how top consultancies worked, and, through MPW, customer requirements. Henrik Nordin from Sweden again came straight from Coventry University in late 1998. Richard Stevens came back on board after completing his course, which had included vacation work with us.

The mid-1990s saw our department under great pressure, as the number of projects – both on-site and off – had gone through the roof. The small team was working excessive overtime, something I'd never been keen on, even though most of my renderings for the Company were done at home. Simon Loasby was, understandably, seeking advancement, and Ian Mckay, a director of marketing and my boss, came up with a cunning plan. I continued to be responsible for the Company's aesthetic solutions and Simon would manage the daily workload of the in-house team. This was a good solution as Simon would also have some hands-on styling work: he'd still have to pay heed to my instructions, but hey, life's sometimes tough.

Head-hunting experienced stylists from other companies was not an option as the Company wouldn't pay the going rate, and even if someone could be persuaded to join the small Crewe team, they wouldn't find the infrastructure they might expect. The only course was to take graduates straight from college and absorb their long learning curve. I guess we were lucky with the people we took on in this way.

Following the success of bringing a team of clay modellers to Crewe for the Silver Seraph family, we decided to use this approach again. The main on-site modelling task, code named Bali, was to come up with a replacement for the Bentley Continental R. Although able to bring in people from our consultants, a permanent formal structure eluded us. For instance, taking on a Chief Modeller/Gang-Boss would necessitate a significant payroll increase, which the Company wouldn't contemplate.

The income from cars specially commissioned during the 1990s apparently allowed the Company to continue. The raison d'etre of these projects was styling, largely, but businessmen wouldn't be in business if they didn't

The Corniche – like Silver Cloud and Silver Shadow – was from the John Blatchley/Bill Allen era. Starting life as MPW's 1965 fixed-head coupé, the curvaceous sides incorporated more of Silver Cloud's DNA than its Silver Shadow relative. Walking the tightrope between old world charm and ostentatiousness, the vehicle remains iconic. Badly missing its original chrome bumpers, it shows what a challenge regulations presented for worldwide sales.

Pininfarina's Camargue suggested that perceived modernity, albeit from an excellent source, might not be the complete answer. Elements of the interior, however, especially the seats, influenced future thoughts. NB: Styling's inherited 1970s heritage was less influential at the time than might now be regarded. Heritage, retro, brand and core values are comparatively recent concepts.

object to the spend involved, which, obviously, would be reduced if more work was done on-site. When improved Crewe styling facilities were proposed, we were charged with justifying the outlay this involved, at a time when a large Brand department was set up by Marketing without question!

The compromise (disregarding the head count issue) was that my long-campaigned-for new studio and outside viewing area would finally happen. This would be money well spent, as previous viewing areas had proved their worth to everyone and were, not least, window dressing for potential buyers of the Company. The new styling facility was a complete success, and for this we took over the large Car Bond building in the north east corner of the site by Pyms Lane. Importantly, I had been able to get Planning to negotiate with Crewe and Nantwich Council for some adjacent land. The ability to view cars in daylight, and in secret, is a fundamental styling requirement.

Working with Crewe Plant and Equipment and a German firm, Simon Loasby organized best-practice measuring equipment which ultimately could also machine clay. Without the new facility the Continental GT and Flying Spur might well have been modelled in Wolfsburg studios.

Styling Department – the team at the time of the VW-appointed Styling Director

Previous to Dirk van Braeckel becoming Design Director at Crewe during 1999, Styling's head count was as follows –

Graham Hull – Chief Stylist
Simon Loasby – Manager
Darren Day – Senior Stylist
Robin Page – Senior Stylist
Crispin Marshfield – VW Designer
Henrik Nordin – Stylist
Richard Stevens – Stylist
Caroline Walley – Secretary
(Steven Piantoni – Stylist, pending Coventry course)

Crispin Marshfield had been seconded into the department on January 1, 1999 by Herr Warkus, head of VW Design. Crispin was the first member of Crewe Styling – apart from myself – to have previously worked in a car company Styling Studio.

Styling Department – overview

If the factory that built Rolls-Royce and Bentley cars was unique, so, too, was the Styling Department. This small Company resource, established in the 1950s, was deemed sufficient to meet requirements for the next fifty years.

There were several reasons for this unusual attitude –

1 The Company was founded on engineering with an acceptance of marketing. Styling was a latecomer: aesthetics embarrassed British management.

2 Top management, like the man in the street, regarded styling as just a body shape, which meant that a new one was only infrequently required.

3 The powers-that-be underestimated the changing requirements of car design, particularly legislation.

4 The success of Bentley greatly increased Styling's workload.

5 The board only eventually realized that unassisted consultants were unlikely to deliver a genuine Rolls-Royce or Bentley.

A separate important issue was that the Crewe workforce wouldn't support industry norm clay modelling and associated fibreglass replicas, as it was seen as usurping traditional methods and involving non-union labour. These techniques were opposed from 1970 until the early 1990s, forcing the functions off-site.

Despite Crewe's Styling Department being so small, end results were of the highest quality. Being so close to the production process, we were able to enhance and complement the craft-skills and techniques the factory was renowned for. VW's and BMW's interest in full ownership was partially influenced by the vehicles' world-class interiors.

Our young team acquired wide experience working with numerous 'outsiders,' which was not so easy with some closed-loop companies. In order to appreciate the overall picture, it's necessary to understand the advantages and disadvantages of the circumstances that Crewe's Styling Department operated under.

Tom Creer's laboratory was a bastion of Sir Henry Royce's legendary materials standards, and Tom made me feel decidedly shady when I requested smoke-tinted chrome plating for Bentley.

CAMARGUE
CREWE BUYS AN ITALIAN SUIT

First impressions

By the time of my arrival at Rolls-Royce the styling and design of the Camargue (DY) was done and dusted, with prototype bodyshells arriving at the top of the factory for painting and fitting out. This Pininfarina design was to be the last Company product executed entirely by consultants. The shape was a surprisingly simple, two-door coupé using Silver Shadow (SY) floor pan and mechanics, although an innovation was Crewe's new, sophisticated air-conditioning system: a Bruce Sutherland project, and probably the most advanced in the automotive world.

Having no experience of trying to style a very large motor car, let alone a Rolls-Royce coupé, 'look and learn' became my creed. Pininfarina had the highest possible credibility and, after all, one of our family cars – the delightful MkII Austin A40 – was from that stable.

I was very impressed by my first sight of the bare bodyshell (body-in-white) with doors, etc. It was obviously more modern than SY, with clean, uncluttered surfaces. Fritz Feller kept his powder dry but the rest of the team was less than enthusiastic. The 'not invented here' syndrome was obviously involved, although it was generally accepted that the interior was not bad.

When the complete pre-production car could be studied my new colleagues' reservations about its exterior shape began to make sense. Whilst vehicles of this size have authority and presence as a birthright, DY seemed a little ill-at-ease. Cars project body language, just like people, and coupés have only one aim: to look slinky or maybe just a little raffish. Whether DY fitted into either category was debatable.

The cabin was light, airy and elegant, the flanks sheer and uncontrived, the tail straightforward and of its time; the front, well, a little Lady Penelope. Late in the day, apparently, the radiator shell was made larger to emphasise the fact that this was indeed a Rolls-Royce, resulting in something significantly larger than that on SY or the Corniche; in addition, the latter's small, round headlamps were overwhelmed when used on DY.

As well as the slightly unfortunate frontal aspect, cars, like people, can suffer from bad posture, and DY's body overhung the wheels, making it look heavy and hardly the svelte coupé it should be. The vehicle was never on an even keel, either, but instead down at the back as if crushed by a great weight the self-levelling suspension couldn't handle. A car's stance is critical: wheels should fill the arches and be as far outboard as legally permitted (BMWs are particularly good in this respect). Additionally, any vehicle looks perkier and ready for action with its nose slightly down and tail slightly up.

Before DY's 1975 launch there was a bit of a panic as Pininfarina's Fiat 130 coupé was thought to bear rather a close resemblance, so a Board of Directors viewing was arranged on the helipad at the Company's sports field behind the apprentice's hostel, although I'm not sure what action could have been taken at this stage with the ship already moving on its slipway. However, although the two vehicles were obviously related, seen together it wasn't a case of two women wearing the same dress at a social function, and the rather nervous gathering learnt that design consultants tend to have a recognizable house style, to the extent, some would say, that at any given time a lack of good, original ideas will mean that what is available will be stretched between as many clients as possible ...

Styling developments – initial input

To promote and reinforce DY's premium pricing, Styling came up with some special paint and hide colours; the hide being Connolly's absolute finest, the super-soft Nuella, superior even to the Vaumol used on other Crewe cars (I was told Italian farmers kept their Nuella cows in the bathroom to avoid barbed wire and insect damage).

DY, unlike traditional Rolls-Royce motor cars, didn't have raised wing crowns, which, from behind the wheel, gave the disturbing impression that the front corners disappeared into infinity. So we shaped two small wing-witness markers showing where the front corners actually finished: Styling's first contribution to exterior style!

Styling developments – suspension

Trying to coax some élan into this very large, staid coupé, we put on an impromptu display for our pre-knighthood MD David Plastow (DP). World Champion motorcyclist Barry Sheen had an SY, and one of his sponsors – Campagnolo – had made some attractive alloy wheels just for his car, at a time when all Crewe product was running on steel wheels with stainless steel hub caps, and alloy wheels weren't even returning pings on Engineering's radar. Barry Sheen's car arrived at the factory for some work, and we quickly purloined the wheels and fitted them to DP's dark blue DY, leaving it outside the directors' dining room one sunny lunchtime for DP to discover.

The effect was pretty convincing, much reducing DY's over-bodied look. Having got DP's attention, we then arranged a viewing to demonstrate the effect of dropping the nose slightly and lifting the tail. In the Styling Viewing Area we had Pininfarina's original mock-up, code named Delta, to experiment with, and when DP saw the effect of re-setting the fore and aft pitch in this way he described it as a revelation. So emboldened was I by this feedback, I stated that DY was currently like a speedboat or motor launch digging in its stern, an analogy that had a profound effect on my subsequent thinking regarding Rolls-Royce in general.

The Engineering Department was extremely nervous of alloy wheels at this time, mainly due to potential corrosion and porosity risks, and alloys were not used until 1985 on the Turbo R. We were more successful with the vehicle's pitch, which was found not to be as per design specification. Tighter controls were ordered on coil spring poundage rates, and production standing height instructions were changed: a small victory, maybe, but one which demonstrated that styling wasn't just about drawing pretty shapes.

Styling developments – body

In the late 1970s it occurred to us that the four rectangular headlamps we were working on for the federal version of Silver Spirit (SZ) might suit and freshen the angular DY. Fritz Feller asked me to do a couple of renderings showing this and other tweaks, which we arranged to show Sergio Pininfarina at the Turin Motor Show. I was nervous about showing the Italians how to improve their 'masterpiece,' but Fritz relished this opportunity for nose-tweaking.

At the Turin show Sergio sent his Chief Designer, Leonardo Fioravanti, to see my drawings, but Fritz stuck to his guns and demanded to see Sergio himself, telling me not to open my portfolio. This greatly embarrassed Leonardo, who pleaded his case, but Fritz looked at his watch and loudly enquired when the next flight home was. After a couple of phone calls we were driven out to the Pininfarina factory for an audience with the great man. Sergio and Leonardo were polite but non-committal about my renderings, and confused by my surname, which they thought applied only to ships. Sergio became quite emotional about DY, declaring that he would "travel through the rain and fog to be with his child." It was clear, though, that they felt there was room for improvement.

Debate continued about how to keep this coupé credible alongside the now-iconic Corniche. At a meeting where possible new initiatives were discussed I suggested that, as MPW was using so much lead loading on the body, perhaps it could be marketed as a luxury mobile nuclear fall-out shelter: how to win friends and influence people ...

We did try quite a radical exercise on DY, grafting on what became the Bentley Mulsanne nose, radiator shell and headlamps, etc. Visually, this was very successful but posed as many commercial questions as it answered styling ones.

A bizarre episode occurred in 1984 initiated by Crewe's first Product Planning Director, John Stephenson, previously of Vauxhall Styling Studios. John commissioned a DY that had every conceivable piece of additional brightwork trim you could imagine 'shot-gunned' at it.

With all the other directors present, my opinion was asked; I rejected everything except some alloy wheels. Stephenson didn't seem to disagree; as I had just taken over from Fritz, perhaps the question was a kind of test.

Although never to receive a face-lift the good ship Camargue did go down with all guns blazing. Working with Bernard Preston, the second director of Product Planning, Styling had everything painted white on the 20 or so remaining bodyshells: body, Everflex roof, Bentley alloy wheels with RR centres; the tyre sidewalls receiving a thin white line. In 1987, DY finally got the alloy wheels it had ached for from day one.

Camargue Days – never a dull moment

After we showed Pininfarina how to improve DY, Leonardo Fioravanti took Fritz and I out for lunch. As I wasn't drinking, Fritz and Leonardo polished off the wine between them, and then the latter declared he would take me out for a run in the Ferrari 308 he'd designed.

A memorable drive into the foothills outside Turin followed. Mid-engine cars on the limit can be twitchy, and at times I was bracing my feet so hard against the front bulkhead that it flexed. At one point we scythed through a flock of chickens wandering about outside a farm, but the highlight was jumping some lights at a big crossroads and power sliding across the path of a Lambretta tricycle van. It was stacked high with chairs, and I glanced back to see it see-sawing erratically in our manic wake. A fired-up Leonardo lowered my window shouting "Induction!" as the engine gave its all.

Our Italian adventure did not end there, however, due to a big art theft. A menacing-looking plain clothes policeman caught sight of my large portfolio at Turin airport, and we were quickly surrounded by armed police demanding that I open it, dsplaying all of our highly secret drawings in a crowded airport thoroughfare. No Mona Lisa, but great alloy wheels. After all the excitement I then had to find Fritz, who had somehow managed to melt away.

Cometh the Turbo

A lasting memory of DY is the advent of the turbocharged engine. A very tired development car was the second mobile test-bed for the turbocharger installation. Whether or not Engineering really foresaw the effect this device would have on the, even then, venerable V8 engine I don't know, but word quickly got around that something special had occurred. Ron Maddocks, Styling's model-maker, knew one of the testers, and got me a ride.

Development cars tend to be pretty unkempt – bits missing, gaffer tape stuck over some lashed-up modification, and so on – and this DY in battleship grey was as rough as they come. The interior was a shambles: test equipment all over the place, wires hanging out of the facia, and a huge turbo boost gauge rigged up beside the driver. The car was also apparently running on open 'silencers' to reduce back pressure on the exhaust gas-driven turbine, but even on idle it rumbled menacingly as we edged away from the factory toward a favourite nearby test route.

As luck would have it we got caught in a spot check by Cheshire Constabulary. The police had an understanding with the Pyms Lane factory: production cars were all road tested and a very familiar sight, locally. R-RMC, a very important local employer, was largely left to get on with it – within reason. Perhaps we could be accused of pushing our luck with this particular hot rod. The slow drum beat of this scary V8 very evident, we tried to tip-toe up to the wary-looking officer of the law, who, running a cursory eye over our street-fighter, asked to see our driver's license. Our man had to apologetically explain that he didn't have it on him. "Just go away," our guardian of the law sighed, and this big bruiser of a car edged down the road, making a fearful racket even though just ticking over.

Reaching our quiet Cheshire B-road straight, our expert demonstrated what a union between a big V8 and a turbocharger could deliver. I've never been in a jet fighter catapulted off an aircraft carrier but I know what it must feel like. The 5135lb (2329kg) car felt as if it was being relentlessly drawn toward the horizon by a fantastically strong rubber band, in a seamless surge of ruthless acceleration based not on screaming revs but awesome torque: an incredibly impressive demonstration. But even in a straight line this vehicle felt a bit unstable and something would have to be done before it could negotiate high-speed bends. Aerodynamics were unquestionably part of the problem as the large bluff front rose ever higher under power. On our onward surge we passed two farm labourers sitting on the narrow grass verge eating their midday sandwiches. To them it must have seemed as if an Inter-city express train had appeared from nowhere. On our return run they seemed to have been stunned in position, their sandwiches the same distance from their mouths as when we first passed. We could imagine them being gently carried away locked in that pose.

It was obvious that turbochargers would change the rules of the game, but we were in a quandary about how best to exploit this transformed engine. A nice problem to have, some might say, but the Company was focused on survival through Rolls-Royce, and such brute power wasn't that marque's forte. Of course, the flat-lining Bentley could be given this massive boost, but would it be wise to let it challenge Rolls-Royce? How would Marketing price it, and what about Engineering's resources?

In my naïve enthusiasm, following the demonstration run there seemed little question as far as I was concerned, and I did a rendering, showing DY with a Bentley radiator shell and 'Turbo' graphics. However, any challenge to the premier marque by one showing so little sign of life would have to wait, although my use of the slang 'Turbo' instead of turbocharger seemed to stick in people's minds, and was used shortly after the launch of the Mulsanne.

The Camargue in retrospect

Commercially, DY may have been quite successful, with its new set of designer label clothes on a proven body, and it was capable of carrying premium pricing and attaining product rarity status. It introduced an extremely

sophisticated air-conditioning system – arguably one of the last times that R-RMC was technically ahead of the rest of the world – and, for the first time, alloy wheels were considered at Crewe.

From a design point of view I began to appreciate the scale factor of large cars: a style that works on a medium-sized vehicle cannot be pumped up to suit a larger package. Drawings and scale models were often submitted that simply could not be scaled up to seventeen feet (5.2 metre) long cars. DY's slightly gauche appearance helped the in-house team, demonstrating that however good styling consultants are, if left largely to their own devices, recognizable and usual DNA can be lost. From this point on, Crewe's stylists were closely involved in any project that reached production.

Regardless of personal views concerning DY, on several levels the model aided my career at Crewe, for which I am grateful, and also helped stimulate emerging debate about what constituted a Rolls-Royce and what a Bentley.

At the time of the DY's launch much discussion focused on car safety; Ralph Nader started this particular ball rolling with his book, Unsafe at Any Speed. *During the American launch a journalist asked how safe Rolls-Royce motor cars were, and was the Company making progress in the way that the Japanese appeared to be? The eloquent response was that Rolls-Royce liked to think that, in a Camargue, it was possible to drive through a Toyota without spilling your drink!*

Rumours of some manufacturers using cadavers as crash test dummies circulated at this time. When R-RMC was queried on this, the journalist was assured that, if ever this was the case, the cadavers would, of course, be titled! Ex-BBC man Reg Abbiss reminded me of this quip. Reg was 'Mr Rolls-Royce' in America, and a rare example of someone who spent a lifetime in media and PR while still retaining his sanity – although he did choose to live in New York.

THE STYLING PROCESS
TRY, TRY, TRY AGAIN

Five steps to aesthetic heaven

Considering the importance of how cars look, the alchemy of transforming base metals into objects of delight is not generally understood, but over a period of 90 years the industry has developed a process of five universal steps to styling cars.

The brief – the package – two dimensions – three dimensions – the replica

What caused the development of this process, starting in the 1920s, was economic pragmatism. Tooling for large, pressed-metal panels is a colossal financial commitment, and requires faith that what is produced will be successful. Techniques and methods change but not the above five stages – established by Americans, not surprisingly – which are used in any product design.

Companies with strong roots in coachbuilding, such as Rolls-Royce and Bentley, were late adopting the American structured styling system. Coachbuilders used a separate chassis, and, as the body didn't need to be load-bearing, shaping the metal by panel beating obviated any need for press tools (the wonderfully anachronistic Morgan Sports Cars employed such traditional methods). As soon as pressed-steel monocoques combined chassis and body, the superstructure could no longer be a bolt-on 'addition.' The way to get strength into thin sheet metal panels is by having lots of shape, which must be decided on aesthetics, amongst other considerations; hence styling. Of course, this line of reasoning doesn't explain the shapely, 1930s,

chassis-based bodies by manufacturers such as Bugatti, or even most fibreglass cars. But the former used unique shapes as a sales feature, and the latter tended to echo mass-produced fashion.

Styling process – the five phases
1 THE BRIEF

Different organizations may call this phase by a different name, but it's simply the reference source for anyone involved in a project. The document is specific in technical specification and marketing expectations, including brand identity.

The brief must eradicate one of life's great perils: assumptions. If you find yourself saying 'I assumed,' you're probably in some kind of trouble. A design brief is similar to a legal document, but one that everyone can understand, and much within it appears common sense. Unfortunately, not everyone recognises this and so framework rules and guidelines are written down. Some areas are difficult to predict, especially future legislation: a pending proposal for pedestrian airbags, say.

The R-RMC Board of Directors earnt their money when it came to briefs for proposed vehicles, and the Silver Spirit SZ family – when being designed in the 1970s – met with a number of conundrums. Existing federal 5mph impact, no-damage bumper requirements might be upped to 50mph collisions you could walk away from! Run-flat tyres were dialed-in at birth (but ultimately abandoned). Digital instruments were championed by the chief engineer, as was the desire to cease using lead loading on bodyshell joints. On top of all that SZ had to look bigger than SY Silver Shadow but use less fuel. SZ's elusive 'brief' eventually gelled as there was only enough money, essentially, to re-skin SY in any case.

By modern standards R-RMC only began employing a sort of formal brief for the small four-door SX project in the 1980s, the Bentley Continental R, perhaps, the last Crewe car not having a comprehensive brief initially. The beauty of the 'five steps to heaven' process is that ongoing activity tests the brief and modifies it, or, if necessary, cuts short a project before any real financial damage is done.

A side effect of corporate globalization and conglomerates is that styling has to be conversant with a product's position in the marketing mix. A company with many brands and variants will try to base as many styles as possible on the same platform (underbody), making styling for product identity more critical than ever. So many briefs are based on the same underpinnings it seems that shape-shifting is becoming the norm.

2 THE PACKAGE

The package is based on elevations of the vehicle showing all of the internal hard points such as mechanicals, occupants and luggage: anything that styling has to accommodate. Wheel movements are critical, as are ramp angles, the latter dictating how low front and rear aprons can be before they foul speed bumps or kerbs. Legal requirements such as fields of view, lighting, etc, are inherent parameters, dictating vehicle proportions before a stylist so much as sharpens his pencil or grasps his mouse. BMW believes there is only about 20mm (three-quarters of an inch) of space around the hard points with which to shape any car, which is not quite as bad as it sounds because human faces have considerably less flesh than this.

With different styles using the same platform, the interface between existing and new has to be millimetre perfect, which can leave one weeping with frustration in the face of implacable purse strings holders. R-RMC established a successful luxury car package in the late 1950s for SY, although developed and refined since its 1965 launch, it dictated certain engineering hard points which affected Styling into the new millenium.

3 TWO DIMENSIONS

This is where the fun begins. The usual process is to muster as much input as possible from Company studios and often anonymous consultancies, creating a brainstorming session based on the brief and the package. Creativity can be sparked by storyboards of lifestyle, fashion trends, competitors' offerings, and so on. This technique wasn't pursued at Crewe until the rebirth of Bentley in the 1980s when differentiation from Rolls-Royce became important.

Car rendering is increasingly done on computers using sophisticated software, but initial thoughts tend to be sketched quickly on layout pads in pencil or Biro. A team of stylists will cover the spectrum from bland to mind-blowing, creating a cloud of ideas with, hopefully, some kind of nucleus. Tom Karen of Ogle Design said that young designers fall in love with what comes off the end of their pencils, so it is useful to get a group critique of the 'wallpaper,' with a project leader to establish and guide a theme.

Many would say that the most important view of a car is the front or front three-quarters, followed by the side and then rear view. True to a point, I don't believe this holds good for medium-sized cars, and definitely not for large cars, the side section or the shape through the doors of which is of paramount importance. The 1991 Mercedes S Class W140 had a featureless side section, lacking any positive sculptural statement, a result of which was that this car went straight from production line to taxi rank. Rolls-Royce and Bentley product majored on strongly-shaped features and surfaces on the sides of their vehicles, which the two dimensional phase took care of.

Size is fundamental in this respect. Smaller vehicles cannot afford much side section due to the fact that sculptured surfaces consume space, the most efficient package being a box. Large cars have the volume to employ more shape. Styling management choose promising ideas from the mass of sketches provided. A style can be sub-divided into front, side and rear; areas can be chosen, such as headlamps from one sketch, and tail lamps from another, for inclusion in the project, but a cohesive theme linking the three views is the aim. At this stage, exaggeration and 'cartoon cars' are permitted, but experienced stylists are surprisingly accurate and realistic: they have learnt there's no point promising what can't be delivered. Conversely, whilst fools may rush in where angels fear to tread, they do occasionally come up with good ideas!

Another factor to consider is the brief's scope: will this be a model year face-lift or all-new show stopper? The former probably requires re-styled bumper/aprons and wheels; the latter, divine inspiration. A big influence will be current trends. As cars tend to be built pretty much the same way, how other manufacturers resolve issues is important information. Of particular interest in this respect are the base of the windscreen A-post and the base of the rear-quarter panel. A history of post-war saloon car styling could be written about these two areas as they dictate overall shape so much, and, again, the larger the car the more scrutiny such areas attract.

Elements of preliminary sketches are re-worked and upgraded to coloured renderings. Computers are increasingly used for artwork as images can be quickly changed, re-coloured, re-skinned, etc. 'Designed by computer' still remains a misnomer as binary codes haven't yet replaced brain cells – well, not creative ones, anyway. Oh, okay, they can beat me at chess.

Once management feel that a theme shows promise, full-size tape drawings or renderings can be developed. Computer-generated projections are also used, and, indeed, any tactic to evaluate and progress aesthetics. These methods allow packaging checks and section measurements for the next stage.

4 THREE DIMENSIONS

This phase offers several options. Many projects begin with quarter-scale or fifth-scale models, and some go to third-scale, but at Bentley World the model is no toy. Something that every young stylist has to learn very quickly is that not everything he can draw can be made, so a model is the acid test, and the surfaces of a style must be seen to work. Stylists can experiment on a clay model to check and develop shapes, often with the help of a modeller. Another big plus is that creating several scale models provides a 'car-park' of comparisons.

Some managers don't like scale models and go straight to full size, because they have been victims of the dreaded 'scale factor': what looks good as a model is rarely completely right enlarged to full-size, and very well known names in consultancies have been caught out in this respect. If you are used to small or medium-sized cars, suddenly having to convert to Rolls-Royce or Bentley scale can fool even experienced people. Typically, a scale model windscreen transferred to full size can be totally out of proportion – an accurate model of a production car often appears too narrow: it's all very tricky. We did successfully copy mill (contour) two in-house, quarter-scale models to full size in the 1990s for an urgent board viewing. By then I almost knew what I was doing, and we only smoothed off the milling cutter's machine marks. This was living dangerously, and the indentation on my temple from the MD's gun muzzle remained for a long time ...

Whether by measuring preliminary drawings or scaling up a model, a full-size mock-up is made. Industry norm is to use synthetic clay originated by the Americans (the Italians had a long tradition of using plaster or plastic wood; their skill in using these materials was exceptional, though clay really is better). Crewe used plastic wood – Epowood – on SZ because Pininfarina used it on Camargue. The deciding factor was lack of a precedent for clay at Crewe and union issues regarding bringing clay modellers on-site.

A humbling fact for stylists is that the classic 1950s cars from Rolls-Royce, Bentley, Jaguar, et al, were shaped in wood. Talk about getting it right first time: any re-working of surfaces or tweaking must have meant that blood was spilled. 1950s stylists used fastidiously accurate scale models and their unique draughting/lofting skills to achieve this. Bill Allen was a master at drawing scale or full-size body sections and 'stacking' them together to achieve smooth transitions, which is how computer-generated surfaces are constructed. With Bill, though, the art of the coachbuilder was responsible.

Clay modelling is in a class of its own and modellers are a breed apart: highly-skilled sculptors are employed by companies or are nomads plying their trade around the world. You can spot them as they often work the clay with one hand while the other holds a mobile phone, on which they arrange the next contract. They get to see all the secret stuff but know if they breathe a word their career is finished. The clay looks like milk chocolate so never accept a piece of Cadbury's from a modeller! These are unique, secret bands of people who have shaped all the cars on the road.

The smoothed clay is dressed in a painted film called Dynoc, and all the details – lights, brightwork, and so on – mocked-up. Silver paint is the usual body colour as it highlights shapes best. Outside viewing in natural light is highly desirable; also having comparison cars, and viewing from a distance. Security is a huge problem and some consultancies cannot offer such viewings, so we eventually managed to create a secure compound at Crewe adjacent to the factory for such occasions.

5 THE REPLICA

Once the full-size clay is approved, a fibreglass replica is made – an illusion of a real car. Top management must not be distracted by any obvious fakery, and it should not be necessary to have to use the imagination to appreciate the proposal.

All details are constructed from metal or plastic, and

The 1980s Turbo R was the first time Rolls-Royce or Bentley used clay-modelled interior elements, which allowed sophisticated surfaces, and the resolution of increasingly complex legislation. Additionally, leather workers and trim engineers could directly input their requirements. Although this work was done on-site, due to intractable industrial relations issues, clay modellers were not fully accepted at the factory until the 1990s.

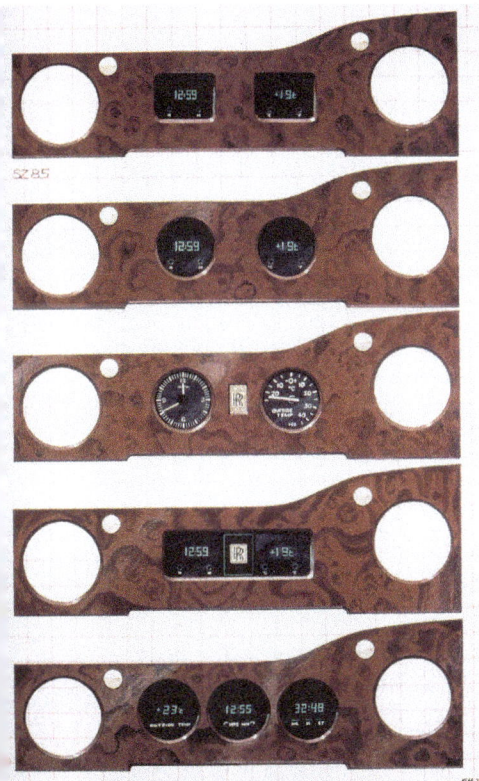

Various ideas proposed for the mid-1985 Silver Spirit facia. Digital v analogue was an issue. Styling's favourite is usually the middle option.

Bentley Continental R styling mock-up. The through rear console was a customer option.

Legislation affected all styling decisions from the late 1960s. Head and knee impact areas were critical. Whilst Martin Bourne would, undoubtedly have preferred to be flying his aircraft, he was also good at cars!

the windows are Perspex. In its final stages, the replica is fitted with an interior.

It is possible to fit electric motors for drive-by viewings, which can also be created on a computer. In the late 1990s we designed a new Rolls-Royce that only existed electronically, though it was possible to watch it 'drive' through a city. A brilliant facility, though not intended to replace the replica: even a hologram can't do that.

Interior styling

A major feature thus far omitted is interior styling, a specialized discipline that follows the same five steps as exterior styling. The big difference is that although exteriors require a few good ideas, the interior needs a whole lot more. A good car interior creates a cocoon of peace and tranquillity in a hectic, noisy world: a haven that is created, like the exterior, amidst a confusion of legislation, ergonomics and conflicting technical requirements.

The facia area alone has been described as the most expensive real estate in the world, and simply to locate all of the functions into the space available is a technical tour de force. To achieve an aesthetically pleasing and unique interior poses a significant challenge which should never be underestimated.

Measures and checks

Keeping a project on course throughout the styling process is the formal review mechanism, when the fruits of all this labour are periodically wheeled out in front of the Company's command structure for judging and guidance.

Regardless of product plan timing, realistically, the launch date countdown doesn't really start until a project gets styling 'sign-off.'

The styling process – Crewe

Although the five steps described previously form the backdrop to Rolls-Royce and Bentley styling, the Crewe operation was, perhaps, the last significant car manufacturer to fully commit to the styling resources that others took for granted. During the latter half of the 1980s and through the 1990s, the site was transformed from industrial heritage to state-of-the-art. New regulations – including those concerning factory and car emissions – German/Japanese production excellence, and team-building initiatives, etc, forced Crewe to stop resting on its laurels. It is a credit to the directors concerned that, although not always understanding this specialized discipline, they nonetheless protected a core resource, despite constant financial pressure. Indeed, although VW dramatically increased Styling's head count and brought in a director to head the department, the new studio facilities were already in use.

Chief Stylist

It's difficult to generalize about the ideal candidate for the position of chief stylist, but regardless of personality and talent a battle-hardened veteran is what's required, who will know what is aesthetically effective but also be practical and pragmatic. It's not advisable to show the board boring stuff, but the fallout from offering exciting proposals that aren't feasible or commercially viable is equally unwelcome.

What's in a name?

We cannot leave the subject of the styling process without asking why, after almost a century, a discipline that is so fundamental to car production hasn't got a proper name. Everyone knows what styling means – hairdressing, right? – and everyone knows that designers are concerned with frocks and catwalks: see the problem? Studying Industrial Design at the Central School of Art and Design it was very simple: you were a Graphic Designer or Textile Designer, both branches of 'art.' The American car world popularized the term 'stylist,' which posh institutions such as the RCA couldn't stomach, which is why I studied 'Automotive Design' there.

Hair-splitting? Quite possibly, but pertinent to R-RMC's attitude to car design. The large Engineering Department consisted of production engineers, development engineers, electrical engineering or design (draughtsman). In 1971 it was impossible for the Styling Department to use the title 'designer' as it just upset everyone. (Particularly true of development engineers: red meat-eaters to a man.) While they accepted that stylists existed, unfrocked engineers were what they were to them: tellingly, Fritz Feller, in charge of Styling, was an engine designer.

If at first you don't succeed

Finally, we must mention the 'three Ts': try, try, try again. Wolfgang Reitzle, a former top man at BMW, once told us that all he knew about styling was that you kept on trying, and manufacturers wouldn't have large styling budgets if it was easy. The process can go through countless loops and cycles, and take many months. The stakes couldn't be higher – very survival may depend on it – so the necessary commitment is a small price to pay.

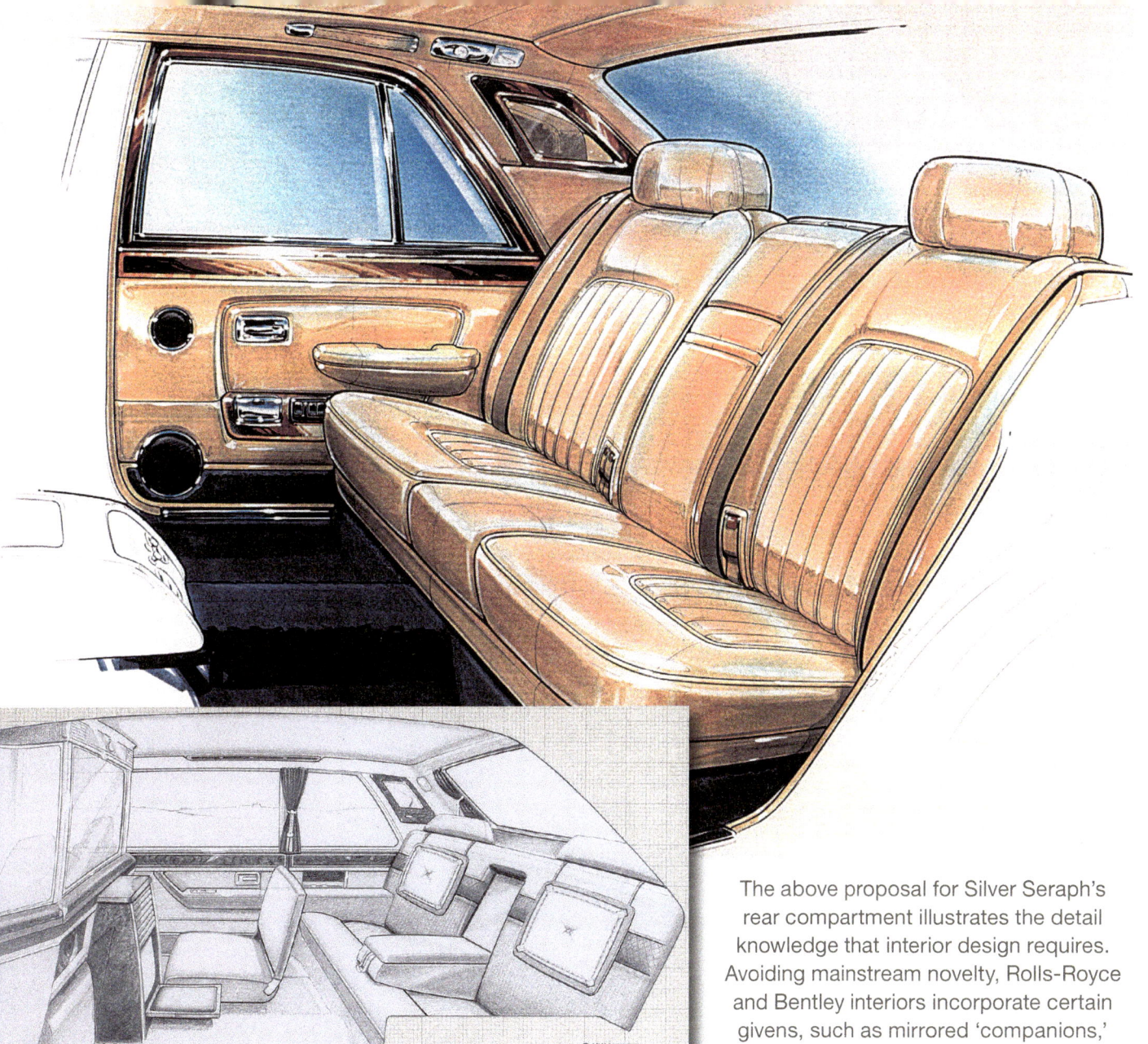

The above proposal for Silver Seraph's rear compartment illustrates the detail knowledge that interior design requires. Avoiding mainstream novelty, Rolls-Royce and Bentley interiors incorporate certain givens, such as mirrored 'companions,' 'Duchess straps,' and chromed 'jewellery.' Hide trimming and woodwork required ongoing dialogue with those possessing production craft skills.

Limousines offer endless permutations for bespoke interiors. When separated from the driver's compartment by a division, rear occupants can feel as if they are travelling on an aircraft or in a train, with ambiance ranging from the genteel Edwardian era to a state-of-the-art electronic office.

Apple Computers founder and design doyen Steve Jobs cared more about getting the product right than the bottom line. Regarding himself as an artist, he encouraged his team to do likewise, apparently telling them that the product should be so desirable you want to lick it. Whilst this is a little extreme, I do admit to somewhat unnatural feelings for Morgan three-wheelers ...

31

SZ
REPLACING A SHADOW

In 1971 the Rolls-Royce Styling Department contained two veterans from the golden age of Silver Cloud, Silver Shadow (SY) and Corniche in the shape of Bill Allen and Martin Bourne. Following John Blatchley's resignation in 1969, Fritz Feller – a very clever, possibly brilliant, engine designer who dabbled in paints and appreciated classical music – was put in charge of the department. Norman Webster, a very experienced design draughtsman, was netted by Fritz as a feasibility engineer, Ron Maddocks was also scooped up due to his model engineering reputation, and yours truly joined this small team. Well qualified on paper, I possessed zero experience of large luxury motor vehicles or, indeed, life in general.

The Board of Directors primarily tasked Fritz to come up with a style to replace the very successful, but somewhat aging SY, and even by that day's standards, ours was a very small team for such a daunting task. The Company had Bert Jeal's and George King's Body and Design offices, but was awaiting Styling's proposal before these departments could get their teeth into the job.

Since the watershed vehicles of the 1950s and 1960s, car design was undergoing dramatic and fundamental changes, and whilst mass producers were accommodating these changes model by model, R-RMC was going to have to swallow everything in one go. Regulation changes continued, affecting every aspect of car manufacture, and Graham Starling and Malcolm Smith at Crewe had to try and predict what the future might hold from a legal perspective. Even disregarding huge social change,

increasingly sophisticated marketing requirements and vehicle dynamics (including aerodynamics), regulations continuously change the car world.

Fritz used the department's veterans for the day-to-day demands of current production cars. For instance, in order to satisfy federal legislation, US vehicles required bumpers that would absorb a 5mph impact without damage (this was the law responsible for spoiling the appearance of MGBs and MG Midgets). Customers also requested certain features; changes to in-car entertainment equipment, etc: one of my first jobs was to design a knee-rest pad for Alex Moulton's SY door trim panel (picture a nicely-trimmed blackboard duster).

Although my arrival at Rolls-Royce barely registered on the Richter scale, new car ideas had to come from somewhere. Sir Henry and the Honourable Rolls were looking to Fritz Feller, Ron Maddocks and myself to conjure up the next manifestation of their noble creed. And no doubt W O Bentley was paying attention, too. Unnervingly, I discovered that a predecessor, Chris Johnston, had wrestled with this unique challenge for a while before leaving to take up teaching.

My original training as an Industrial Designer underlined the need for a design brief agreed between client and supplier. Fritz cheerfully disregarded my suggestion, however, dismissing it as legal mumbo jumbo: he wanted a long-haired, inspirational approach. However, a brief, of sorts, did exist in the form of gradually disclosed Company assumptions.

SZ – game rules, as understood by Styling
- A new, 4-door Rolls-Royce saloon worthy of the marque
- SY underbody and mechanics
- Standard wheelbase (SWB) and long wheelbase (LWB)
- Style to be suitable for all markets, both visually and legally
- Designed to accommodate Denovo run-flat tyres
- Eliminate lead loading between body panels, etc
- Use of curved side glass
- Greater boot capacity than SY
- Greater presence than SY and Corniche

This last requirement was significant as current product in the USA didn't have the visual impact to dominate house and hotel drives and forecourts. After the UK the States was hugely important for sales.

In theory it was easier to re-skin SY if the assumption was that SZ should appear larger. The main challenge in maintaining the SY package was how to modernize that vehicle's dated perpendicular style. All proposals for a new shape had to accommodate 'hard-points' –
- Front and rear headroom
- Bonnet height over engine
- Base of windscreen (scuttle) – air-conditioning and wiper spindles
- Wheel positions – including new Denovo run-flat tyre envelopes
- Fuel filler position – height dictated by legislation
- Energy-absorbing bumper envelopes

Establishing SZ's styling theme
All the stylists, modellers and computers in the world are useless if you don't know in which direction you're heading, and, thankfully, the number of decision-makers at R-RMC was quite small as Product Planning or Brand Management had yet to discover the north. In practice, Fritz was answering only to Chief Executive David Plastow (DP) and Chief Engineer John Hollings (Hgs).

In the Styling Office/Studio were quarter-scale models of Silver Cloud, SY and a SZ proposal. Perhaps surprisingly, all of these models had been in the wind-tunnel. Although beautifully made, the rather conservative SZ proposal hinted, in its fullness of form, at the Mk1 Ford Consul of the fifties. It was easy for me to criticize: given the challenge could I do any better; why did my predecessor walk away?

I searched for inspiration from favourite large, modern saloon cars, though my confidence level was low. There weren't many, or indeed, any limousines in my album. The sporty Jaguar XJ6 was proving a big hit, and the 1967 NSU Ro80 had impressed stylists generally. The Jaguar was very low-slung, its cabin pressing down between a wide track and muscular rear haunches. The NSU remains difficult to pigeonhole, but was based on an aerodynamic wedge. Luckily, Ron Maddocks shared my interest in both these vehicles. Fritz, very much in tune with the human condition, knew that Rolls-Royce owners inhabited a different planet to Mr Average. David Plastow, too, possessed a deep understanding of the Company's clients, having sold so many SYs.

I had an affinity with the NSU Ro80. My maths teacher at Lascelles Secondary Modern School in Harrow had a NSU Prinz. During my transition from aircraft adulation to car worship, a small group of us were taken to the Beaulieu Motor Museum in the Prinz. Our teacher, a German-speaking car enthusiast, regularly visited the NSU factory, and explained the Wankel rotary engine premise to us, using a model the factory had given him. Crewe had bought an Ro80 because of Fritz's team's ground-breaking development of the military 'Cottage Loaf' diesel Wankel (one small chamber compressing the fuel for it to be fired in a larger one). The Company also studied large, front-wheel-drive cars, and ran an American saloon of this layout: Austin 1800s had been used at Crewe, and the Austin Princess was in common use by directors and for chauffeured airport runs.

Fritz seemed to think it reasonable to pursue some of my sketches based on a wedge shape. Although Harris Mann's wedged Princess didn't have to encompass a visually separate boot, the Ro80 did. It was assumed, needless to say, that SZ would be a three-box shape. A quarter-scale model was quickly fashioned over SY hard points. The conclusion rapidly reached was that, regardless of our enthusiasm, the wedge formula wouldn't work; not even a wedge softened by a waist line that was allowed to dip slightly as it climbed from nose to tail. The famous radiator shell could accommodate the indignity of being lowered, but the problem was the high scuttle. Visually balancing it all meant that a rising waistline at the back resulted in a vast rear. In an effort to reduce this we tried various bumper treatments (see TR7 and 1997 Jaguar XK). An additional concern was how to stretch this wedge four inches (100mm) for a long wheelbase version.

The approach tried by my predecessor and Ron Maddocks didn't encounter these problems, and so, allowing pragmatism and fear of failure to rule my heart, I suggested to Fritz that we abandon the tricky wedge and look again at this more conservative model. Even with my limited experience I knew that we could develop this styling theme and reduce its visual weight, coupled with which Ron had spent a fair amount of time on it, so his commitment was essential. Apart from anything else it was now clear that developing surfaces on a full-sized clay wasn't an option at Crewe, and that the practically extinct method of pattern makers carving the shape out of blocks of wood, or wood substitute, from sections measured off the scale model, would have to be used.

The Americans had established best styling practice, tending not to scale-up from models, but resolve shapes at full-size using modelling clay and specialized modellers. We had no choice but to go with the right-first-time, one-shot William Tell approach.

We checked that the earlier SZ model was holding SY's hard points. Whilst maintaining this model's basic side section, every effort was made to get the surfaces more taut and contoured. Using large, circular wheelarches helped to reduce body mass and emphasize the wheels (this had worked on one of my student projects – often, simple ideas are the best). One advantage of the overall style was the ease with which it could be stretched: the extra four inches in SZ Silver Spur's rear door are never obvious.

Let there be light – SZ's illumination
Styling the front and rear lamps presented both a problem and an opportunity. In the 1970s, it was assumed that car styling would continue along a linear evolution line, and the idea of classic marques overtly cherry picking elements from previous models not really considered. Some echoes from the past persisted – such as Crewe's superb structural stainless steel glass frames – but what optimists call retro and pessimists call 'turning our back on the future and facing the past with confidence' hadn't yet emerged.

Previously, Crewe cars' large, bright bezels made the most of ordinary five-and-three-quarter inch (145mm) round headlamps, which, even in the early 1970s, were 'so last year.' SZ's radical front-end solution and departure from tradition came about quite easily, thanks, in part, to Camargue (DY), whose completely overpowering radiator demonstrated that, even on a Rolls-Royce, you could have too much of a good thing. SZ's large rectangular headlamps were technically the best that money could buy, and big and bold enough to complement and help integrate the radiator shell. The adjacent, wrap-around corner lights completed the assembly, and happily did away with a previously irresolvable area of body pressing.

The rear lamps were difficult because, apart from anything else, European and federal regulations were not in sync (my first white hair made an appearance whilst I was trying to satisfy the legal demands of both markets). The final solution of a wall of lamps running across the car enabled the necessary lit areas and separations to be achieved.

The remaining fly in the ointment posed a real dilemma: how to achieve the low boot opening of SY? Large areas of rear lamp would have to move with the boot lid, so would slamming the lid break lamp filaments? We weren't sure if anyone else had found a solution to this particular problem. Happily, tests proved that all was okay, which was just as well as there was no Plan B ...

SZ boldly sported front and rear lamps radically different to anything previously seen on the marque, helping to project a contemporary and upbeat image. Having stumbled toward these lamp styles I had to learn about the grim reality of getting ideas into production. It's not great to get a styling sign-off from the MD and Board, and then not being able to deliver!

Our proposed lamps were visually and technically ahead of the curve. The lit appearance of tail lamps that I'd seen during my regular runs to London fascinated me. Most reflector bowls were round, giving the 'fried egg' effect when illuminated. If the external graphic was square the mismatch looked amateurish. Fritz Feller organized a convincing demonstration of this issue for Lucas, our supplier, which was well aware of this shortcoming, and that it meant a lot of hard work for its designers to resolve, entailing many trips to Lucas in the Midlands by me and Crewe's electrical people, such as Mark Spice. After one long session of stressing to Lucas the need for aesthetic excellence, its designer walked with me to the car park, and was genuinely outraged to discover I was driving a Citroën 2CV. Somewhat defensively I commented that one doesn't necessarily expect a signpost to proceed in the direction it's pointing.

Lucas did a brilliant job – literally – with front and rear lamps. The large headlamps, in particular, were incredibly powerful, and actually had to be de-tuned before production. Driving at night in Germany I noticed a Mercedes' hazard warning lamps flashing some way in front: I'd inadvertently left the headlamps on full beam and probably cracked his mirrors.

SZ body – a pressing issue
Car shapes, although possibly considered the result of a

1980: the dichotomy of a marque – Mulliner Park Ward's Phantom shown against its preferred background epitomised public perception of Rolls-Royce. With Bentley yet to reassert itself, some styling thought was given to an aerodyne Rolls-Royce sports saloon. Even with the extreme example of the 1976 Lagonda, could a Rolls-Royce radiator shell be dramatically reduced in size and still be credible?

stylist's whim or fancy, are, like everything, affected by rules and regulations, and also the experience of those responsible for the pressings. Stamping shapes into metal is the most expensive element of car manufacture.

Press Steel Fisher (PSF), part of British Leyland, was the supplier of Rolls-Royce bodyshells. People who press metal want lots of curvature or doming in the panels to avoid 'oil-canning,' and the bigger the panel the bigger the problem. SZ's roof, rear-quarter panel and boot lid were right on PSF's limit but it achieved the necessary result. The rear wing trailing top corner was 'impossible,' however, and PSF demanded we change it. Fritz refused. David Plastow backed Fritz and at a highly-charged, top level viewing PSF finally agreed to employ extraordinary tactics to create what was wanted – but not before its boss 'playfully' threatened to throw a punch at DP.

Worse still was how to fix the roof to the lower body. As it's not possible to press a bodyshell in one go, because it's an assembly, the usual method is to press the side of the car to the front wing, and have a visible joint somewhere along the edge of the roof. A popular solution

was to style a joint at the base of the rear quarter, as on the Citroën DS, Rover 2000 and NSU Ro80, or simply use a separate finisher, as with the Jaguar XJ6, etc. A third – to be avoided at all costs – alternative was to make the joint invisible by using lead loading, plastic fillers, mash welding or brazing: all bad news for mass production as they required highly-skilled hand working. Guess which method we wanted? Due to the relatively low number involved, PSF was able to use its best men to braze and finish the joint. It was important that a Rolls-Royce projected the image of strength and integrity – the antithesis of mass-produced vehicles – and David Plastow, Fritz Feller and John Hollings knew this.

Again, in an effort to be different, SZ's front and rear lamps weren't 'planted' on the surface but fitted into apertures, and Bert Jeal, Crewe's Chief Body Engineer, told me they would have to use mallets on the production line to get the lamps to fit! To disguise necessary clearance gaps I styled some delicate bright tracery with which to edge the lamps, but found that I was suggesting solutions

Rolls-Royce was the subject of debate, inside and outside of the Company. *Car* magazine, in 1973, queried how much longer Silver Shadows would be an investment. R-RMC leaked information pre-positioning the big styling changes (for 1980 Silver Spirit) in 1978. (Courtesy *Car* magazine)

to Fritz which, in some ways, were more problematic than the original difficulty. These jewel-like elements were desperately hard to engineer, although their effect was unique and special, subtly conveying quality. Fritz loved that sort of thing, but I found it hard to look those charged with making them in the eye.

I continually tried to anticipate the implications of styling proposals for the engineering and production departments, although Fritz had no such qualms: simply put, we had to make its appearance worthy of a Rolls-Royce, and it was up to the rest of the workforce to find a way to achieve this objective. The old adage goes 'Form Follows Function,' but the clever bit is understanding what the product's function really is. Fritz did.

SZ – the bumper system

Due to the American habit of parking by touch, the SZ's bumpers – like those of the SY – had to be able to absorb 5mph impacts without damage, but a 5040lb (2286g) car takes a bit of stopping, even at low speed. This requirement hugely affected styling in these areas; apart from insanely complicated dampers, sliding linkages, and so on, black rubber impact areas were de rigueur. Engineering built an evil-looking, mediaeval siege engine-type testing rig, which swung a mighty pendulum at various angles at an unsuspecting SZ. On impact there was a horrible dull 'crump,' a cloud of dust, and the car jerked away with all the indignation of a goosed Great Aunt. Needless to say, anything over 5mph meant the repair bill would be significant. Considering the engineerng constraints, bumper style camouflaged their distasteful work well.

Subsequent impact criteria almost eliminated visual bumpers.

SZ's boot – how many golf club bags?!

There can never be enough boot space in a luxury saloon,

as testified by previous vehicles receiving criticism for not being able to carry enough luggage for five people. The Peninsula Hotel, Hong Kong, used fleets of Rolls-Royces as taxis to go to and from the airport, but luggage tended to follow in a lesser vehicle as wealthy people don't usually travel lightly.

Golf club bags have always been the elephant in the boot corner: big and awkward, and often travelling in groups. Chief Engineer John Hollings also had a thing about accommodating school trunks, obviously reflecting his public school background. Having lived near Harrow School, I knew that trunks usually arrived in the back of battered old Austin Maxis and the like (4x4s, subsequently); Crewe product was reserved for speech days. Ironically, 26 years later, the boot was on the other foot when explaining Bentley luggage parameters to VW's Dr Piech. He favoured the swoopy tail of the 1950s R-Type Continental, and when I mentioned that our boot space took into account the hard corners of several large Samsonite cases, his response was to favour me with the famous Dr Piech 'look.'

SZ jewellery – John Hollings' 'entrinklements'
Ron Maddocks made a superb, jewel-like, polished exterior door handle to my sketch. John Hollings tried it with his shovel-like hand and demanded we increase knuckle clearance considerably. I made a mental note that although there were some fine people out there buying these cars, to always assume they had all the dexterity of an arthritic Orang-utan. As a microcosm of Rolls-Royce design, this handle is a good example. It had to have a base, or slipper, to prevent nails and rings scratching the paint, and mustn't break fingernails: a doorman must be able to quickly master it, and it should provide sufficient grip to control a big door on a windy day. That handle was in production for 30 years and counting.

SZ – in the flesh
Portraying what we wanted in a full-size block of Epowood was not easy. This two-part 'plastic wood' could be worked by the skilled Experimental Woodshop people with chisels and gouges, but any modification required applying a pancake patch ... I'm going to stop describing it now as the smell and frustration has flooded back. Suffice to say, without Ron Maddocks negotiating with body draughtsmen and shop workers we couldn't have done it. Ron used every trick in the book, including creating a device that would reinflate the forever-leaking hydrolastic suspension on Leyland cars. This saved a fortune at the

1977. A radical, stainless steel superstructure, with glass roof and alloy wheels (the concept became the original Bentley Mulsanne scale model).

garage, and once he had this hold over anyone wanting to borrow the device, they were much more helpful.

Running prototypes were made from early styling lines. John Fox, Manager of the Experimental Garage, arranged a drive-by on a quiet country lane. The vehicle was approaching us at high speed when suddenly the bonnet flew open. Being forward hinged, luckily, aerodynamic forces stabilized the bonnet just below the top of the windscreen. Our little group stood open-mouthed as the car shot past, the driver standing up, head cranked and pressed into the headlining in a desperate effort to see the road.

SZ – interior
Given the radical departure from SY of SZ's exterior, it was assumed that the interior would be very much the same: a reasonable expectation that didn't take into account certain developments. Martin Bourne, in particular, had to work hard to seamlessly accommodate SZ's greater internal width, which affected many SY elements. Seats were re-contoured, and a nod to modernity was a digital display on the facia centre (if John Hollings had had his way the entire facia would have been digital). Fritz's opinion of this latter possibility was a cartoon of Big Ben with digital clock face.

During its lifetime this interior was continuously re-worked, especially for Rolls-Royce/Bentley differentiation, but it evolved gradually because, basically, earlier iterations of both marques were what customers liked.

SZ – gently Bentley

A later result of the styling programme was the creation of a Bentley version of SZ: almost an act of charity on the Company's part after Bentley had been practically ignored in the 1970s.

Ron Maddocks grafted a very convincing clay radiator shell on to Styling's SZ mock-up. This necessitated a different, more curved, front bumper to protect the peaked shape of the Bentley shell. Although SY had a specially-shaped bonnet to match the rounded corners at the back of the Bentley 'header tank,' the funds were not available to do this for SZ. The radiator shell was styled to look right from the front with a slight mismatch at the back:

The Rolls-Royce and Bentley factory became adept at broadening the SZ product range:

Main: Turbo R. By 1993 even four-wheel-drive was under consideration.
Left, top: 1980s Silver Spirit.
Left, bottom: The 1991 MPW Silver Spur II Touring Limousine.

a compromise that latter came home to roost when MD Peter Ward pointed out the mistake to me.

SZ glides to centre stage

At Nice in 1980 the SZ Rolls-Royce Silver Spirit, Silver Spur and Bentley Mulsanne were launched to the world's press. The Mulsanne name had been in David Plastow's locker since my styling proposal of 1977, and Fritz told us on his return from the apparently successful launch that the Bentley had received a lot of attention.

The three variants then went on display to the public at the Geneva Motor Show, where, lurking amongst the crowds, I got the impression that we hadn't disgraced these legendary marques. Reaction from fellow stylists is always interesting, as they are among the few who really understand this particular discipline. Bruno Sachs, Chief Stylist of Mercedes, had a deep conversation with Fritz. Sergio Pininfarina said to us, "Well, it's not what I would have done but it is a Rolls-Royce." On the forecourt of a Cheshire country inn, Giorgetto Giugiaro stared, apparently fascinated by the rear lamps acreage, but said nothing. Sitting next to Peter (McLaren F1) Stevens at a 1980 Design Centre gathering, Peter said to me, "Carved out of the Solid," which was pretty astute, as SZ had been. The style was destined to be the mainstay of production for 18 years.

SZ – the later years

The SZ family received numerous styling tweaks and modifications, often linked to Bentley criteria, and stretched versions of various lengths and heights. There were big changes to the interior, including different passive restraint systems. Alan Dutton had to resolve the mad federal requirement of automatic seat belt deploy, a device worthy of Rowland Emett, that automatically travelled the seat belt from the top of the A-post and along the cantrail, to lash passive/helpless front occupants to their seats.

From my totally biased point of view the best SZs were those of the 1996 model year. We finally managed to persuade Engineering to abandon the old front door quarter-light, and create a small glass guide, or 'cheater,' which also carried a modern, integrated mirror (we had been campaigning for this since SZ's conception!). The latest federal bumper regulations permitted the previously black impact zones to be colour-keyed, which meant that completely new bumper/aprons could be used, even those which were as much as 2 inches (50mm) higher, covering more of the bodyshell. In turn, we reduced the radiator shell in height and made the Spirit of Ecstasy slightly smaller. These treatments freshened and visually lightened both Rolls-Royce and Bentley models.

Memories are made of this ...

In the history of motoring it is hard to think of any other bodyshell that carried such graphically diverse front-end treatments as did the SZ. Using different headlamps, radiator shells and bumper/aprons, the unique personas of the two marques were instantly communicated.

Like SY, SZ was easy to drive and position due to its commanding driving position and visible front wing crowns; the Rolls-Royce Spirit of Ecstasy added to this sense of location on the road. Regarding Bentley, anyone who has driven a Turbo R knows what a revelation it was. The near-brutal bottom-end torque means you can lift off the throttle before you've actually completed an overtake. I always felt a ride in a Rolls-Royce or Bentley should be available on the National Health. Our family doctor had a Turbo R; instead of giving potions and pills to anyone suffering from depression he could have taken them out for a little drive instead.

One time, we sat astride a pedestrian crossing in a busy Midlands town in an SZ that 'refused to proceed,' George Ray trying to coax the Spirit's recalcitrant experimental induction system back to the land of the living. After waiting patiently for a time a very polite school crossing 'lollipop lady' tapped on my window to enquire whether we intended to stay there much longer. Thanks for the memory ...

RE-BIRTH OF BENTLEY
LIFE IN THE FAST LANE

When the curtain finally fell on SY in 1979, barely three per cent of production had been Bentley. The 'Bentley Boys' legend of the 1920s/30s Le Mans and Brooklands era persisted only in the form of an *Eagle* annual schoolboy-type yarn – and one for home consumption only. In the most important export market, America, Bentley was barely acknowledged.

The Crewe factory had been all about Rolls-Royce: locals worked at 'Royce's,' and it was the magic of this famous marque that generated their sense of privilege and pride. Fritz Feller had been charged, along with Engineering, to create a new Rolls-Royce saloon, period. This was no easy task – more of a burden – generating nervousness and not much in the way of fun: nothing less than 'The Best Car in the World' was expected. Camargue had been done elsewhere and, although something of a sideshow, overtly majored on that imperious radiator shell.

Against this oppressive and demanding backdrop, Bentley was an irrelevance, and continued to be so up to the SZ's launch in 1980. The Engineering Department had been straining every sinew to meet the market's towering expectations of a new Rolls-Royce. With Bentley's survival hanging by a thread, Styling and Marketing managed to mask the marque's vulnerability with just a radiator shell and the name Mulsanne.

Mulsanne – what's in a name?
Fritz Feller asked me to do a futuristic rendering for David Plastow's office. Duly executed and framed, it never got past DP's secretary, however, who said the colours clashed with the curtains! Because the shape seemed worth pursuing, undaunted, Ron Maddocks and myself began making the model as a 'lunchtime special,' and it turned into a typical Maddocks tour de force. The cabin was in polished stainless steel with a glass roof panel; Ron made some wheels at home in turned aluminium. We thought it more fun to put a Bentley radiator shell on it. Although loaded with interesting jewelled detail, writing Mulsanne on the rear number plate was one of my better ideas: the famous straight at Le Mans had seemed the obvious name for a Bentley. Finished as an official project, Fritz presented it to David Plastow as a model for his desktop, and there it stayed from 1977. DP said it took his mind off all the daily problems. The name was soon registered.

The Mulsanne Turbo – it's mainly about what's under the bonnet
The turbocharged engine development, if not exactly Skunk Works status, seems to have been done off-piste. One of Fritz's ex-Wankel team, Jack Read, was the key man. A radiator shell and name ensured it was still a Bentley, but the advent of the turbocharged engine was going to boost that marque into orbit.

Integrating the radiator shell by painting it in body colour had been a rare customer request on previous Bentleys, and this was resurrected on an early rendering as the only instant external Turbo cue, apart from badges, that I could think of. It became a major distinguishing feature

continued page 44

There are few sights and sounds to equal the charismatic Cricklewood-built, four-and-a-half litre Bentleys. Transcending mere mechanical elements, these machines projected a sense of occasion and lifestyle that formed the core of the marque – whether as W O Bentley intended or supercharged. (Author collection)

The wonderful 1938 Jules Vernesque Embericos Bentley Pourtout Coupé. Comparison between this shape and the Cricklewood Bentley brings to mind that between a conventional steam locomotive and streamliners such as the Mallard. (Author collection)

GH.10

GH.10

and rapidly the norm for Bentleys. The psychological reasoning behind such visual elements is complex: okay, the Bentley was a big, expensive motor car, but did not make the same overt statement as the Rolls-Royce radiator shell. In 1982, the Mulsanne Turbo was launched and 'Crewe's missile' achieved lift-off.

Light at the end of the tunnel?

The Falklands War, IRA bombings and other issues made for difficult days for the country and the Company. In 1983, the Board had a big shake up when Mike Dunn took over as Chief Engineer, Peter Ward as Marketing Director, and John Stephenson as Director of Product Planning. A moody, Mafioso-style photo of Crewe's new order featured in *Car* magazine.

Peter Ward and John Stephenson didn't seem traditional Rolls-Royce types. Like most people they probably found the marque slightly intimidating, and were unsure how to handle its contentious social image. Peter Ward (Wrd) remarked, "Don't expect to see any more publicity photos of our cars outside Castle Howard." There was no such apprehension about Bentley, however.

Mike Dunn and John Stephenson had worked with large, world-class styling departments, and Stephen Bayley had put on a terrific exhibition of Mike's Ford Sierra in the V&A's Boilerhouse, showing what massive styling effort went into just one model from Ford's range. John Stephenson had worked under Wayne Cherry at the fabulous roof studios of Vauxhall, Luton. Consequently, Mike and John appeared understandably bemused by Crewe's tiny styling resource.

We managed to find another model-maker – Brian Hassall – following the departure of Ron Maddocks in 1982. Although Brian was ex-Experimental Woodshop, there was still no union agreement regarding staff working on full-size styling mock-ups or using professional clay modellers. Jaguar, who, like Crewe, traditionally used wood for styling mock-ups, had changed to the industry norm of using clay, employing around eight specialist clay modellers. Brian efficiently sculpted some Bentley clay seats for us, but in a tense atmosphere.

Fritz was suffering increasing periods of ill health, and, from February 6, 1984, I was formally making more styling decisions in his absence. Dick Perry had been doubling up with running Mulliner Park Ward in London, and took the helm from George Fenn, David Plastow's successor, during 1983.

Fritz retired due to failing health, and on 6 May I

officially became responsible for the Styling Department. To say this caused me some trepidation would be putting it mildly: these were far from calm waters, and the new directors were obviously going to make big changes.

The Marketing Department began to align with Engineering in terms of product direction, requesting an 'entry model,' if so humble a term can be used at such a rarefied altitude. The result was 1984's Bentley Eight: essentially a Mulsanne with a woven wire mesh grille, straight grain veneer, and other minor interior differences, which allowed a price drop that tempted new customers into the family. By offering a cloth option instead of leather, the starting price fell below £50k. The strategy worked but if there were any Eights with cloth upholstery they were rare.

Turbo R – the heavyweight boxer in a tailored suit

The famous Bentley Turbo R was a happy amalgamation of Marketing, Styling and Engineering. The Mulsanne Turbo needed a suspension upgrade to help it go around bends, and Marketing wanted a top-of-the-line Bentley. Satisfying these requirements began to separate Bentley from Rolls-Royce. A soft ride had always been a Company prerogative; the R for roadholding now heralded a change with a soft ride taking second place to firm and sporting. The Turbo R was also the first Crewe product to use alloy wheels: hitherto, reservations existed about metallurgy, corrosion and damage, but the industry had vastly improved these concerns. Strangely enough, a clincher for the engineers was that alloy wheels are truly round, whereas steel ones aren't, and so alloy wheels were soon adopted by both marques.

The Turbo R sat on very wide tyres which tended to dwarf the Company's 15 inch wheels. The design I drew tried to emphasize the expanse of alloy. Martin Bourne regarded alloy wheels as boy racer nonsense, but generously described this design as "reasonably civilized." These massive wheels and tyres triggered the whole debate about spare wheels. SZ carried the spare in a cradle under the rear bumper, but the Turbo R's tended to be too visible. It wasn't unknown for the police to stop cars, believing that the wheel was about to fall out. Eventually, we styled a rear apron with a flap in it.

Aerodynamic work on the front air dam improved stability and drag. There was some upgrading of the interior with extra instruments, new driver's console, and a leather-trimmed, padded steering wheel. This sort

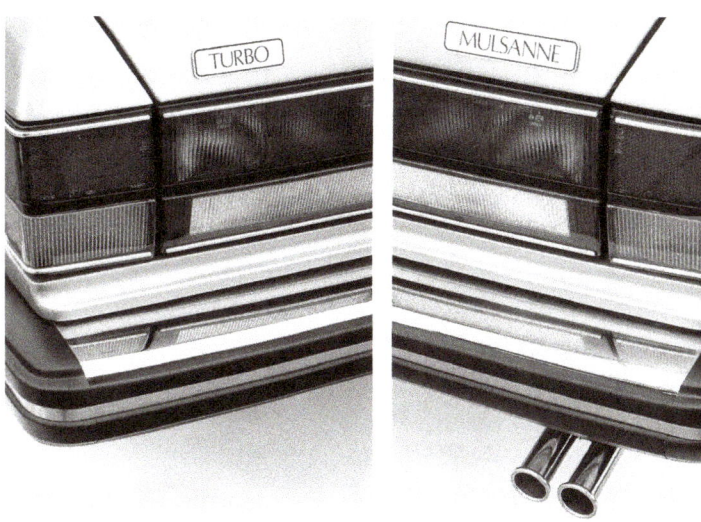

Extreme British understatement: 1982 black and white press pack photos for the Mulsanne Turbo launch. Turbo badges, twin tailpipes, and the leather-covered steering wheel gave the nod to those in the know.

BENTLEY M5 COUPE

The face of Bentley:
Above, left: 1984. A sporty two-door was considered highly desirable. Silver Spirit-style headlamps were still state-of-the-art, as were traditional radiator shutters.

Above, right: Late 1992. Concept Java explored a radical alternative to the production Bentley's round headlamps; shutters were unchanged.

Below: Mid-1990s. Styling's face of Bentley: round headlamps and sculptured grille matrix.

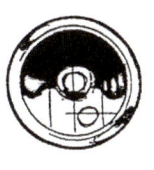

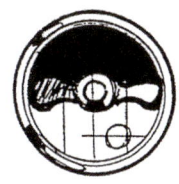

of work – which had to be implemented quickly – was ideal for the small, in-house team. Familiarity with factory processes and access to specialist experts achieved practical production solutions.

The first Turbo R, in Vermilion Red, was in Car Bond, the holding area for finished cars. Dick Perry was there to check over a Rolls-Royce, and we found ourselves looking at the Bentley. I remarked to him, "It's good news, isn't it?" in answer to which he simply smiled: everyone knew it was going to be a winner.

Turbo R 1989 – the tough gets tougher

Peter Ward took over from Dick Perry as Chief Executive in 1986. With little notice I was asked to show the Board further visual changes to Turbo R. That evening hasty ideas were scribbled on my sketch pad: it was one of the roughest drawings ever, but, sensing that subtlety was no longer the order of the day, the design was practically a cartoon, suggesting even larger, negatively cambered wheels packing out the bodywork, 'Desperate Dan' chin dam, and body-coloured sills. Perhaps the most obvious change was to replace the large, rectangular headlamps

with four round ones. When I presented this tatty piece of paper in the boardroom Peter Ward described the proposal as a "hairy-looking beast" and we were turned loose on it. It's a cliché but often the best ideas are drawn on the back of an envelope.

Due to the amount of clay development involved we worked with Peter Horbury's team at MGA Coventry. Peter had been at Volvo and later returned there before going to Ford in America, eventually returning to Volvo. He had a great sense of humour, and his account of being involved in an armed robbery at a Dutch filling station is a classic.

It had been assumed that the round headlamps fitted to SY and Corniche would be used, but on the mock-up they didn't quite work. One morning I walked into MGA's studio with four 7-inch cardboard discs I'd cut out that could just be squeezed into the apertures. It was a rare eureka moment when my black belt in flower arranging really paid off. The headlamps were immediately incorporated into concurrent Continental R work.

The big headlamps and extra body colour below the bumper line freshened the car, and appeared to lower it. SZ's front end was transformed and, watching the reaction

Late 1990 saw separate SXB Rolls-Royce and Bentley saloon body styles being viewed when Styling was asked to quickly generate a back-to-back presentation of the two proposals. The only possible way to achieve this was to make very accurate quarter-scale models and machine them to full size. The Bentley proposal is seen alongside a Continental R.

The clay is having its machining cusps removed; the Rolls-Royce version is being prepared in the background. Replacing the Silver Spirit family with two new bodyshells would have had profound financial implications.

of younger potential customers at motor shows, seemed to have a Thomas the Tank Engine-like appeal. Usually seen storming up the outside lane of motorways, it was Bentley's bold and inspiring new face which persists to this day.

Turbo R became the car to be seen in. When the famous boxing promoter Frank Warren was shot getting out of one, the resultant publicity did sales no harm at all. There was a slightly dangerous romantic air about the vehicle: getting carried away one day I told a London dealer that early development cars regularly returned from testing on the Continent with 2CV debris stuck in the grille ...

These vehicles didn't need any hype. Flying down to International Automotive Design (IAD) at Worthing with Peter Ward and Mike Dunn to see how the Continental R was getting on, we ran into trouble. One rev counter in the twin engine helicopter suddenly began fluctuating wildly. Returning to Tatton Park, there was no choice but to use Peter's Turbo R to transport us quickly to the south

coast. Wanting me to arrive fresh and relaxed (and if you believe that ...) Peter and Mike shared the driving, and the long, fast journey was an awesome demonstration of what the Company had achieved with this big bruiser of a car. I've never driven anything else that felt remotely like it. Tom Purves enjoyed the Turbo R and called it an Edwardian sports car. At that time it really was the 'Best Car in the World.'

Styling work on interior differentiation between the marques continued apace, with Rolls-Royce and Bentley sharing DNA that was presented quite differently. Bentley was more of a cockpit car with a large, floor-mounted console featuring the gear change. The featherlight Rolls-Royce column gear control was a delight to use, but not exactly macho. By the 1990s, opportunities for bespoke interiors had increased dramatically, and Styling's Simon Loasby, Darren Day and Robin Page were kept busy creating schemes for individual customers.

Bentley blood line 1929-1998.

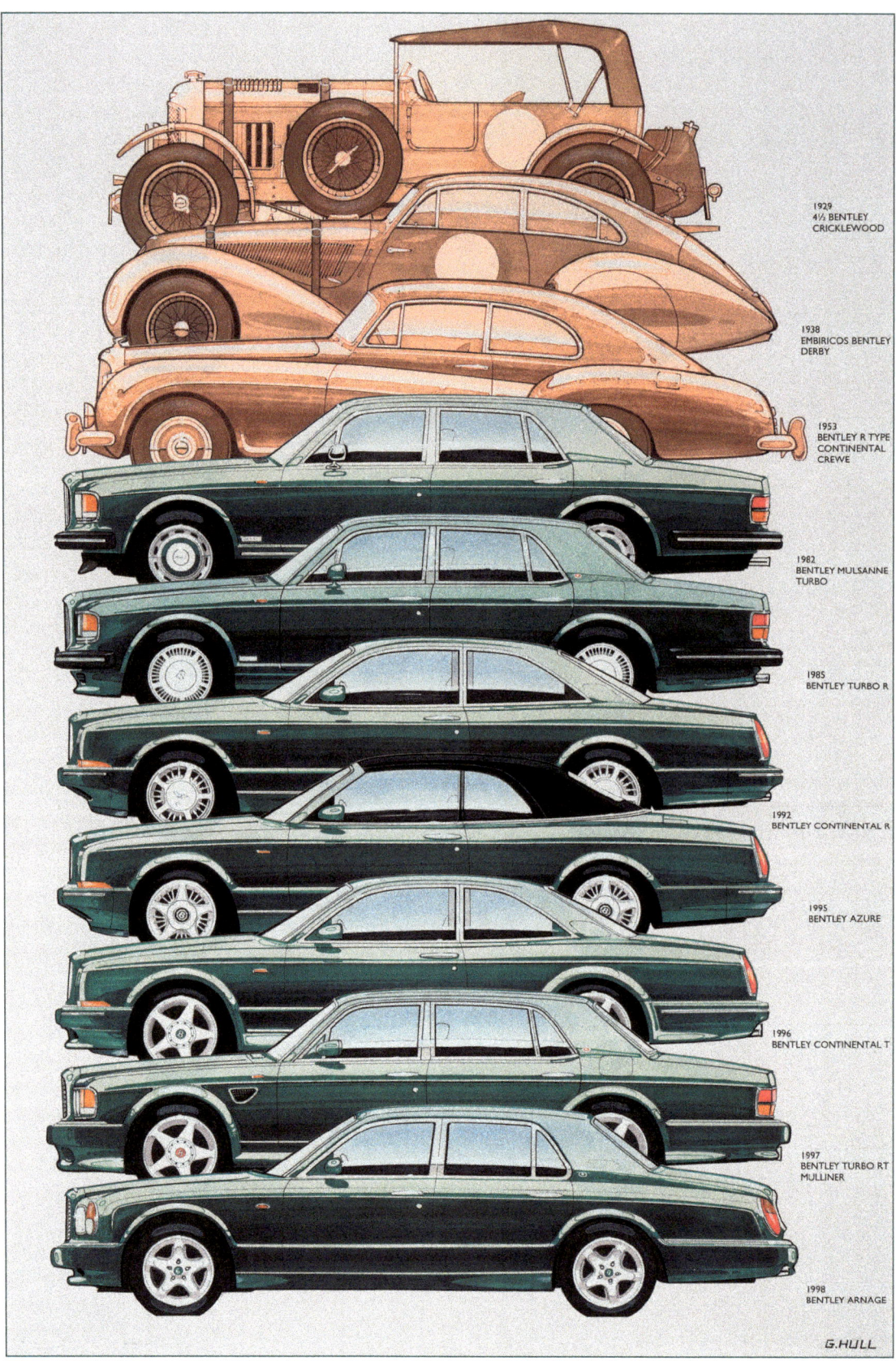

1929
4½ BENTLEY
CRICKLEWOOD

1938
EMBIRICOS BENTLEY
DERBY

1953
BENTLEY R TYPE
CONTINENTAL
CREWE

1982
BENTLEY MULSANNE
TURBO

1985
BENTLEY TURBO R

1992
BENTLEY CONTINENTAL R

1995
BENTLEY AZURE

1996
BENTLEY CONTINENTAL T

1997
BENTLEY TURBO RT
MULLINER

1998
BENTLEY ARNAGE

G.HULL

The 1989 model year iteration of the Turbo R effectively completed the re-birth of Bentley; it just remained to give that marque its own unique body style, which arrived in 1991 with the Continental R. At the end of the 1980s, sales of Crewe product reached 3333 units, a pinnacle for some years either side of that date. Just over half were Bentleys: an increase of more than 47 per cent in nine years.

From the launch of SZ in 1980 the Company couldn't put a foot wrong with Bentley, and this was partly due to the fact that no one was uptight about the marque; everyone involved in decision-making felt confident and relaxed. Success breeds success – and confidence. Rolls-Royce was a much trickier proposition: imagine being on a planning committee to add a new wing to Buckingham Palace or, heaven forbid, signing off a new Windsor Castle. It was sweaty palms stuff for those at the top, though for Bentley it was simply a case of its time had come.

The Crewe factory regularly hosted Institution of Mechanical Engineers evening lectures. On one such occasion the speaker began by saying, "I'm told Rolls-Royce lectures are inaudible and go on for ever."

This certainly wasn't true of another speaker introduced in the 1980s by Mike Dunn. Dr Harvey Postlewaite was then a Ferrari F1 Chief Engineer. After a superb lecture, questions from the floor were slow in coming, so I asked him, if regulations permitted, would he use variable geometry aerodynamics while in motion? After explaining just how restrictive the rules were, Postlewaite asked me to see him afterwards if I had any ideas. It took more than twenty years for McLaren to come up with the 2010 F-Duct, which allowed the driver to modify airflow to the rear wing by moving his body; thus circumnavigating the legislators.

Visiting the TWR-based Arrows F1 team in the 1990s tended to reinforce my opinion that studying the construction of these exotic racing devices at least matches watching them in action: having said that, being in Monaco's Harbour Grandstand in 1997 watching M Schumacher dealing with the rain was a revelation.

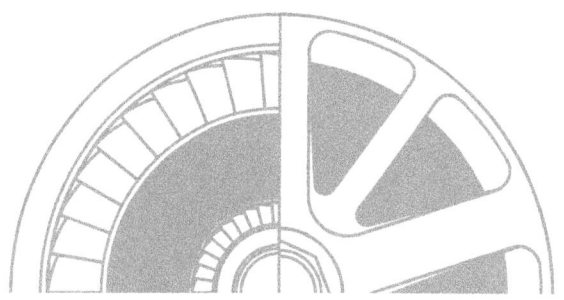

THE COLOUR COMMITTEE
ANY COLOUR AS LONG AS IT'S BLACK (OR BLUE)

One would think that if you could afford a Rolls-Royce or Bentley the choice of colour would be anything imaginable, and, to an extent this was true. The quality of the Company's paint was legendary in respect of both number of coats used and superb finish attained; the interior's leather and carpet was simply the best. Indeed, all of the materials used were subjected to tests way above the norm.

In practice, there was a fine balance between offering a bespoke service of anything the customer desired, and avoiding an impossible number of 'one-offs,' and anything of less than ideal quality. The resultant system at Crewe comprised an extensive range of well-tested paint and trim. The worldwide dealer network was given a comprehensive colour and trim kit of various swatches to ensure customers were spoilt for choice. Strangely, for apparently innocuous subjects, colour and trim were not without potential pitfalls and occasional drama, and were responsible for my grossly unfair threatened sackings.

The Committee

One of my predecessor's, Fritz Feller's, early moves was to set up a Colour Committee of interested parties, which met several times a year to deal with ongoing topics such as model year changes, technical and supply issues, etc. Typically astutely including a lady on the committee, Val Scott, from old-school Sales and Marketing, was no shrinking violet, and would ruthlessly demolish any lightweight views. Membership of the committee carried high status and meetings were very well attended, if only for the coffee and biscuits that were served. Secretary Bill Allen possessed a photographic memory for paint and leather names and their references, which I simply could not match when I eventually took over the position: a shortcoming that Fritz delighted in commenting on.

The committee had three different types of customer to satisfy –

1 THE MAINSTREAM CUSTOMER

It would be wrong to refer to average or even normal customers when talking about Rolls-Royce or Bentley because they were all unique. The comprehensive colour range was aimed at people who would take great pleasure in selecting their new motor car's specification from the Company's swatches; an experience that, importantly, wives and partners could share in.

2 INDIVIDUAL DEALER CHOICE

Dealer choice was a hard-nosed affair because if you buy for stock, you buy to sell; the Americans, in particular, sold product off the showroom floor. Customers would point to a car and say, "I want that now."

No American dealer would order anything for stock unless it was a 'safe' colour, and told me, with their love of understatement, that green was 'sale proof:' so much for British Racing Green. This, of course, hopelessly skewed the Paint Popularity Chart, so American cars had to be listed separately.

3 Unique personal choice customers

Different-at-any-price customers considered 'standard' to be anathema. Customers in this group gave rise to many R-RMC anecdotes: Arab princesses would send in the top from a perfume bottle to match paint to, and Princess Margaret, in Silver Shadow days, forwarded a green carpet from her dog's basket, complete with hairs, for reference.

Chairman of the Committee

On Fritz's retirement, I found myself Chairman and Secretary of the Colour Committee. As the colour and trim range had to be approved by the Product Policy Committee at Styling Reviews, I was also the obvious person to pull together the samples. Other styling departments had full-time teams servicing less complex ranges, but in a weird way I enjoyed it.

Initially, colour and trim was a blind spot in this engineering-based Company (engineers don't mind what colour the paint is as long as it stops things going rusty). Colour is also very personal; one director criticized a new metallic light blue because it reminded him of an old lawn mower! (presumably, he'd been forced to cut the grass as a boy and the hang-up remained). Manufacturing generally hates paint: it's a world of pain for that department, with the potential for things to go wrong.

Individuals involved

Understanding colour and trim got you very close to what made the Company much more than just a nuts and bolts factory. A great character from my earlier days was Don Simmons, who was in charge of Production Paint. Ex-Fleet Air Arm, he was a bear of a man, and perfect at understanding the gentlemen of the shop floor. He was showing me round his empire one day when he had someone literally falling down with laughter. A group of painters were pushing a Camargue bodyshell with the bonnet open. Going over a bump, the large bonnet crashed down onto the hand of one of them. There was a ghastly, shocked silence: surely the guy had lost some fingers? His mates whipped the bonnet open to discover he'd been saved by the deep drainage channel, and Don casually remarked, "Lucky it wasn't his pecker," which one of the group found so funny that he sank to his knees laughing hysterically, and keeled over. Don calmly carried on with the tour. Shortly after, Don went up to a paint sprayer working on a car and pointed out that he didn't want any runs; normally that sort of comment wasn't conducive to good relations, but the old brigade knew their men.

David Walker was responsible for the paint laboratory; he looked a little like William Haigh with a college scarf. A pleasant enough chap, but whenever I showed him a new colour he regarded me with barely concealed hostility.

New paint test panels had to spend months undergoing field trials in the Florida sun to check quality: Rolls-Royce and Bentley motor cars were expected to have the best paint finish in the world. Perfection really was the only acceptable outcome, and if this was not achieved, heads could – and did – roll.

Brian Lofkin was a stalwart of the Paint Laboratory, and a key, long-term member of the Colour Committee. We relied on his analysis of market demand for individual colours shown on his paint charts. Despite his proximity to this career-threatening discipline, he always delivered the goods. Apart from anything else he spoke fluent 'Crewe,' and managed to get Production to test-spray large panels: some clever metallics and micas had very lively flip tones that could shade a car beautifully or diabolically, leaving no choice but to have complete bodyshells painted if the colour was tricky. Occasionally, we managed to get perhaps six bodyshells painted in proposed new colours for the Product Policy Committee viewing (I'm not sure the directors appreciated the heroic effort that went into this).

You can't call it that!

Technically complex, paint was available in various forms from cellulose to acrylic to water-based two-pack, clear over base, and so on, and the Company offered solid colours, metallics, micas and pearlescents, plus others. Fortunately, paint technology was continuously improving, and with established formulations the test cycle was much reduced. But the Colour Committee always assumed a certain failure percentage, testing more colours than were required.

As well as choosing new colours the committee named them. Due to the sophistication of the product, common names wouldn't do, so light blue would have to be Seychelles, dark grey Tsunami, and so on. Marketing was usually helpful with this but I was once desperate enough to have *Voice*, the Company newspaper, run a colour-naming competition for the workforce, some of whom simply went to Halfords and suggested the names of the touch-up paints there. Other suggestions were wincingly rude, but we were able to award some nice ties and scarves, despite that.

With the launch of Turbo R we decided to offer a colour option of bright red (actually, for technical reasons, a red with a fair amount of blue in it), which we named

Vermilion, mistakenly spelt Vermillion (guess who). This went right through the system, one journalist assuming it was a play on the word 'million.' We bluffed it out for a bit then quietly changed it. Hey ho.

Despite a range of some 26 or so colours, the main business was done using surprisingly few. For instance, of 590 early 1994 model year cars in the ten most popular colours, 58 per cent of them were Royal Blue, Peacock (blue mica), Black (basecoat) or Royal Ebony. Black or dark blue were inevitably the most popular colours. Silver and shades of metallic grey did climb the popularity charts towards the new millennium.

Due to Sales and Marketing wanting to offer repeat customers a fresh palette, the Colour Committee often had to tweak a popular colour and rename it (it's amazing how many names you can think of for black and dark blue; Black Sapphire (blue) was a masterstroke). As an example of this turnover of paint colours and names, in 1996, of 26 colours, 18 were new, including Arnage Green: a name which pre-empted a car of that moniker by 18 months.

General working of the world of colour

Styling held a large number of paint samples, covering standard and non-standard ranges, and also all the leather, carpet and binding colours, and for many years our office was the only place where large samples of these colours could be seen. The clatter and clank of metal paint panels being lifted on and off the walls was a regular background noise.

Sales and Marketing became especially interested in any new offerings with which to tempt a special customer, which resulted in my occasional contact with Richard Charlesworth from that department. Visually a mixture of a Russian Embassy employee and comedian and character actor Terry Thomas, Richard was the buccaneering ingredient of Sales and Marketing. Furtively visiting the paint laboratory he would purloin rather extreme colour sample panels with which to tempt his Middle Eastern clients, stowing said panels in an inner jacket pocket, just like contraband goods. Everyone seemed to turn a blind eye to this brazen circumnavigation of the Colour Committee. Still, the colours concerned would never bother the horses of Cheshire. Richard became the Crewe PR guru and general pillar of the Company.

Our Committee recommended preferred colour and trim combinations for the dealer colour selection kits. Like paint, there was a large range of Connolly hides, all of which required suitable names. Stitching colours, carpet binding and fine lines all needed care and thought, and that's not to mention the wonderful 'forever 1970s' world of Everflex roof coverings.

All styling studios paint their mock-ups in silver as it's great at showing off surface contours. Due to the popularity of dark blue cars, I took the unusual step of always viewing and presenting the Silver Seraph in that colour, as it also made the brightwork easier to study. If the style looked well in dark blue, silver would do it no harm.

Colour keying

The Colour Committee – apart from offering a huge range of colours and materials – also offered advice on which colours should go with what for the dealer kits. We developed a good spread of 'mixers' for the interior: Cotswold Beige hide and carpet went with lots of exterior colours, for instance. Carpets did tend to be a bit of an issue as suppliers didn't want to carry big stocks that had a small call-off. We did try a new colour, Wildberry, throughout the car – paint, hide and carpets – which was quite successful but cross matches were very restricted. Colour-keyed seat belts seemed a given, but pre-VW's purchasing power we were struggling to offer anything but black, apart from maybe a gold/beige. Sales and Marketing were wary of any 'adventurous' individual specifications, and would politely extract a sizeable deposit against the order: if the customer who ordered a purple car with lime-green leather should disappear, who would buy it?

A classic example of a special order was the all-black Turbo R. The customer wanted everything black, including the alloy wheels. Subsequently, all interior wood veneers were replaced by piano black; a final, surreal flourish being a black coachline. We had tried to dissuade the customer from black wheels, and when his car was finished he asked for the wheels to be changed back to production silver. The interior was quite effective, if you're into sensory deprivation. His cheque was good, apparently.

Occasionally, requests for non-standard exterior colours were rejected outright if considered bad for the Company's image, especially if intended for the home market. This was the MD's prerogative: "Standards, old boy, standards."

Given all the possible permutations – including dual paint schemes – customer and dealer choice was actually usually excellent. Maybe it was something to do with the fact that the vehicle's value was on a par with the average house which focused attention. The Colour Committee was charged with choosing and maintaining an aesthetically and technically sound colour range for the benefit of customer and Company. A Rolls-Royce or Bentley customer could be charged extra for a unique paint formulation or some-such, but the Committee left it to Sales and Marketing to bully the paint laboratory into complying with said request. Marketing also tried several times to corral certain colours and trim for a model or marque, the logic of which escaped me and led to a little unpleasantness between Marketing and myself.

Like Corniche, Camargue was launched with its own colour range, and used Nuella hide – Connolly's finest – with the objective of reinforcing its status above that of the Silver Shadow: not a very robust strategy, as it happens. Nuella was a gorgeously soft, dyed-through, natural hide that Connolly couldn't have supplied for all production cars, anyway.

This issue got me into trouble with Peter Ward in the early days of his reign as MD. A Marketing request was submitted to the Colour Committee for Rolls-Royce and Bentley to have separate, dedicated colour and trim ranges: ie two unique colour collections. This seemed impractical and, as Chairman and Secretary of the committee, I responded in the negative, explaining why we preferred not to pursue this idea. Peter sent one of his enforcers, a menacing Scot, to tell me: "If you won't see to it, we'll get someone who will!" Doubling the committee's workload wouldn't have fazed Peter Ward, but doubling the price of the already-expensive dealer colour selection kits eventually did. Not the best start to my relationship with the new Managing Director. Mind you, if the individual sent to 'persuade' you is a big fish, you know you're considered worthwhile: the enforcer that Peter sent to see me was Tom Purves, who went on to become firstly Marketing Director of BMW, and then MD of Rolls-Royce Goodwood.

In general

Normally, looking after colour and trim could be a pleasant job, but if model year changes and new projects overlapped it became very demanding. To some extent it was possible to delegate these duties to the Laboratory, Production Paint and Marketing departments, though the work really needed a full-time driver. It was just one of those conundrums: small-scale production, but large-scale expectations.

Whatever the highs and lows of trying to marshal the best colour range for the 'Best Car in the World,' there were, occasionally, some magic moments, for example, walking across the factory yard on a sunny day and spotting a design you'd been involved in, resplendent in colours you'd helped create. For a stylist, there really is nothing better.

It was a Bahama Yellow Porsche 911 which opened my eyes to the emotional impact that car colour can have. As a youth I daily walked our Labrador past racing driver Piers Courage's flat in Pinner Road, North Harrow, where Frank Williams (later Sir Frank, and founder of the Formula One team) would also be seen. E-type Jaguars and other exotica would howl off down Pinner Road, and sometimes a certain 911 in this unique and stunning yellow ochre. Subsequently, Minis, Maxis and Marinas appeared in a 'me too,' sadly diluted version of this hue.

SX
THE DOOMSDAY SCENARIO

Background

In 1980 the SZ family of Silver Spirit, Silver Spur and Mulsanne had been launched into the teeth of UK and worldwide economic problems, not least of which was the Middle East oil crisis. Simply getting SZ to the marketplace was a huge effort for a small company, and most of its system's bearings were running hot. All credit to the MD and Board of Directors, because as soon as they could snatch a breath they looked to the future. The great concern was that the world stage scenery was still being moved around: assuming a market still existed for large, luxury cars, what size and fuel consumption might be deemed acceptable?

The Crewe factory effectively relied on one product – the good ship Silver Spirit. It was a brand new product with a new name, to be sure, but so was the Titanic. If holed below the waterline by legislation or social mores, what was available to act as a lifeboat for the Company? Debate rapidly boiled down to how small and light could a Rolls-Royce be, and still retain its credibility? Once this had been established, should circumstances change, it was possible to stretch a smaller car, but shrinking a larger car would prove almost impossible.

John Cooke's people in the Design Office (Engineering) drew package layouts aimed at achieving projected weight and mileage targets, which involved reducing overall dimensions of various engines, including a favoured straight-six. To give an idea of the down-sizing, SZ was 17.3 feet long (5.27metres) and SX 16.16 feet (4.93 metres).

Once track and wheelbase dimensions began to gel, quarter-scale models began with Ron Maddocks as model-maker, and myself as stylist.

With Styling experimenting around this reduced package in early 1981, Ogle Design and Ital Design were commissioned by Fritz Feller to submit rendered proposals, and subsequently Tom Karen of Ogle and Giugiaro of Ital presented their work to the board. Ogle's ideas were very attractive, as good as anything a GM division could do, but Ital's were 'Lancia meets enlarged Volvo 340.' The board chose Ital's offering, perhaps because its work had been the most expensive.

Ron Maddocks made a quarter-scale clay model to Ital's drawings. Viewing this very accurate model against same-scale models of SY and SZ really unnerved the directors. As the board stood in stunned silence at the unveiling of maestro Giorgetto Giugiaro's proposal, they realised what a challenge SX presented.

By mid-1981 we managed to negotiate an extra two inches (50mm) on SX's proposed overall length. With a slightly wedged nose, a long cabin and a fairly high longer boot, proportions were beginning to look a little more reasonable. This in-house model achieved Cd30 in the wind-tunnel, and could tolerate being stretched for a long-wheelbase version. My big concern was that no one – and especially Marketing – really appreciated what down-sizing SX's package represented, compared to SZ. The style would be almost irrelevant compared to the impact of seeing the full-size version against other vehicles.

The first ever full-size Rolls-Royce modelled in clay

The most important service a Styling Department can render its Board of Directors is the full-size styling replica. For a few thousand pounds the board can look at – perhaps sit in – the object that will cost millions to bring to the marketplace; in many cases nothing less than the future of the Company, and the associated thousands of jobs, depends on the experience. Replicas are beautifully finished, fibreglass time machines that momentarily transport decision-makers into a possible future.

In the second half of 1981 we got the go-ahead to proceed from our in-house scale model to a full-size mock-up. The techniques Crewe used to achieve Styling sign-off with the 1980 SZ were already dated in the 1950s: the Company needed to adopt the industry norm of full-size clay modelling and subsequent fibreglass replica. It was time to bite the bullet with SX.

However, established shop floor practices and trade union issues, apparently beyond the control of the directors, were major obstacles to this objective.

How to create full-size clay models at Crewe?

Options were –

PLAN A

Ron Maddocks, our ace model-maker, would work with a team of professional clay modellers contracted for the job: this was a non-starter due to union objections.

PLAN B

Ron Maddocks would work with Crewe's Experimental Woodshop personnel: this didn't wash, either, as Woodshop was 'Works' and Ron 'Staff;' anyway, our Woodshop colleagues took instruction from their own manager. We tried this compromise and a couple of ugly scenes resulted. Appealing to Personnel to resolve this issue resulted in demarcation, with 'Staff' working on scale models only and 'Works' on full-size ones!

PLAN C

I would give instructions, via a supervisor, to Woodshop personnel: this unlikely-sounding scenario was the only show in town. Our Woodshop people were highly skilled, but had no experience of working clay. I knew and appreciated the skills of these guys, even the awkward, cross-threaded ones, although my face must have said it all when one of them said, "We're a necessary evil, Graham."

In a better industrial climate we might have pulled it off more easily at Crewe: as it was, in the 1970s and early 1980s the UK was anything but settled, the unrest eventually culminating in the pivotal miners' strike of 1984.

SX full-size replica

I was philosophical about the situation as my prime aim was to achieve Crewe's first full-size clay and fibreglass, see-through model, regardless of any and every obstacle.

No challenge to Michelangelo, SX – resolved by Maddocks and Hull in quarter-scale – was pretty simple without any tricky curves. At first everyone in the Woodshop wanted a hack and a scrape at this strange new clay material, but once the novelty had worn off things settled down a little and Ron Maddocks was able to get involved. As with SZ, without Ron's exceptional abilities the situation would have been practically unworkable.

Fritz Feller had little enthusiasm for a smaller Rolls-Royce, feeling he'd given the Company the motor car – SZ – it needed for some years ahead. His counter proposal to SX was to have six inches cut off the boot of the original SZ styling mock-up! Fritz was probably just telling the board what he thought of it, as this suggestion wouldn't have saved much weight and looked – well, you can imagine. Fritz had little input in the full-size clay work as his health was becoming a problem. I had tapered SX's tail for aesthetic and aerodynamic reasons, but Fritz asked me to widen it again to echo SZ's treatment.

Aerodynamic capers

In the pursuit of better fuel efficiency, aerodynamics had become a major consideration. Mike Dunn's Ford Sierra had been launched in 1982 with a coefficient of drag (Cd) of .34, which was almost immediately bettered by the Audi 100's Cd.30 (the average around this time was Cd.40-plus). Fritz invited in MIRA aerodynamicist Geoff Carr for a chat. Geoff regarded the Rolls-Royce radiator shell as a nightmare for air management: the best approach, he suggested, was to simply streamline the rest of the body as much as possible; advice which may have been rather tongue-in-cheek as we hadn't paid him for any SX testing at this point.

The Company had acquired an Audi 100 which Fritz was using as his company car. Mulling over Geoff Carr's comments, I suggested to Fritz and Macraith Fisher, Head of Development Engineering, that we simply test a Rolls-Royce radiator shell and bonnet on the super-slippery Audi. No one could think of a reason not to and the Audi,

Opposite page:
Economic uncertainty and threatened USA fuel economy legislation resulted in the 1982 SX project, with reduction in weight, size and aerodynamic drag the key drivers. It was the first full-size clay made at the factory. Approval was given for a see-through fibreglass replica shown on May 18 the following year.

Top: On the right MD George Fenn (with back to camera) talks to MPW's Richard Perry, who was preparing to take over at Crewe. Fritz Feller is on the left. Viewing in the Experimental Garage.

Middle: Chief Engineer (body) Nick Colbourne has a good look.

Bottom: A drawing is worth a thousand words, but a styling mock-up speaks volumes. The Dynoced SX clay eloquently demonstrates the challenge that a large BMW presents. (All author collection)

with its mocked-up plywood radiator, recorded around Cd.32 in MIRA's wind-tunnel in January 1983, increasing to Cd.34 with all cooling ducts open. This simple test proved that Rolls-Royce and respectable aerodynamics weren't incompatible. Air flow is complicated, and Greek temples weren't designed to travel at 100mph-plus. Tests on previous cars actually showed a reverse flow phenomenon immediately behind the header tank. However, I'd got the impression from various sources, including Spen King of Leyland Cars, that greeting the air at the front is less important than how you say goodbye at the back.

SX replica

My wish for a fibreglass replica from the SX clay was granted, although, as there was no question of this being done on-site, we approached Specialised Mouldings. World-class in this field, apart from one-off work, this company made production shells for the Unipower GT, Lotus Europa, replica Spitfire and Tornado aircraft, and pioneered the use of carbonfibre. Working with its staff was an education and a delight; the end result looked like a real car.

On May 18, 1983, Styling presented SX to the board on the Rolls-Royce sports field, alongside offerings from Mercedes, Jaguar and Audi, and the Silver Spirit. One side of the vehicle demonstrated pressed door frames; the other more classic stainless steel separate frames. Everyone

preferred the traditional side but the future belonged to the better sealing – and easier to make – pressed alternative.

The directors and staff gathering around the cars represented an all-change at Crewe. David Plastow had moved to Vickers, and George Fenn was MD, although Dick Perry of MPW, soon to be MD at Crewe, was present. Mike Dunn, recently arrived from Ford, took over Engineering when John Hollings retired.

Although Mike Dunn was used to viewing fully dressed replicas, the others present were able to appreciate how powerful this aid to decision-making was. As I'd guessed, size – or lack of it – was the key SX issue; particularly how narrow this package was. Nigel Cornelius of Marketing succinctly summed up this exercise as "... a stage we'd had to go through." At the following SX review it was proposed to increase length by six inches (152.4mm): four inches (101.6mm) to lengthen the cabin, with width increased by one inch (25.4mm).

At this point I felt the credibility of the SX programme began to unravel. Generous seating was required by those who travelled in Rolls-Royces, and so, to keep the car as compact as possible, the bonnet and boot had to be compressed (when a car's packaging becomes awkward, Americans call this 'dressing the hunchback'). Apart from in-house, Ogle and Ital Design proposals, Peter Horbury's MGA studio had made a couple of scale models: it wasn't as if we hadn't tried, and doubtless we could have come up with a pretty enough solution eventually. Whether the Vickers board would have signed off a vehicle of a size that could compete in what Sir David Plastow referred to as the BMW/Mercedes bear-pit is another matter.

The Bentley Mulsanne Turbo of 1982 was beginning to attract a fan club, and it seemed reasonable for Styling to help meet the rapidly growing interest in Bentley SZ. With impressive pragmatism Mike Dunn agreed with my slightly left of field proposal that Engineering directly supervise any ongoing SX mock-ups, and a further full-size clay was made at MGA to latest Engineering schemes. With no Styling involvement this device was reminiscent of Volvo's Cubist period. Shortly after this the dust sheets were kindly pulled over SX.

It was a steep, vital learning curve for all, and a fundamental issue began to concern me: was genuinely efficient packaging compatible with high style? Space-efficient people carriers are essentially boxes: interesting and charismatic shapes burn up space. The generous shape of the iconic Rolls-Royce Silver Cloud resulted in relatively poor interior space, given overall vehicle size.

Conflicting legislation

Much of the impetus behind SX was the suggestion from the USA that car fleets should achieve an average of 25mpg. In the event, after some anguish, American car companies claimed it couldn't be done and the proposals were dropped. In complete contradiction, American legislators also went through a phase influenced by Ralph Nader's 'Unsafe at any Speed' campaign, the basic premise of which was to create cars that occupants could walk away from after 50mph crashes. All R-RMC could do was to tread water and hope the industry could get the federal agencies to see sense, despite the fact that, at times, Styling was making scale models of SZ with grotesquely extended noses intended to soak up 50mph 'head-ons,' as well as the models with six inches (152.4mm) chopped off the boot to save weight! As Barnes Wallace once said, "When dealing with governments and bureaucracies, it helps to have a sense of humour."

Afterword

In December 1982 Ron Maddocks applied for a severance package and left the Company.

Ron Maddocks with a quarter-scale SZ model in a MIRA scale wind tunnel; the turntable allows testing in yaw. A model Greek Temple on the front might appear problematical, but vehicle rear ends are the key for drag and stability aerodynamics.

When it was suggested to GM's Bill Mitchell that the 1975 Cadillac Seville appeared heavily influenced by a Rolls-Royce, he replied, "Well, my Daddy always told me that if you're going to steal, steal from a bank, not a grocery store."

MULLINER PARK WARD
HOSCARS AND OSCARS

The coachbuilders

Rolls-Royce and Bentley have a long tradition of building bespoke motor cars for connoisseurs. However, the two companies came about in an era when a chassis was often produced for others to fit their own special bodies.

John Blatchley, my predecessor's predecessor, learnt his trade at coachbuilder Gurney Nutting. Other UK coachbuilders included Barker, Hooper, James Young, H J Mulliner, and Park Ward. The famous Embiricos Bentley was built by Carrosserie Pourtout, and Van Vooren of Paris also built unique Rolls-Royces and Bentleys. Significantly, many of these vehicles were financed by individual enthusiasts.

Coachbuilders thrived in the 1920s and 1930s chassis era. With the advent of monocoque body construction, trade shrank rapidly. Occasional exceptions – such as Pininfarina – survived over the years, but most of the remaining 'coachbuilders' became mainly modifiers of existing pressed steel body shells. H J Mulliner and Park Ward, two companies bought and melded together by Rolls-Royce, were true coachbuilders, who managed to survive in their North London, Willesden factory, and continued to function as a separate entity, even after eventually moving to the parent company at Crewe in 1991. They continued to thrive when Bentley became part of the VW portfolio.

Mulliner Park Ward (MPW)

In the 1970s, MPW was building Rolls-Royce Phantom Head of State cars (Hoscars), the Corniche convertible and fixed-head, and, later, Camargue. Like many centres of creativity the company's somewhat inauspicious premises belied the wonderful craftsmanship that occurred therein: on my first visit I had to wait while a chap pushed a Corniche bonnet on a costermonger's barrow down the middle of the narrow road (at that time the works straddled Hythe Road; separated from Wormwood Scrubs Prison by only railway lines). The nearest thing to MPW's setup, albeit on a slightly smaller scale, is the Morgan factory at Malvern. Whilst, unlike Morgan, there was no cat sitting on the receptionist's typewriter, both concerns were typical of 1930s car production

Due to the usual restrictions of space in London, activities occurred on more than one floor. I never fully understood the complex layout but it wasn't hard to imagine MD Dick Perry storming around demanding, "What the bloody hell is going on?"

As well as the highly-skilled business of building Corniche convertibles, the one-off Phantoms were fascinating, the inner structures of some closely related to Lawrence of Arabia's famous Silver Ghost-based armoured cars. Although capable of surviving exploding mines and small arms fire, the Phantoms appeared quite normal. The skills displayed by the workforce made you believe it could build anything, but don't ask for a wiring diagram, as you'll probably be met with a blank stare.

An early visit to MPW was to discuss the possibilities of a Phantom replacement based on SZ. At Crewe, we had looked at drawings and scale models of several variations of this type of vehicle. MPW always maintained an excellent small team of design/draughtsmen, under George Mosley originally and later Bernard West. Peter Wharton's evocative renderings of this period occasionally appear in reference works, and engineers such as John Lake and Bob Watson had to sort out a multitude of issues on a daily basis. Crewe's George Ray was a liaison engineer helping to keep the London and Cheshire sites in sync.

Limousines

With the rising tide of the celebrity cult in the 1970s, it became de rigueur for Oscar nominees and suchlike to arrive in stretched limousines, creating an upsurge in demand for these vehicles. Extended Rolls-Royce SZs began to appear, and, in the UK, the late Robert Jankel exploited this niche, much to the interest/consternation of the Crewe factory. Jankel at Weybridge, Surrey, had been cutting the cars in half and welding in new centre sections. The extra space could allow a division between front and rear occupants, and a lot more legroom in the back. Not especially high spec internally, they did the job. I've sat in one in America, the owner of which assumed it was built at Crewe. R-RMC wasn't too relaxed about this situation and decided to work with Jankel.

Let's raise the roof!

There was virtually no limit to the potential for lengthening an SZ, but, beyond a certain point, the 'stretched toffee' illusion kicked in. I went to the London showrooms at Conduit Street for a meeting with Robert Jankel and Bernard Preston, Crewe's Product Planning Director, and presented some renderings of raised-roof stretched limousines, which achieved a complete car look rather than an obvious adaptation. Nick McGrath, a Crewe engineer who had crossed over to Marketing subsequently, worked with me at Jankel's to help develop this rather more sophisticated offering. It was a complicated conversion process: to some extent working in the Italian manner of solving any issues as and when they occurred. And like the Italians it was usually better to let the Jankel men get on with it.

Robert Jankel was a true entrepreneur, with workshops in the courtyard of a mediaeval fortified Manor House, surrounded by pastures full of deer for his venison production. Like so many in the world of Rolls-Royce and Bentley, Robert was a one-off: his specially-tailored shirts had a semi-circular cut-out in the cuff to make reading his watch easier. Bordering on eccentricity? Perhaps. But how many people would have the nerve to cut a new SZ in half with an angle grinder?

Eventually, the whole limousine operation was carried out at Crewe in the MPW workshops, and a particular configuration was promoted as the Mulliner Park Ward Touring Limousine. This Silver Spur, SZ long-wheelbase-based version was a six-light, 24 inches (609.6mm) longer and with the roof raised just over two inches (50.8mm). The model was quite successful and, despite the extra work, profitable. The fact that, like SY, SZ was styled to accommodate a long-wheelbase version greatly helped the general appearance of limousines.

Limousines are all about the rear occupants, and you can never give these too much room. It's the case that Formula One racing car designers resent the space taken up by the driver, and so it is with limousines. Chauffeurs had to put up with restricted seat travel and very thin seat backs: this went with the territory.

A true, Silver Spur-based, Head of State car was supplied to the King of Morocco, complete with all the classic elements such as small backlight, flag masts, unique interior features, and so on. Martin Bourne of Crewe Styling employed traditional draughting skills to resolve the complex curvature of the raised-roof option limousines. These substantial panels weren't fashioned in clay but by the traditional method of making wooden formers from drawings and forming metal over them – pure coachbuilding.

At Crewe, with Martin Bourne and Ryan Lewis, a furniture designer from the RCA, we were able to consider very special unique interiors for limousines. Rear compartments with up to an extra three feet (914.4mm) and the roof raised by over two inches (50.8mm) were more than equal to the later Maybachs. A whole range of fittings and options were available, such as drinks cabinet and television, etc. Phantom-type, rear-facing seats could be fixed or folding from the central division, which could have a separate air-conditioning unit that was controlled from the rear seats. This was also the natural environment for non-standard trimming techniques such as ruched, diamond pattern and buttoned. A wide selection of alternative veneers to the standard burr walnut could be supplemented by superb examples of inlay and marquetry work. Carefully concealed lighting created magical effects.

However cleverly stretched limousines are styled, they always bear witness to the host vehicle, and this was especially true of the SZ family, with its distinctive front and rear lamp treatments. Ideally, Head of State cars should be completely unique styles, and extraordinary examples of this came out of 1990s Crewe (discussed in a later chapter). Limousines were another world, and the only limitation was the imagination of the customer, stylist or salesman. Coachbuilding in general engenders a most

heartening 'can do' attitude: nothing is impossible, it just takes a little longer, and, of course, costs a little more. Billy Connolly's joke about an optically-ground prescription windscreen certainly wouldn't have been dismissed out of hand at MPW!

Hardly a limousine, but this 1990s P460 mid-engined proposal would have been a natural candidate for an MPW special commission build.

Nick McGrath and I shared a similar sense of humour. Driving back from Jankel's, what looked like a character from a horror film was trying to thumb a lift. Driving past I commented that if I looked like that I wouldn't trust anyone who gave me a lift, in response to which Nick quoted Groucho Marx, "I wouldn't join any club that would have me as a member!"

There was always a contrast between factory life and 'Rolls-Royce' life. In the mid-1970s I had a lift from the Geneva Motor Show to our splendid hotel by the lake. Sitting in my Burton's suit in the front of a Silver Wraith II, we diverted to collect someone at the airport. As they got in, assuming that they were from Crewe, I turned round and grandly said, "Hallo, I'm Graham Hull." "Hallo, I'm Lord Stokes," the head of the British Leyland Motor Corporation Ltd (BL) replied.

BENTLEY CONTINENTAL R
OLD WINE, NEW BOTTLE

Phase One – Project 90

In the mid-1980s the Crewe Styling Department was fully engaged with ongoing production cars and model year (MY) requirements, whilst yours truly was wrestling with the issues involved in trying to run R-RMC Styling. Dick Perry (Chief Executive), Peter Ward (Marketing Director), and John Stephenson (Crewe's first Director of Product Planning) wanted to expand Bentley's model line-up.

They commissioned consultants to style a two-door coupé, code named Project 90, which was a surprise exhibit at the 1985 Geneva Motor Show, attracting a lot of interest. Crewe Styling had no involvement with this, other than supplying alloy wheels and door handles, and the suggestion not to paint it black. But black it was painted, and hence the Company nickname of Black Rat, though I called it Stephenson's Rocket (Martin Bourne thought this too complimentary). Apart from witnessing how independent consultants tackled a Bentley, this exercise underlined the necessity for specialised mock-up facilities. Working at IAD (International Automotive Design) in Worthing, Crewe could exploit world-class concept show car techniques.

P90's stylists, John Heffernan and Ken Greenley, had been at GM's Luton Styling Studios with John Stephenson. Although I was feeling left out of the P90 loop, I'd always regarded GM Styling as the most advanced in the world. Heffernan, Greenley and Stephenson had been at Luton when the superb 1970 Vauxhall SRV was built under Wayne Cherry, and, apparently, John Stephenson had

come up with the clever hinges on the clamshell doors. Exhibited in the year the Turbo R was launched, P90 was obviously a contender for production, and Mike Dunn asked for my written views on it. My response, dated May 29, 1985, supported the idea of a Bentley coupé, but with reservations about this particular style. An RCA graduate writing in *Design Magazine* rather savaged it, which seemed a bit over the top. Some R-RMC comments mentioned similarities with a Lincoln of the time: I simply thought that P90 lacked character, and felt that a replacement for Corniche needed our attention more. Given its limited resources, the Company might be wiser to produce a convertible and coupé from the same body, and P90 didn't seem to lend itself to this.

Some reports suggest that John Stephenson resigned over the board's decision not to proceed with P90, but I think it was because he had a bit of a hard time at Crewe establishing Product Planning, which Engineering thought a lower form of life than the Styling Department, even! Bumping into him on the stairs, we shook hands and he simply said, "I'm off." Oh dear: one less person at Crewe who understood Styling …

Phase Two – a Rolls-Royce Convertible

Dick Perry, previously MD at Mulliner Park Ward, knew that the factory depended on the ageing Corniche, and wanted a replacement for it.

He chose a Heffernan and Greenley proposal from a full-size rendering. The duo was able to take advantage of a temporary studio facility at MPW in Willesden using 'hired gun' clay-modellers.

Considering the Corniche's character and shape, the style chosen by Dick Perry appeared rather 'extruded.' Crewe Styling had enough on its plate without getting involved, but with John Lake, a very keen MPW engineer, overseeing things, a well-finished, full-size clay mock-up was made, and, fully-dressed, viewed at MPW on February 10, 1986. I restricted my comments to noting it looked very high-waisted, and should be photographed with other cars in order to better understand its style. Dick Perry put things on hold until feedback was received from the key market of America.

A month later the temporary theatre in Crewe's old design office was used for a board slide show of the Corniche proposal, alongside some 'competitors.' Reaction from the board was rather muted; no one was rushing to comment. Finally, I said that the shape didn't have enough character to replace the classic Corniche, whilst Dick Perry added that the proposal was "very English." The consensus was that it looked too big compared to Silver Spirit and Camargue; neither was the front-end liked, and the boot looked heavy. A side-groove found few fans either.

I felt that in order to reduce the apparent bulk of our large vehicles and make the style more interesting some strong sculpting was needed, particularly in the car's flanks. Coke-bottle styling was a well-known American theme, which I had tried with some success on a scale model when at Chrysler UK Advanced Styling Studios. Essentially, the car's waist is pinched in at the middle, so that what mass remains is focused around the wheels: a good thing. Some quarter-scale convertible models had been worked-up in-house, all focusing on sculptured sides. We had also approached an American agency for some drawings of a Corniche replacement, and its recommendations pretty well echoed ours. A car featuring a dipped lower side-glass line and slightly concave sides seemed the way to go.

At a boardroom presentation on April 9, 1986, I went over the American suggestions, including my own interpretation of the American theme. Also shown were my illustrations of the existing clay mock-up morphing into a pinched waist solution. I stressed the need to reduce apparent weight, using tactics that included a dipped lower glass line emphasizing a pinched waist, as well as raising the sill. Given the existing temporary studio at MPW, I suggested to Dick Perry that Heffernan and Greenley be retained to re-work the current clay. This was agreed and I was asked to work closer with John and Ken.

Phase Three – Rolls-Royce Convertible 'take-two'

For me the next bit was a little tricky because, in reality, John and Ken had been independent of, or actually in competition with, Crewe Styling, but now we'd been told to work together. John and Ken probably wouldn't have walked away from this proposition, but life would have been very tricky if they had. However, they seemed to tolerate my suggestions, particularly as I took care to stress the American input. Showing John my morphing sequence of side views, he said it was a nice drawing. We agreed to do the usual technique of variations on each side of the clay, with both sides placing emphasis on the wheels.

Work started in mid-April, continuing through May. A typical visit to MPW resulted in the following builds –
• SZ type waist overhang side section doesn't work as well as the alternative side's ledge
• Curve sill-line in plan
• Soften 'Vauxhall Nova'-style hips
• Soften wheelarches
• Lower side feature line too heavy

At MPW later in May, I asked why there was no evidence of the dipped waistline as previously suggested, and John and Ken told me that a Crewe board member had popped in and said he didn't like it! It sounded as if the dip had been overcooked so I asked them to reinstate a more subtle version.

June, July and early August saw the basic shape established with main Crewe Styling input during this period –
• Shape on offside is right direction
• Combine nearside waist feature and lower side details with offside theme
• More splay on catwalk
• Protect for hard top version
• Reduce 'Harold Macmillan' eyebrow effect above headlamps
• Rear lamps to be more formal

Crewe's big guns gathered round what was obviously our best shot at a Corniche replacement. Previously, Mike Dunn had told me to be more outspoken at viewings, so, thus emboldened, I stood by the clay and stated that we were now working on the wrong project; the shape being developed would suit a Bentley coupé. It was a bit surprising to see Peter Ward, still Marketing Director, looking rather annoyed with me. In hierarchy terms, possibly Peter thought that Styling's tail was trying to wag the dog, but I didn't even have a designated parking space!

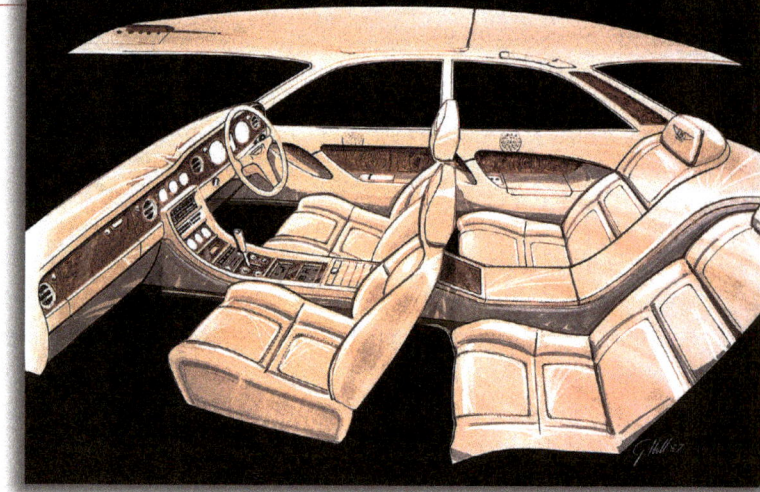

1986 rendering presented to the board for an all-new Bentley Coupé body. At this stage Styling had only been asked to investigate converting a Turbo R to two doors. Project Nepal (Bentley Continental R) came about shortly after this. The interior featured a through console with gearlever, continuing the distinction from Rolls-Royce with its column change. Managing Director Peter Ward included both renderings in the Continental R's launch brochure.

Justifying my belief in the Bentley marque, the Corniche, despite its age, had become a classic, and, like Porsche's 911, seemed to go on and on. At this time the Turbo R was showing all the signs of being a hit and we were developing it further. Limited funds dictated that creating a new dedicated Bentley body was the best bet for growth.

An ongoing distraction for Styling was a request from the Product Planning director to investigate making a Bentley two-door out of the SZ saloon. This we duly explored, making a quarter-scale model in-house, but, put bluntly, little more was envisaged than simply deleting the rear doors and increasing the length of the front ones. Considering a coupé's raison d'etre is to look chic and even stunning, SZ's Bank of England persona was not the place to start.

However, in January 1987, possible solutions were presented in the boardroom. My final, unofficial rendering was for a completely re-bodied coupé, which I suggested could be based on the re-styled Corniche work. I had drawn two views in 1986, trying to convey the charisma such a vehicle should exude. The tapering tail included a fence spoiler as employed by the Audi TT in the next century. The new Product Planning director's reaction was to point out that this rendering was outside my brief for an SZ coupé.

Phase Four – as you were, it's a Bentley coupé

By the end of March, Mike Dunn informed me that a replacement for the Corniche was not going to happen, and the model would continue as a Bentley coupé. During a meeting at MIRA on April 2, 1987, Mike Dunn, Howard Mosher, John Lake, IAD representatives, Heffernan, Greenley and myself discussed this change in policy. The official statement read, "Due to the success of recent modifications to Corniche and strong sales, the current exercise to replace Corniche has been postponed."

As the work was now based at IAD in Worthing, Howard Mosher, my boss, and I visited there on May 27 that year to discuss the new package for the Corniche; particularly rear head clearance. John and Ken felt the side-glass, etc, needed to be pulled out at the waist, which would involve major surgery of the 'Corniche' mock-up. However, appearance is all with a coupé, so there was no question. Peter Ward was closely following the project, as, too, was Mike Dunn. A list of agreed modifications issued by me on July 1 is typical of how such projects progress –

• Radiator shell – make as low and as wide as possible, and pull centre-line forward. Run top of bumper straight through and fill in gap under radiator shell
• Headlamp/bonnet shutline – reduce 'Harold Macmillan' eyebrows
• Front apron – too extreme: refer to 89 MY Turbo R solution
• Mirrors – new pod-type required in body colour
• Roof/cantrail – check crowning on roof and refine cantrails
• Rear quarter/D pillar – slimmer offside version preferred but nearside chamfer
• Rear end – try undercut boot spoiler; new line under lamps. High stop lamp required and featured winged B
• Rear width – car okay over lamps but bumper sides and apron need to be checked for feasibility
• Rear bumper – awkward line adjacent to side of rear lamps
• Fuel filler door – check feasibility
• Spare wheel – check body contours
• Door frames – 'cut-through' pressings on one side and traditional stainless steel SZ type on other

By this point I had managed to have the larger, 7 inch round headlamps fitted to the 89MY Turbo R, and John and Ken were asked to use the same light units.

Interior

Towards the end of 1987, the 'who does what and where' question was causing some head scratching. Exterior styling development and packaging was being handled down on the south coast at Worthing, which required frequent trips from Crewe. Occupant packaging was making Crewe a bit nervous, as it's easier to make coupés look superswish if headroom, particularly in the rear, is allowed to be compromised somewhat. Several other models were looked at to establish a market norm, and these included the Mercedes 300CE, Audi Quattro, BMW 635Ci, Jaguar XJS, and Porsche 944S. In final form the Bentley came out pretty well, although, considering its size, it needed to.

I showed the board a rendering of a cockpit-type interior style, stressing the sporty nature of this coupé, the main thrust of which was a centre console running from the facia through the car into the rear seat cushion and squab. The through console made the vehicle a four-seater but the rear part of this could be removed, if necessary. The gear change was moved from the steering column to the centre console as with the 89MY Turbo R. This interior theme was accepted by the board.

We wanted to do the interior at Crewe to make use of the factory's wood and leather know-how. Engineering and Production needed to be fully involved with Styling's work to ensure the smooth transfer of ideas to production reality. Exteriors get all the attention but it's the interior that is really very complicated. Unfortunately, the issue of Crewe works and staff demarcation regarding styling mock-ups was still unresolved. Heffernan and Greenley recommended we modelled all of the 'A' interior surfaces in clay, which was industry norm, but we still couldn't bring clay modellers on-site. I lost count of the number of meetings – official and unofficial – we had over this issue between September 1987 and February 1988. MPW engineer John Lake hadn't experienced this problem before, and was understandably frustrated. I knew the Crewe workforce would eventually arrive at some compromise with Styling, but a frontal assault wasn't an option.

Martin Bourne, the last survivor from John Blatchley's Silver Cloud/Shadow era, was, thankfully, still with us. He was brought up on the 'give us a drawing and we'll make it' shopfloor philosophy, and so with Martin's ability and others in our tiny team, we were able to begin fitting out an interior mock-up for the Bentley coupé, now code named Nepal. Like so much of life at Rolls-Royce and Bentley, personality mattered a lot. Everyone knew and liked Martin, the pilot and dance band musician with the large, ginger moustache. I asked Martin to stay with the interior mock-up in the Experimental Garage as the man on the spot, feeding information and smoothing ruffled feathers as necessary.

The working arrangement arrived at to achieve Nepal's interior cost us Brian Hassall, Styling's modeller, who, quite understandably, felt unable to make a full contribution due to the, by now historic, dispute regarding hourly-paid workers and salaried staff sharing any hands-on tasks. He moved to another department to avoid this frustrating situation.

Although Nepal was based on SZ's platform, the upper monocoque was all new. Car interiors have to interface with the body's hard bits: for instance, before the headlining can be styled you have to know where the inner box sections are, and here an element of catch 22, or chicken-and-egg, occurs as head clearance can't be signed off until a compromise is agreed between occupant packaging and engineering structures.

Establishing head clearance can burn time ferociously as re-designs to win back a couple of millimetres are common. Life would have been much less complicated if all styling, package engineering and mock-up work had occurred at the same location.

Nepal's interior was largely finalized by early July 1988; work then began to validate the approved style's feasibility. This is where experienced interior stylists are worth their weight in gold because the more they have collaborated with Production en-route the more robust the proposal.

Gaining permission to draw up a 16 inch (406.4mm) alloy wheel for Nepal indicated that years of nagging the board about our wheels being too small were finally paying off. Actually, wheel size is not the problem: it's the expensive rubber bit that goes round it. A new Aston Martin tyre had became available, so development engineers were happy as they could squeeze in bigger brakes.

The final stages

The Nepal clay had been made into a fibreglass, see-through replica and taken to Crewe (there were still some outstanding issues with the exterior styling).

I felt the front end looked a little pug-nosed. The radiator shell leant back quite a lot, eating into bonnet length, and the side lamps abutted rather abruptly to the radiator shell. No doubt Bentley radiator shells would gradually develop a more laid-back attitude but the degree of slope now apparent on this replica was too much in one go. John and Ken visited Crewe to discuss this and other areas, including a new treatment of the front side lamps preferred by the in-house team. John Heffernan didn't agree with making the radiator shell more vertical; Ken Greenley didn't think making it more vertical would compromise the style. Eventually, all of the various changes – some feasibility-driven – were agreed on.

John and Ken were in slightly unusual positions compared to design consultants generally. Consultancies tend to contribute to larger company studios, whereas these two – with their excellent Panther Solo work – had gradually worked closer and closer with Crewe's in-house styling department. I think they came to realize that I was trying to do the best for the Company rather than there being any issues with ego. Towards the end of the programme I dropped John at Crewe railway station after a brief visit. As we shook hands he rather sympathetically said, "The perfect car is yet to be designed."

Sir David Plastow had viewed Nepal on April 1988, and the Vickers Board, then including The Duke of Kent, formally approved it on June 23, 1988.

The launch

Nearly five years after the second Corniche proposal began, Nepal – now Bentley Continental R – was launched at the 1991 Geneva Motor Show, Peter Ward pulling out all stops for the car's debut.

Next to the Styling Department at Crewe, a mock-up was made of the planned area round the Company's Geneva stand. A driver practiced manoeuvring the car from behind curtains, along narrow walkways and onto the stand. At the show, waiting journalists were so excited by the car's arrival that they rewarded Peter's showmanship by making it the star of the show. So stunning was this new, bright red Bentley that The Sultan of Brunei made Peter Ward an offer for the actual show car that he couldn't refuse, which, no doubt, didn't do Company coffers any harm, although Mike Dunn must have been shocked to lose the only finished car from his programme. I didn't attend the launch but Crewe's styling involvement was acknowledged by my original renderings of a coupé exterior and interior appearing in the brochure.

Big coupés are not that common; big, attractive coupés are rarer still. Such was the style's success at disguising its bulk that no one realized the coupé was actually longer

The 1991 Bentley Continental R demonstrated that the marque was now very capable of sharing the limelight with its more famous stable-mate, Rolls-Royce. A new paint plant at the factory enabled Styling to exploit body-coloured composite bumpers, etc. The wheels were the latest iteration of the effective 'sub-spoke' theme: Styling had long campaigned for larger diameters, and had finally gone from 15 inch to 16 inch – Rome wasn't built in a day! The interior had generous rear space despite its coupé style.

than the saloon it was based on. There can't be too many cars with such a complicated gestation period, but the end result was worth it.

The Azure – finally, the new convertible

The Bentley revival was in full flow, and a convertible version of Continental R was a given. Corniche's fabric roof, when lowered, had the old-fashioned 'pram-hood' stack. Modern convertibles are expected to hide everything, and this involves a huge tear-up in the area behind the rear occupants to insert an automatic opening and shutting hood stowage box (rear occupants are also squeezed together by the narrowest part of the folded hood).

Hood material is not the flimsy piece of canvas from yesteryear, but a multi-layered sandwich, which makes it akin to trying to fold a mattress. Much later, after VW took over the reins, I asked the German chief engineer if he'd seen much of England. His reply was that he had had to engineer two hoods recently; the implication being that he'd hardly had time to see his wife and children, let alone go sightseeing.

It was decided to commission Pininfarina to convert Continental R into a soft-top, and it was soon apparent that the car would have to suffer the indignity of having its rear decking raised to conceal a folded hood. Happily, the Italians can do this sort of thing with their eyes shut. Needing to justify the cost of visits to Italy, the close-coupled rear seat was an opportunity to suggest some novel sculpting. The new front safety seats with built-in seat belts were also interesting.

Working with the Italians is an education: they are much more intuitive than the Germans, and even the British. A well-known British stylist who eventually gave up on them said the Italians have a low attention span. That's a little harsh, I think, though must confess to being a touch concerned whenever they said something was 'no problem,' as this could mean no problem, because soon you will return to England, or no problem, we always beat you at football anyway. There was 'no problem' about how to resolve the tricky, curving, waist line brightwork, so I asked that we sort that out at Crewe, which we did.

It was always enjoyable working with Pininfarina's Chief Designer, Lorenzo Ramaciotti, and when he realized I was a Fiat Abarth fan I couldn't go wrong. Lorenzo went on to head Fiat Design in 2007.

The Bentley Azure was launched in 1995, and no one realised they were looking at a redirected Corniche replacement.

The Bentley Continental T – less is more

In theory, Product Planning/Brand Management guided Company product, and the Continental T is a glorious example of old-fashioned, back of an envelope-inspired improvisation.

Jim Orr was the slightly menacing Scotsman in charge of MPW's 'one-off' customer specials. One day, he walked into my office and asked if I'd seen the shortened Continental. This was a development hack (literally), quickly modified to test a shortened chassis for a special new project. A 4 inch (101.6mm) slice had been cut from behind the front doors, and the 'eyebrows' pulled out to cover wider tyres: rather drastic surgery that had transformed the elegant Beau Brummel Continental R into a real bare-knuckle fighter. By compressing the sculpted sides, the muscle around the wheels was emphasized and further enhanced by the wider eyebrows. The truncated rear side-glass, instead of looking unbalanced, stressed the hybrid's rather roguish nature: it all looked great.

Peter Hill, the engineer responsible, told me it had been quite a complicated job. Knowing he'd appreciate my knowledge and understanding I sympathized about the work involved in shortening the handbrake cable ...

Crewe couldn't afford to tool a true sports car, but suddenly we had the next best thing. Okay, rear occupants had it tough, but this more extreme offering allowed Styling to turn up the wick on the 'Bentley Boys' image a little more. I'd always liked engine-turned aluminium dashboards, and coupled with new chrome bezels for the instruments, the interior looked dramatically different. 'T' interiors often had dual or triple colour schemes, and separate, red starter-buttons to rouse the beast into life added even more theatre. The 'T' was responsible for the rebirth of the starter-button; an anachronism that several other manufacturers copied. Having championed this device, the first time I drove one I turned the key and couldn't understand at first why the engine wouldn't start! Thankfully, I was on my own at the time.

We tidied up the 'eyebrows' a little and modified the front bumper/apron. The vehicle looked very macho on approach, and the interior had a definite 'WOW!' factor. In addition, the engine was modified to give 590lb/ft of torque: probably the highest of any production car at the time. Bigger wheels allowed bigger brakes, and stopping from a speed of 100mph was achieved in 4.96 seconds. Marketing expected to sell a few to hard-core enthusiasts, but word spread and demand soon outstripped supply. The Midlands company responsible for modifying the bodyshells became very agitated, as what began as a 'knife-and-fork' sideline soon demanded more and more skilled workers. I was asked to visit to see if we could simplify the troublesome compressed sill area. Launched in 1996, the 'T' was quite something, and it was easy to appreciate how Nigel Mansell came to lose his licence whilst driving one.

Bentley Continental Sedanca Coupé (SC) P966

There were many variants of the Continental R as one-offs or limited batches. The 1999 Bentley Continental T Mulliner had various enhancements, including stiffer suspension. The final mainstream model was the Sedanca Coupé of 1999, the first Crewe project mainly driven by Brand management. A niche within a niche, the SC was based on the 'T' with removable roof panels over the front occupants, leaving the rest of the roof fixed. Instead of the 'T's' extended eyebrows, Styling re-sculpted the entire side section. Front and rear wings were flared, emphasizing the pinched waist, and the sill was re-shaped, and christened the 'baguette.'

P966's clay was created in the UK and Pininfarina made the bodywork. In late 1997, issues arose over the transfer of styling intent to metal. I had to go to Italy, and requested that project engineer Alan Fairless ride shotgun. The Turin shop floor was a world apart from Pininfarina's 'smoked-glass and coffee' empire. Due to timing and spend pressure the discussion became a little heated, and Alan had to ascertain at one point whether his opposite number understood what 'bollocks' meant ... As the verbal fisticuffs continued, Alan stated that I was the most realistic stylist he'd met: strangely touching as even opposite camp engineers can adopt a "you hold him and I'll hit him," attitude toward stylists. Alan was a good egg who raced Austin 7s.

Engineering had a major challenge (for challenge read 'tearing your hair out') making the removable roof sections watertight and rattle-free. Engineering, still experimenting with Project Teams, were effectively 'bringing in' other disciplines such as Styling. It felt a bit strange at times but the Triumph GT6-owning team leader, Robert Upcott-Gill, was a pleasant enough type, even bordering on the intellectual.

The Sedanca was not for introverts and ideal for wafting around California. Brand management chose to put one on the launch stand in one of our more adventurous colours, a metallic orange, with chromed wheels. Mike Tyson, the boxer, toured the Crewe factory with his entourage, and bought one, of course.

The Continental R – on reflection

If the Mulsanne kicked off the Bentley rebirth and the Turbo R established it, the Continental R completed the process, and Bentley was once again recognized for its own unique body style. We considered a four-door version for mainstream production, as sporty four-doors have a rakish charm, but how would Marketing position it alongside the Turbo R? Pragmatism is often boring, but it beats shooting yourself in the foot. Many commissioned specials were built, including estates, limousines, and even SZ limousines with the Continental nose grafted on!

The vehicle's final contribution to Crewe was to form the basis for the four separate headlamp treatment that the Arnage finally received, courtesy of VW, and echoed in the 2009 Brooklands Coupé. While elegant and even graceful, it was necessary to remember this vehicle's power. The only time I really turned one loose was at Bruntingthorpe test facility, totally losing it in a lurid, tyre-shredding spin.

The Continental R family was in production for eleven years. Perhaps the last word can be left to Styling's Darren Day. Driving to Coventry in one he was stopped by the police. The officer told him, "Nothing wrong, sir, I'd just like to say this is the most beautiful car I've ever seen."

My mid-1990s boss, grey-bearded Chief Engineer Chris Cernes, gave me his views on dealing with consultants. "When preparing a brief for consultants, don't put too much detail in because if you leave something out it's your fault. If it's all left out and the consultants don't query it, it's their fault!" At times I wondered if I had a proper grasp of the business world.

HIS MASTER'S VOICE
IF MY BOSS PHONES, GET THE NAME

Background

How a car looks has always been a major consideration in the buying process, and will remain so whilst consumers have free choice. Although the number of independent manufacturers has shrunk, variation and choice of model has increased, with conglomerates often perilously close to competing within their own ranges. Platform sharing is now so common that the main differentiation is often style and image. Huge financial resource and economic structure can depend, somewhat nervously, on independent souls with a pencil and sketch pad.

Automotive corporations tend to mask and deny this unpalatable dependence on flaky, artistic types, and company heads have been known to monitor the efforts of their stylists, even at junior level. Conversely, some engineering designers never even speak to a managing director throughout their entire career! Author Arthur Hailey recognised this special relationship between chief executives and stylists, basing a key part of his best-selling novel *Wheels* around it.

Despite its rather olde-worlde characteristics, the Styling Department was located in the top corridor of the Rolls-Royce and Bentley factory at Crewe. The post-war period had the Managing Director, Engineering Director and Chief Stylist in virtually adjacent offices in 'Mahogany Row'; an arrangement which persisted throughout first John Blatchley's reign, and then Fritz Feller's. I managed to cling on to these desirable territorial rights until the early 1990s.

Chain of command

Despite the close relationship between MDs and Styling (again, for Styling read Design, even if 'Design' requires a rider), the reporting line is not usually direct, and, from the mid-1980s at Crewe, it became flexible and frequently changed, reflecting the tectonic plates shifting within the Company.

Sir Henry Royce and The Honourable Charles Rolls were a memorable union of engineering and marketing. Sir Henry's primary approach was to adapt/improve the best engineering available, and Crewe still embraced this philosophy of finesse and development; more so than innovation, even. It didn't take a genius to recognise that Development Engineering still pretty much ruled the roost in 1971. The Silver Shadow was selling successfully on the Company's reputation, so 'Marketing' was essentially a wining and dining function for prospective customers.

Whilst Crewe had a large and competent Engineering Design team, it was Development Engineering which seemed to have a direct line to Sir Henry's thinking. The top men involved were Macraith (Mac) Fisher, Derek Coulson and Jock Knight (Mac Fisher was Chief Engineer John Hollings' right-hand man), and theirs are the most frequently mentioned names in the SY (Silver Shadow) and SZ (Silver Spirit) story, although there were, of course, numerous other key players. Development tended to regard Engineering Design drawings as just the starting point for 'its' motor car. Phil Harding, a Development Engineer was put in charge of the Silver Seraph/Arnage programme, and Tony Gott, who took over from Phil, was possibly the first engineer with significant drawing board experience to reach the position of Chief Engineer on the site. This bias within Engineering continued right through into the VW era, with Styling traditionally pitching its tent in the Engineering camp.

Directors 'responsible' for styling managers

John Hollings was Chief Engineer and board member from the late 1960s and into the early 1980s, and Fritz Feller – my predecessor as Chief Stylist – pretty much coincided with his reign. Fritz reported directly to Hollings (it was impossible to ever think of him as John; even calling him Mr Hollings to his face seemed risky, such was the feeling of intimidation), and from them I learnt that clever and intelligent people can be completely different.

Fritz was not a tall man; Hollings was. Fritz was mercurial; Hollings heavy artillery. If Fritz won an argument he would jump up and down on the wreckage of his opponent, whereas Hollings would simply clean his gun and move on. Fritz was one of the brightest people at R-RMC, with a deep understanding of the human condition. John Hollings used his military bearing to cow the toughest engineer. John Coyle, in charge of Electrical, was once summoned to Hollings' office due to some electrical problem on the car. John Coyle said, "Good morning," to which Hollings snarled in reply, "Pleasantries won't save you!"

Innocent bystanders such as me could occasionally get caught in the Feller/Hollings crossfire. Our workers were being poached by Jaguar, so Hollings drew up retention contracts for certain individuals to sign. Fritz talked me through my form, skilfully suggesting that there was no real need to sign it. Shortly afterward Hollings appeared, looked at me, declared that all stylists were "awkward bastards" and stormed off, leaving Fritz beaming. I avoided Hollings for a while after that.

On another occasion we were discussing SZ's roof panel at a viewing, and Fritz said he couldn't see anything wrong with it, whereupon Hollings indicated a modeller's stool and told Fritz he needed to stand on it, implying that he was too short to see! Never a dull moment.

Despite this running battle, both men were very experienced engineers with a real understanding of what Rolls-Royce customers expected. Hollings was happy for Fritz to get on with the mystical world of car aesthetics in the knowledge that Chief Executive David Plastow took a close interest in all proceedings.

This 1970s balance of power endured long enough to get the SZ family of Spirit, Spur and Mulsanne into production, from which point, for almost twenty years, all bets were off as this great British institution struggled to regain equilibrium in a rapidly changing world. With Vickers taking over R-RMC in mid-1980, David Plastow was increasingly engaged in London, and George Fenn became Managing Director at Crewe. Both Fritz Feller and John Hollings had health problems, and the latter asked me to stand in for Fritz as required.

John Hollings retired in the early 1980s, and he showed me the write-up of his departure in *The Daily Telegraph* before he went. I was surprised and quite touched that he also bothered to explain to me that his leaving was an amiable parting of the ways. He later asked me to give a lecture to the Rolls-Royce Enthusiasts Club at Paulerspury.

A new broom

Mike Dunn replaced John Hollings as Director of Engineering in 1983. Like a stick of rock, Mike had automotive engineer written right through him: working at Alvis, a disciple of Spen King at British Leyland, and then Chief Engineer on the Sierra – quite a radical style – at Ford of Germany. Tall, with powerful glasses and cropped, grey hair, Mike had the appearance and manner of a German-speaking Jesuit priest.

Mike centrifuged off the Catherine Wheel that was Ford to the quiet cloisters of Crewe; the cultural difference must have been immense. His core brief was to instigate a step change in how the Company tackled Engineering. Styling, part of his new flock, probably wasn't very high on his agenda, and it became apparent that Mike wasn't a great fan of chief stylists in any case.

As 1983 progressed, Dick Perry came up from MPW in London to replace George Fenn. It really was all-change at Crewe, as Peter Ward also arrived as Director of Marketing. Later in the same year Rolls-Royce and Bentley got its first Product Planning Director in the shape of John Stephenson from Vauxhall. Between them Perry, Dunn, Ward and Stephenson had to find a way to keep Vickers – well, the recently-knighted Sir David Plastow – happy with the finances.

The new Crewe boys were featured in a moody pop group-type photo in *Car* magazine. Although it might have seemed that their master plan was the re-birth of Bentley, they benefited somewhat from synchronicity. The outgoing order, although weighed down with keeping R-RMC viable, created the Bentley Mulsanne and Mulsanne Turbo, and it was blindingly obvious to the new guns in town that this was the marque to concentrate on. Apart from anything else, perhaps it was only Dick Perry who could really feel at ease in a Rolls-Royce.

It is better to travel hopefully than to arrive
Fritz Feller's increasingly poor health resulted in his retiring in 1984. Once telling me that I needed an agent more than a manager, one of his last comments was that I'd never gone behind his back: obviously no small thing to him.

I was now theoretically in charge of the Styling Department, answering directly to Mike Dunn. While most stylists would be gagging to hold such a position, I was not one of them. The image of a chief stylist languidly sketching his next masterpiece, handing it over to grateful worker ants who scurry away to build it, is not totally accurate. Modern styling departments are usually very large, multi-layered complexes, and Mike Dunn and John Stephenson, familiar with the setups at Ford and Vauxhall, must have been shocked by Crewe's resource. I had, however, three factors in my favour when it came to running the department: the second-to-none reputation of our products; the fact that Styling's budget barely registered on Mike's monthly print-outs; arrival of the new team of directors coincided with Styling's SX Rolls-Royce 'concept car,' so at least the department was productive.

Mike hadn't been responsible for a styling department before. While reviewing a car I would studiously write down his comments, as I genuinely respected his opinion. He, however, thought I was extracting the Michael and asked me to stop doing it. Luckily, on a trip to the Midlands we realised we both appreciated the comedian Al Reid, and the eccentric Ivor Cutler. I've found it to be the case that you usually get on with someone who laughs at the same things you do.

Mike had a huge task integrating the specialist elements and disciplines of Engineering into a harmonious team. Consultants were brought in for various team-building exercises, and a big issue was how to make meetings more productive: 'There's no such thing as a bad idea;' 'There's no 'I' in team,' and so on. The motor industry, traditionally, was pretty macho, with intimidation and heart attack-inducing confrontation the norm: Desmond Morris and David Attenborough would have been fascinated. Engineers simply enjoyed being combative: one exasperated consultant said that even if they did agree, they did so violently!

I suggested to Mike that stylists and engineers were different animals: he didn't disagree but wanted to keep Styling. Dick Perry apparently suggested I should report directly to him, but Mike wasn't keen on that idea. Electrical Engineering became responsible for the Styling Department, which may seem bizarre but Dereck Best, the engineer in charge, who admitted he couldn't tell one alloy wheel from another, was good with people. I was left to attend to aesthetics and he kept me in touch with inter-departmental activities, salaries, etc.

When the music stops ...
The next individual to have the dubious pleasure of taking Styling under their umbrella was Chris Cernes, another good-with-people, avuncular, experienced engineer bought in from the world of lorries by Mike.

Chris had been involved with early work on tilt-forward cabs, and told me one problem had been the windscreen falling out when the cab was tilted! The courtyard of his Cheshire farmhouse was full of unfinished Austin 7 specials, a partially restored charabanc, and general enthusiast paraphernalia – it's easy to like someone who occasionally thrashed a tiny Lambretta van down the country lanes to nearby Crewe. Chris was trying to kick-start the moribund SX/B programme, for which Tony Gott was attempting to design acres of plastic bodywork. In my presence a frustrated Chris gave Tony a raking for not chasing up a supplier.

Mike Dunn got on well with a new Commercial Director: American Howard Mosher. Mike had moved most of his people into the new Engineering block on the NNW side of the factory, leaving Styling on Mahogany Row. As Howard was literally next door I was asked to report to him.

Although a hard-nosed businessman, Howard was also a Barbour jacket-wearing Anglophile, and like all Americans, believed that if something looked good it probably was, a philosophy very compatible with aesthetics in general. Quick-witted and with a great sense of humour, Howard helped bridge the gap between a humble chief stylist and the chief executive when Dick Perry handed over to Peter Ward in 1986. At one meeting I said that Engineering needed to take its shoes and socks off in order to be able to count the spokes on the latest alloy wheel style, and Howard commented as we walked away, "You can never go back to Engineering now."

One of the tasks of my immediate superiors was to remind me that the Company was actually profit-based. If I was arguing the case for some aesthetic nuance Howard would say, "If someone was riding past on a horse, would they spot the difference?" Howard went back to the USA to take over the Sales and Servicing facility in New York. He had a wealth of experience and eventually joined BMW's Rolls-Royce factory at Goodwood as Marketing Director.

Next in line for the debatable pleasure of having Styling in their portfolio was Peter Middleton. Peter had taken over from Dick Perry at MPW, and was brought into Crewe on the commercial side; this also saved MD Peter Ward from having to look after Styling directly. Peter Middleton was a very helpful chap who tried to get Styling a new studio/viewing area. The fact that we continued to report to Marketing underlined the profound sea change at Crewe: a Company legendary for its engineering heritage was becoming marketing-driven.

Bentley's heady success meant the Company had a marque that Marketing could do something with, which didn't sit easily with its Rolls-Royce stablemate, whose cars could only be offered as convertibles, coupés, and long-wheelbase versions with specific prices. Bentley was perceived differently: using the same bodyshell, an entry model could extend right through to the top of the range – classic marketing territory. The Rolls-Royce ship of state steamed on at its own serene pace, regardless of what Peter Ward did at the helm. Bentley, on the other hand, was more reminiscent of a nippy frigate, darting here and there.

Crewe was beginning to lose its advantage with product specification, where once it had led the world with fully adjustable powered seats, electric windows, and air-conditioning, etc. Engineering worked hard but lesser marques were catching up fast, requiring greater marketing effort to promote more esoteric elements of the product, in addition to creating an engineering legend. Styling's aesthetic contribution became increasingly important, appealing as it did on an emotional level.

Styling and Engineering go their separate ways

My next boss, Mike Donovan, was the Commercial Director responsible for all marketing and associated resources, and Peter Ward's right-hand man, in effect. Ex-Land Rover, Mike had been a key player in the hugely successful and market-changing Discovery programme; also responsible for the imminent arrival of Jim Orr, another Discovery man, more of whom later.

Mike had insight and knowledge beyond his years. Something of an enthusiast, he'd tried his hand at racing single-seater cars. His 'Unique Selling Point,' in my opinion, was that he'd once owned a Messerschmitt KR175 Kabinenroller; any follower of its creator, Fritz Fend, was okay by me.

Mike was pretty bright on aesthetics; well, bright enough to give me the benefit of the doubt on a couple of occasions. With the dynamic duo of Ward and Donovan at the helm, Engineering was becoming a service facility more than a leading light of the Company. Mike Dunn, maybe sensing the inevitability of events, had let Mike Donovan assume full responsibility for the Styling Department on July 9, 1991. The following year, perhaps not surprisingly, Mike Dunn decided to leave the Company.

Mike Dunn had been extremely reasonable in his handling of Styling's shaky situation following Fritz Feller's departure. I'd always found it difficult to read marketing people, and Peter Ward was no exception. It seems quite likely that Mike saved me and Styling during Peter's early period as Chief Executive.

Mike Donovan could think outside the box, and when we visited the old Vauxhall Design Centre at Luton, he demonstrated how radical he could be. GM had left perhaps the best design facility in the UK – this huge, multi-floored block had fantastic roof-top styling studios. The engineering facilities were equally impressive, including superb test rigs, etc. As we left, Mike suggested that Rolls-Royce Engineering could move here en mass, and he wasn't joking. I said I thought it was too far from Production at Crewe, although it would, of course, have helped with the ongoing problem of coaxing experienced people up north. This exchange also demonstrated that, with Mike Dunn gone, Mike Donovan was in a very powerful position. A particular highlight of the Donovan years was when a group of us accompanied him to Italy in a Lear jet. Surprisingly small inside, it went like a fighter.

Efforts to make the Company more efficient were relentless, and an across-site head count reduction of around ten per cent was planned. Mike told me I had to secure voluntary redundancy of a senior employee in our department, so, not only could the department not expand or even regain lost ground, we had to absorb a 25 per cent reduction in manpower! When I pointed this out to Mike he became quite agitated and asked me to credit him with some intelligence. Shortly afterward, Martin Bourne, the last member of John Blatchley's old team, decided to depart, although, having set himself up in business as a freelancer, we worked together whenever possible.

Mike Donovan supported all my endeavours on various projects, joining me at numerous locations around the world, usually when finance reared its ugly head. Having a heavy-hitter from Crewe always proved very useful in foreign fields. Mike was subsequently head-hunted by BAE, and joined the world of aircraft, much to Peter Ward's undisguised chagrin. To my mind both Mike Dunn and Mike Donovan were fair-minded, clear-headed types, who gave Styling a lot of elbow room. Although Rolls-Royce and Bentley were experimenting in the 1990s with stand-alone project teams, losing individuals of such calibre was not a good thing. A company doesn't need too many top players, as they end up fighting each other, but it needs a few.

So who should be responsible for the Styling Department now?

It seemed to me that cutting out the middle man between me and Peter Ward wasn't an option. Peter was an outstanding marketing man, but got very irritated if his ideal world didn't mesh with reality. Results are one thing but marketing folk can tend to be biased towards the singer, not the song. Peter actually told me he wanted people like cricketer Ian Botham: "... someone to kick open his door." Peter had his hands full anyway maintaining the Company's glamorous image whilst running a not-always-glamorous factory.

Vickers Personnel came to me on April 11, 1995 to ask who Styling should report to. What to say? There was no one in Engineering. Jim Orr, running MPW special projects, was someone I respected greatly, but his bulldozer had the throttle jammed open. This left Marketing: less than ideal but, given the circumstances, the only player in town. Keith Sanders, Director of Sales and Marketing, declined to be directly responsible, so I reported to Ian McKay, a chap Mike Donovan had appointed as a pure marketeer. Well, Styling knew all about smoke and mirrors as its facilities had been run on a shoestring for years!

In the 1990s the factory's output of non-mainstream production vehicles greatly increased, with many and varied one-off and small batch manufacture of customer specials, including projects such as the Java concept car. This work tended to be outside of Marketing's remit. Mike Donovan and Jim Orr were successfully running an operation quite foreign to the more usual 'you build 'em, we'll sell 'em' relationship between Manufacturing and Marketing.

With the Company split between mainstream production and commissioned specials, Styling was also divided, and, with such a tiny team, I developed a dual personality: one week jumping continents to service Jim Orr's numerous programmes; the next supplying Crewe Marketing with its Styling service.

Jim's projects resulted in small batch production of Rolls-Royce and Bentley vehicles that were fully resolved, unique designs, necessitating the same aesthetic input as for any new car, giving tight schedules with little room for procrastination. Marketing, on the other hand, had little appetite to step behind Styling's shop window into the messy backroom, and was more comfortable with graphic design, so instrument faces and renderings for individual customers kept it happy.

The latter was particularly relevant to the bespoke production Rolls-Royce or Bentley. Our little team could set up a one-man styling studio at international motor shows, to illustrate how our vehicles could be tailored using the large palette of colour and trim schemes and specification options available. A picture is worth a thousand words and customers were entranced and delighted to be part of this creative process. In addition, renderings could be sent to customers who had approached their local dealerships, and might benefit from such a service. Not everyone could be offered this facility but enough were to make a difference. Man cannot live by pictures alone, of course, and the small team's absolute priority was new production hardware.

Essentially, I had two bosses: Jim Orr and Ian McKay. Jim's main interest was having enough lead shot to wipe out the grouse population of Scotland; Ian was into what sort of music and lighting would create the right ambiance when presenting cars. I always spoke to these two separately as their only common ground was that they were both bipeds.

'Strike up the brand'

Peter Ward resigned unexpectedly in late 1994, his role of Managing Director taken on by Chris Woodwark, who had run Cosworth Engineering, but had previously been the marketing man at Rover. Chris immediately set up a large Brand unit at Crewe, which further complicated Styling's activities as these –mainly – newcomers were divided into Rolls-Royce and Bentley camps, each of which was serviced by Styling, a smaller department. The Company still didn't have an engineering chief to balance the ever more powerful Marketing.

Chris Woodwark did, however, appreciate that Styling, as a core function, should have a larger facility, including an outside viewing area, but money was still too tight to accommodate any additional staff, other than possibly a college leaver. I continued to report to Ian McKay.

Chris Woodwark left for Vickers in early 1997, replaced later that year by Graham Morris, who had been an Audi marketing man. A little earlier, Ian McKay had suggested I concentrate on my role as Chief Stylist, allowing the oldest of my young team to tackle everyday administration. This seemed a case of renaming the same horses pulling a rather large carriage, but it helped the team to see some progression.

The late 1990s saw Styling's position at Crewe become more and more interesting. Apart from the fundamental issue of Marketing running an engineering company, having separate, cross-discipline engineering teams posed problems, not least of which was that a small, relatively inexperienced styling team simply couldn't be sub-divided amongst several projects.

Marketing put a huge effort into the 1998 launch of the Silver Seraph, and this, coupled with major changes and upgrading of the factory, served as a shop window for Vickers to sell the Company. Marketing wanted me to be 'Mr Rolls-Royce' for the Seraph's launch, and one of my team to be 'Mr Bentley' for that of the Arnage. Apart from the fact that this was sprung on me by Ian McKay at a Marketing meeting, it was such a falsehood that I refused to go along with what was akin to instructing an artist to step away from the picture he'd just painted to allow an apprentice to present the work as his own.

In the event Styling wasn't at the Bentley Arnage launch at Le Mans, or the later Rolls-Royce Corniche launch in America. Styling continued to report to Marketing during the 1998 sale process to VW. Just prior to a major presentation to VW I was publicly informed by Graham Morris that I wasn't going to present both marques. Possibly, Marketing wanted to suggest that the Company had a greater depth of Styling personnel than actually existed; although we were just about to commission an excellent new studio and outside viewing area, the team could still be counted on the fingers of one hand.

Back to Engineering ...
After a gap of over five years Rolls-Royce and Bentley Motors again had a 'Member of the Board for Engineering' in the shape of Tony Gott, who had previously inherited Seraph/Arnage as Chief Engineer. Tony then took control of Styling on July 30, 1998, when Graham Morris resigned, immediately following separation of the two marques between VW and BMW. On December 15 that year Tony became acting Chief Executive at Crewe. VW had a fundamental philosophy that engineers should run engineering companies, which included the Styling Department, of course.

Tony preached the Gospel according to cellular, project-based teams, and our meetings regarding Styling's rôle were a bit fraught. He'd obviously been impressed by Jim Orr's MPW/Blackpool teams, but Jim had been both ringmaster and lion tamer, his teams performing around his chair and whip.

Styling gets a Design Director
Tony Gott told me a little while after he'd officially taken the helm in 1999 that he was bringing in a Design Director from the VW group – Dirk Van Braeckel – to take over Styling. Dirk had the advantage of our freshly-commissioned Styling Centre, and was able to pull in experienced people from the VW Group, increasing staff ten-fold plus. Once again, yours truly was reporting to a director, which I continued to do until my departure in 2001.

Overview
Over the period 1971-2001 there had been no fewer than seven Managing Directors at Rolls-Royce and Bentley Motors, all of whom kept a close eye on Styling. For twelve years I reported to Fritz Feller, Head of Styling, and then nine different managers over the following fifteen years (five from Engineering and four Marketeers). During my final couple of years I reported to Crewe's first Director of Design (Styling), Dirk Van Braeckel.

Traditionally, UK manufacturing has had an ambivalent attitude toward aesthetic design. Neither Blatchley, Feller or I were made non-board member directors – possibly Fritz requested a directorship, but I didn't – although VW immediately appointed a non-board director. Because of the politics at Crewe over the three decades from 1970 with regard to such positions, it wouldn't have been a bed of roses in any case.

Considering the huge changes and challenges that occurred internally and externally during those thirty years, aesthetic standards were maintained due to key people at or near the top appreciating their importance. This was one of the reasons that the two marques survived until the significant injection of VW and BMW funds and resources in the late 1990s.

Given that no chief stylist/designer has ever run an automotive manufacturer, they have to report to someone

– directly or otherwise – and this has to be the managing director/chief executive. Engineering solutions often have to be taken on trust by company board members, but not so styling. A car's appearance is always the first to make an impression with potential customers: mechanical parts can be modified over time, but body shapes are fixed for years. We'll see how the various top men at Crewe approached their styling duties in another chapter.

> *Someone suggested an audio speedometer that would inform its driver of speed limits. Above a certain velocity a voice would intone, "Saint Christopher speaking [the Patron Saint of Travellers] you're on your own now, good luck."*

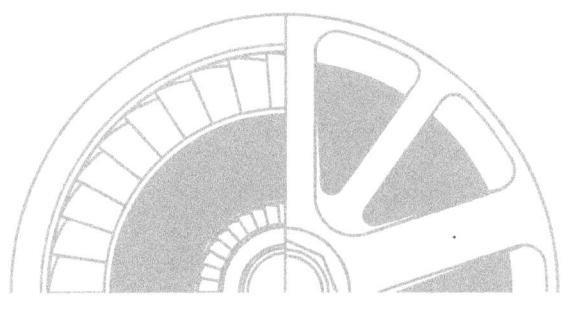

JAVA
THE EYES HAVE IT

A little complicated but worth the telling

The Java saga illustrates that not only was Rolls-Royce and Bentley Motors a rather special company, it was even more special than people imagined.

In 1991, the Bentley Continental R was the surprise star of the Geneva Motor Show. In 1994, again at Geneva, Bentley repeated the trick with Project Java. Peter Horbury, Head of Volvo Design and later Ford, said to me, "You've done it again." (referring to the company as a whole). The Crewe car factory always presented itself well to the world, but those in the industry knew we were now successfully punching above our weight.

What caught everyone's attention was that, in Java, the resurrected Bentley marque was showing a willingness to enter a very different market, with a radically downsized Bentley that was not looking to past glory but reaching for the future. Peter Ward and his right-hand man, Mike Donovan, took a deep breath, ran the flag up the pole to see if anyone saluted, and were rewarded by a cheering crowd.

Although using existing running gear, the vehicle on the show stand was a mock-up: in Styling-speak, a Concept Design Exercise. The chain of events triggered was exceptional: it spanned the reign of three managing directors, led to a follow-up programme with a major manufacturer and, separately, the building of several variants for special commissions. It also influenced the circumstances which led to the sale of Rolls-Royce and Bentley Motors four years later.

The start of Project Java

By the end of June 1992, Mike Donovan – now my boss – called me in to discuss Styling's workload. With Mike Dunn's recent departure, Mike Donovan was effectively Chief Engineer, based in Marketing.

Mike told me we needed to think through a programme for a smaller Bentley saloon or coupé based on a BMW 5 Series-type package. Previously, I'd half-jokingly suggested to Fritz Feller and Mike Dunn that we could clay-up over an actual BMW or Mercedes to kick-start Project SXB, the replacement four-door. However, this reference to a 5 Series had profound implications. Peter Ward wasn't one to waste time and money on a whim so this wasn't simply an amusing distraction. The 5 Series was highly rated in the industry, and, as Charles Matthews, Personnel Director, ran one, the interior space and packaging were quickly checked out.

As the small, in-house Styling team was fully engaged in ongoing tasks, tackling a fresh one required some thought: apart from anything else, paranoia over security for such a sensitive project upped the pressure. Following an earlier and productive SXB four-door replacement exercise with Design Research Associates (DRA), we phoned boss Roy Axe again. Ostensibly a Rover satellite, DRA would eventually become independent. Previously allowed to work on a Rolls-Royce because it wasn't a competitor to Rover, the two companies were connected in any case, through our mutual bodyshell supplier. Mike Donovan obviously had an inside line on Roy Axe's circumstances.

As far as 'Honest-Joe-Hull' was concerned, the BMW was just the best package in that class; we simply wanted to explore a Bentley four-door and coupé using its dimensions. During August 1992, Mike went to Warwickshire with me and told Roy Axe that BMW was more than just a reference point. Roy blanched as he was tasked with supplying Rover with a quota of styling ideas and mock-ups before being allowed full independence, with BMW a definite competitor. However, bigger cogs were turning in the background and Roy got the all-clear. Confidentiality was about as tight as it could be, and Crewe never quite acknowledged that Java sat on BMW underpinnings.

Experience with the downsized Rolls-Royce project of the early 1980s told us that a small Bentley would not be easy. Jaguar's X-type proved how tough it is to make a credible, compact, luxury car: superbly executed aesthetically, but was that Jaguar ever really convincing as a premium product?

Initial DRA sketches of a small Bentley saloon weren't reassuring. I had briefed the designers on our current thinking about the marque's visual values. They had done a lot of work for Rover on what constituted 'Britishness,' and were pretty much in sync with Crewe's product. Adrian Griffiths, DRA's Director of Design (later at Bertone) was very professional in his approach; although a novice at consultancy, he appreciated that the customer was always right, or should be allowed to think he was …

A Bentley's frontal appearance is critical. Since Turbo R, the marque had adopted four round headlamps as a signature feature to differentiate it from Rolls-Royce. Unfortunately, reducing the size of these headlamps to fit a smaller car dimished their visual impact, creating the same 'toy-like' effect that the 2001 Jaguar X-type suffered from. We were heading towards a scaled-down 'proper' Bentley, emphasized by the four-door requirement. Luckily, my masters began to recognise the commercial pitfalls of a small luxury saloon, and we were allowed to concentrate on a coupé.

Although the project had suddenly become much simpler, we still needed a new front end for the smallest-ever Bentley. On one of my regular visits to DRA, Roy Axe, Adrian Griffiths and I viewed a wall of sketches, as usual ranging from the sublime to the ridiculous. From this mass of ideas something jumped out at me: what were to become Java's unique signature 'eyes.' Roy and Adrian agreed: this wasn't sycophancy, stylists are wired much the same way, and this was a genuine eureka moment. Part of Bentley's DNA was raised front wing crowns, and the new

headlamp proposal accommodated and beautifully resolved the tricky junction of the wing crowns and front corner. The lamps were big and bold and complementary to the scaled-down radiator shell. This solution was so radical I made sure, via a bright red rendering, that the folks back home knew where we were heading.

By the end of 1992 we'd told DRA to proceed with a full-size clay based on the sketches, renderings and full-size tape lines. Work progressed with me visiting once a week, occasionally with Mike Donovan; Peter Ward attending key viewings.

With hindsight Peter and Mike were making it up as they went along; actually, this was no bad thing, much in line with Styling's thrashing-about-in-the-dark approach. One problem was that they wanted a show stopper, just as authors want best sellers. No doubt we could arrive at a decent coupé, but what was the point of it alongside the Continental R? We needed a selling point that was unique, apart from it being a smaller Crewe product. Folding hardtops were on our radar, although somewhat unproven at the time. In the mid-1990s we worked with ASC (American Sun Roof Company) in Detroit and associates Metalcrafters in California, building a folding hardtop for a special customer; but this was an idea too far for Java.

By late 1992 I was concerned about not giving Peter and Mike what they wanted (the fact that they didn't know what they wanted was irrelevant). I showed Mike Donovan some exciting examples of recent sports car concepts, smaller than the current Java clay, with no pretensions of being conventional coupés. This seemed to clear the log-jam. At the next viewing Peter Ward told me to cut six inches (152mm) off the back!

The next few weeks were very exciting as the full-size clay took on a life of its own. We abandoned any traditional cues such as the Corniche/Austin-Healey rear hip reference, and the nose was lowered even further, regardless of a shrinking radiator shell. The proposal became a style in the round with any view naturally flowing into another, and instead of a coupé it became a convertible with a removable hardtop. We never quite took those six inches off the back but the shape was a tighter fit on the BMW package than previously, facilitated by a lot of packaging and feasibility work by DRA's engineers. Finessing – ironing-out wrinkles and alloy wheels, etc – took several months.

Time was money, as Roy Axe occasionally pointed out, but no corners were cut. By the end of May 1993, Peter and

Mike had decided they'd show Java at the Geneva Motor Show in 1994, and during September 1993 the clay was signed-off and a fibreglass mould taken for the show car. My weekly visits to Warwickshire continued as the interior had to reflect the Crewe factory's enviable reputation. By British standards, Java was a fairly compact four-seater, the interior of which it would have been easy to 'over-stuff' when trying to convey real luxury (which is most effective when understated and subtle). My diary entry for November 19, 1993 records: "Interior signed-off: sad day for project as playing with clay has to stop." Attention now switched to our old friends at MGA Coventry, where the beautifully-finished Geneva show car was built. Richard Carter of DRA was key in pulling together this stage.

Surprise, surprise: it's a small Bentley

Journalists often write about the 'Star of the Show,' and at the 1994 Geneva Motor Show the Bentley Java concept couldn't have received more attention than it did. Resplendent in a metallic dark green with Harvest Gold leather, the model looked truly stunning. Peter Ward and Mike Donovan could not have asked for more.

Peter and Mike, Roy Axe and Adrian Griffiths unveiled the car to the waiting press. Ian McKay, my boss, had explained that Peter wanted DRA's involvement highlighted, because if the concept went down like a lead balloon he could laugh it off as a consultant's try-on. Certainly, at that time the financial cost of such a speculative exercise would have been eased by allowing DRA's involvement to be credited as part of the deal.

May's *Car* magazine featured Java on the cover, and asked, 'Just what makes a British car?' Art critic Brian Sewell came up to Crewe to see me. Despite his caustic reputation he understood Java's design-in-the-round style completely, describing it as: "... no line is disrupted or suddenly superseded."

Up until the Geneva show the project had several titles – MB (Medium Bentley); P220 (a DRA code), and Java, a previously-used Crewe project code. What followed made an unusual project unique.

P700/P705/P710

Just as Continental R at Geneva in 1991 particularly excited certain individuals, so, too, did Java three years later. Since the early 1990s Crewe had been building exclusive vehicles for particular customers, above and beyond the previous bespoke operations of MPW. We protected the design rights to Java convertibles, saloons, coupés and estates. To get serious about small batch production of these cars required feasibility to be double-checked and maximisation of interior space.

I'd imagined Java appealing to women: John Lennon's 'other half of the sky.' American women in particular were attracted to Mercedes' compact convertibles, so why not more so to Bentley? Currently, Rolls-Royce and Bentley were male owner preserves. Female drivers are responsible for one of the trickiest packaging problems – sun visors – as moving the seat forward and raising it so that the controls are within reach brings the head so close to the sun visor that it may not be possible to use it: a particular problem with Java. Making the windscreen a little more vertical; re-profiling the roof, and lowering the seats was necessary to cater for small ladies and large men. More space was also found for rear occupants. DRA re-worked Java on what was now P700, under Jim Orr's special commissions programme.

Both Peter Ward and Mike Donovan had left in 1994, and their baby was now in the hands of new Managing Director Chris Woodwark, who reviewed Java in 1995 and declared it "pretty." Due to other demands on Crewe's Engineering resource it was decided to move Java/P700 to MGA at Coventry, which was virtually an MPW satellite at this time, offering flexible capacity for prototype/ production work.

continued page 82

Overleaf, page 80: Perhaps the most audacious Bentley project ever, Java, was revealed at the 1994 Geneva Show. Based on a BMW 5 Series platform, this convertible/hardtop – a joint effort between Crewe Styling and Roy Axe's Design Research Associates – challenged many preconceptions. Creating great interest amongst public and industry alike, later, convertibles, estate and coupé versions were built to special commission. The headlamp solution was quite unique at the time.

Overleaf, page 81: Java's interior style successfully built on the Bentley Continental R's approach, its general appearance avoiding the 'over-stuffed' impression that was often an issue with compact luxury vehicles. Particular attention focused on the facia/through console which increases perceived interior size. The junction between facia and console proved tricky to resolve, but influenced future thinking.

Concept Java

Concept Java

Early in 1995, my old RCA chum Geoff Mathews was running a styling studio at MGA: so, Geoff, how about becoming involved in a convertible, coupé and estate based on concept Java? Given the usual 15-year life cycles of Rolls-Royce and Bentley, the idea of three new cars at the same time would have been a shock to the public at large.

Anyone who has engineered total hood stowage for luxury convertibles knows it's no easy task, especially with full four-seaters. Transforming a Motor Show tease into a real car is not an overnight job, even if based on a working platform. We had to deepen the vehicle's sides, and there were issues with the exhaust system, fuel tank and rear suspension. Apart from Crewe Engineering running the overall project, UK talent was drawn in as required, as well as hood design input from Europe and America. DRA packaging stayed involved, and I was visiting the Midlands once or twice a week.

The convertible was the key; once this was resolved the coupé (P705) and Estate (P710) could be tackled using full-size clays. Each vehicle had to have a unique interior due to different layouts. The estate was quite complicated as it was a four-door, and the rear load area received extra special treatment. The classic veneer, hand-stitched hides and solid brightwork – the envy of the world – were carefully employed.

The engine bays, which were non-standard, Cosworth twin-turbo units, reflected the attention to detail expected of such vehicles. Ironically for a programme that involved exacting packaging issues, the simplest of the three variants – the coupé – took the longest. Customers were always shown work-in-progress for the special projects, and, whether good or lucky, we rarely received negative feedback: with the Java coupé, however, we had to undertake several major re-works. Being a perfectionist, I welcomed the chance to carry on with the work, particularly as the customer's comments were spot-on! Of course, Styling never has a completely free hand, and, apart from different package requirements, Jim Orr hoped for maximum carry-over from the convertible and estate. In the end, accepting that the coupé couldn't accommodate anyone of Harlem Globetrotter dimensions allowed us to lower the roof and considerably slim the entire body side. We lengthened the wheelbase and fitted the largest wheels to this member of the trio, and, whilst each vehicle type had its own persona, those charismatic headlamps remained the star on all three.

In August 1996 I met Nigel Cornelius and Jim Orr on the Art Deco forecourt of MGA by the A40. Nigel was one of the few people trusted to look after Java customers. A super-smooth salesman from the David Plastow era, Nigel had the silver hair and tailored persona of a Harley Street consultant: the sort who could empty your wallet without you feeling a thing. He had been helicoptered in from holiday on Anglesey, and Jim had just flown in from the States to allow us to agree that the exotic coupé was now on course to satisfy the most exacting expectations. This we were able to do, and Styling was finally dragged away from the coupé project on November 19, 1996, and from the estate on April 15 the following year.

The Java P700 family was an exceptional achievement, even by Rolls-Royce and Bentley standards, and, apart from anything else, demonstrated what British design, craftsmanship and manufacturing could achieve when an unique opportunity presented itself.

BMW and P1000 – the big boys get interested

While the programme for small batch production of the three Java P700 variants progressed, a completely separate Java exercise began.

BMW had been sending flowers to Rolls-Royce and Bentley Motors for some time, and I visited that company in the early 1990s when Crewe's Mike Donovan and BMW's Carl-Peter Foster initiated a Crewe interior for the BMW 8 Series Coupé. Peter was then in charge of BMW's Experimental Department, and went on to head-up first GM's Opel, and then Jaguar in 2010. We modified a car; presented it in the Crewe Styling area, and BMW took it back to Munich, apparently pleased.

BMW became excited when it realized that Java was sitting on a 5 Series platform. BMW Chairman Bernd Pischetsrieder came to Crewe, and I was asked to show him our current work on the four-door replacement, and Java. He compared the Rolls-Royce radiator shell on the four-door to a ventilation duct ... Still musing on his – hopefully mistaken – English, I led him over to Java and opened the door. He could hardly wait to get behind the wheel, and like any true enthusiast soaked up the special ambiance that Crewe interiors possess. There was little point saying anything: he knew we knew he was hooked.

By February 1995, a proposal for Java production in 1999, based on the 5 Series, had been agreed: a dedicated British and German team based in Munich would develop the Java style to suit the next generation BMW M5.

While BMW resources could easily muster a multi-disciplined team, the British side had no spare people at all. As the raison d'être of the programme was style-driven it was assumed that Crewe would take care of this. Unfortunately, the whole of Crewe Styling didn't have enough people to man even one typical BMW project; apart from model year changes, we were also working on four-door replacement and numerous customer 'one-offs,' including the other P700 Java projects.

BMW's Chief Stylist, American Chris Bangle, and James Batchelor, a British project man, visited Crewe in mid-1995. When my boss, Ian McKay, asked him what he thought of Java, Chris replied that, perhaps the front didn't match the back! Despite this crassness, and subsequent nonsense about flame-surfacing, etc, I've found it difficult to really dislike any of the top stylists I've met. And in any case, when my umbrella was subsequently stolen from a German restaurant, Chris replaced it for me.

Chris explained that one of the reasons he got the BMW job was the 1993 Type 175 Fiat Coupé. When Chief Designer at Fiat, his and his team's designs always lost out to Pininfarina and others, and so with nothing to lose, so to speak, he just 'went ape' on the Type 175 proposal (note the strange slashes over the wheelarches). Much to his surprise, the design was chosen, and may explain some of the, arguably, wilful quirkiness of subsequent offerings from him.

Crewe's Tony Gott would be P1000 Project Director and Graham Lendon of Brand would ensure Bentley was in accord with BMW, leaving me to figure out how to manage the styling in Munich. Rolls-Royce and Bentley simply didn't have the resources to interface with a company like BMW, whose culture had evolved a multi-layered structure suited to the mass production of many different designs. My best possible strategy was to 'busk' the styling aspect as, hopefully, we would only need a clone or close relative of the existing, successful design.

One of my team, Simon Loasby, was stylist-on-the-spot at Futura Design in the Midlands. That project, P240, had parallels with P1000, as we were putting a special order, 1950s 'Cloudesque' style on to SZ underpinnings. Simon's father was Mike Loasby, an engineer who'd managed to make some sense of the De Lorean adventure. Simon had bags of self-confidence, and with a reasonably supportive clay-modelling studio, stood a good chance of achieving a Java MkII/ P1000.

Crewe Styling in Munich

BMW set up a satellite studio for P1000 in Munich, near its headquarters. On one of my work-in-progress visits I attended a weekly meeting of the British/German multi-discipline team, sitting through a couple of hours of mind-numbing progress reporting, little of which concerned Styling. Tony Gott, sitting opposite, asked for my opinion of the meeting: "Absolutely fascinating." I shamelessly lied, the comment bringing the house down with thigh-slapping Bavarian hoots of laughter. Apparently, with typical efficiency, BMW had organized classes in cultural differences between British and German people, where it had been explained that 'absolutely fascinating' was English for 'bored brainless.' Oh, well, better to leave them laughing.

German efficiency was also in evidence in the establishment of a temporary Design Studio near to BMW's Fitz Engineering citadel, which included a new surface measuring plate, computer terminals, and so on. I arranged for Geoff Mathews Design to lend us its Jonathan Gould to supply initial styling cover in Munich. Simon Loasby followed.

Although we had successfully re-worked the original Java show car as a fully resolved road vehicle, P1000 presented fresh issues. The new BMW 5 Series had a longer wheelbase and different packaging, particularly around the rear suspension. Again, due to the practical constraints of a fully concealed hood, the vehicle's height had to increase. And unlike P700, the wheel envelopes also had to accommodate snow chains. Progress was quickly made in establishing a clay shape, cloning Java around the new 5 Series package. Parallel to this we'd created some 40 per cent scale models which incorporated the latest technical requirements, reaching even further into the future.

I asked DRA to provide one of the new models, and Chris Bangle suggested its Californian Studio Designworks USA create the other. Unable to travel to the States, a live audio/visual conference link was set up, which turned out to be especially memorable as I was trying to brief three American stylists who may as well have been sitting on Mars, as the satellite signal lapse made picture and speech hopelessly out of sync, bordering on the surreal. A difficult situation was made worse by Project Director Tony Gott, sitting beside me but off camera, completely cracking-up and laughing uncontrollably throughout. The mike must have picked it all up. I managed somehow to keep going but our American friends must have concluded that Monty Python's Flying Circus really was a documentary, after all!

After several visits to Munich I felt we had achieved all we could. It's not always easy to coax a group of modellers to re-work clays, and Simon achieved good quality viewings of the various iterations. The new BMW package had subtly morphed the original Java into a slightly less attractive sibling. The parts bin philosophy was dictating and restricting styling options, which opened up the whole debate about shared platform limitations. If a company is charging a premium for a unique product, at what stage is the customer being sold short by a less than ideal solution? Interestingly, VW later showed great sensitivity to this issue on the Corniche 2000.

James Batchelor tackled me about doing an interior for P1000 but I demurred. Obviously, BMW was keen to see how Crewe's magic was worked, but what would we gain? Doubtless, we could have rummaged in BMW's parts bin to see what we could use or modify, but we had neither the time nor the resources. If P1000 flew, the interior would be as close as possible to the original show car in any case.

Back at Crewe

Having completed our exterior programme with BMW, the dressed clay arrived at Crewe at the end of January 1996, and we also had the 40 per cent model of Java MkII developed, with DRA incorporating latest package updates. The other model styled in California was not deemed suitable.

The P1000 team realized that without direct Crewe Styling supervision, a Crewe product would not be possible. We showed the P1000 work to Vickers on February 26, 1996, Chris Woodwark and Tony Gott doing the honours. It was only fair to let Simon Loasby present the styling aspects, as he'd not had it easy. Of course, had P1000 been an absolute stunner I would have felt duty bound to humbly step forward to accept all the accolades. We also presented composite photographs of P1000 against current Crewe product, to ensure its size was appreciated.

It always seemed to me that P1000 never had much water under its keel, and it gently beached following this viewing. Certainly, Chris Woodwark had enough on his hands with factory upgrades and the Silver Spirit replacement. The Medium-Sized Bentley (MSB) concept remained alive, and a replacement for Continental R became the next key project.

Overview – Java – P700/P705/P710 – P1000

The circumstances surrounding these projects resulted from some of the strengths and weaknesses of Rolls-Royce and Bentley Motors. While the P1000 team was grappling with getting a potential mainstream car onto the starting blocks, MPW was actually building variants of the same

vehicle, which were delivered to customers (these were not experimental/development vehicles but fully finished cars). The engineering section, controlled by MPW, was a company within a company, and mainly separate from mainstream Crewe Engineering. The two cultures involved were different and largely incompatible, with Styling one of the few common links.

Crewe didn't have a packaging team, mainly because the vehicle platform had essentially been based on the 1965 Silver Shadow for so long. Packaging is an awkward mix of engineering/design/styling, more aligned to industrial design than everyday engineering. It caused a major problem, even at the temporary studio in Munich. Everyone wanted to see quick results in the clay, but the hastily assembled BMW packaging team required a steep learning curve, needing to get up to speed with the latest 5 Series and see how it related to Java; with Styling so far ahead, clay re-working was inevitable, even without purely aesthetic requirements. This weakness regarding vehicle packaging and feasibility had caused fundamental problems at Crewe for years, and continued to do so. One of VW's early actions in 1998 was to set up a specialist unit in the new Styling area that was well versed in this critical discipline.

P1000 was created during the years that the Company didn't have a chief engineer. Apart from those at MPW, there were no wise engineering grey-beards keeping an eye on overall Company resources. Instead, there were project team engineers tightly focused on their own tasks. Having a chief stylist meant that the Company did not easily fit into the 'stand-alone' project team format. It wasn't possible for each team to have its own chief stylist, and my superiors expected me to be the 'eyes and conscience' of the Company as a whole. The fact that this key element was outside of the control of the P1000 Project Director didn't sit easily; while his team was struggling, the Chief Stylist was happily helping MPW resolve its versions of Java. Inevitably, tensions arose.

On the plus side Java/P1000 demonstrated how attractive Crewe product was to one of the most successful car companies in the world, and there was no lack of mutual respect. Whilst there was no comparison between the size and facilities of the two companies, it was still apparent just how much the British had achieved on a much leaner burn.

Conclusion

Would Java have worked in mainstream production? With Crewe limited to a little over 3000 units a year, a completely different animal was needed to facilitate the Company's ability to generate more funds, a conclusion that VW had also reached and acted on quickly with the Continental GT.

At the risk of taking Mandy Rice Davies' "He would say that, wouldn't he" quote out of context, Java was ahead of the game and about as good as it got. Echoes of its style and general proportions can be seen in many subsequent models, particularly the numerous folding hardtops of the mid-noughties. Great minds think alike, and Volvo's attractive C70 of 1997 was also not too dissimilar. Certainly, Java's original and unconventional headlamp solution is now a familiar sight on the roads, with Mercedes and Jaguar, to name but two, using a similar shape to resolve front wing corners. Those charismatic eyes were used again on a larger, one-off coupé based on Continental R running gear for a customer special commission.

The Java was conceived as the smaller sibling of the Bentley family alongside the vehicles seen here – a replacement saloon SXB and Continental R – but couldn't appear merely as a compact Continental R. The blue dressed-clay reflected Rolls-Royce and Bentley saloons ideally having different bodyshells.

After an illustrious career as a Design Chief in the UK and USA, Roy Axe, in his 2010 autobiography A Life in Style *put Java on the cover. You can't ask for more than that.*

85

CHIEF EXECUTIVES
FROM SIR DAVID TO TONY

The rôle of the top man

In the period between 1971 and 2001 there were seven managing directors at Crewe.

Styling departments need a special relationship with the people running a company because one of the requisites of an MD is to ensure the company's survival for the future. If the guy at the top isn't close to the futurists, the prospects aren't good. Aesthetic direction can be decided by committee, but whatever the decision-making structure is, the fewer the people involved the better. You can have a dictator-type MD with a good eye, or someone who trusts the chief stylist: a little of both is best.

Working within the same company for a long time, one's perception of those in charge changes. First regarding them as Gods, commonly, this impression gradually fades to something much less until, finally, an understanding is reached that these are mere mortals after all, in much the same way that we come to appreciate this fact about our parents.

Those entrusted with Rolls-Royce and Bentley motor cars had a tricky job. Outwardly purveyors of the ultimate carriages for gentlemen; in reality having to deal with all of the everyday problems of any car manufacturer. Balancing image with actuality requires a special talent, and because of the extraordinary heritage and expectations of the market about this factory's product, it seemed as if the men at the top had a tiger by the tail.

Tremendous changes occurred in the thirty-year period that this book deals with, particularly in the UK.

Without getting too political, the UK 'us and them' culture of unions versus management cannot be ignored. Apart from such issues as demarcation at Crewe, we worked closely with British Leyland, where industrial relations were the stuff of nightmares. Things could get pretty lurid in the 1970s, but, by the early 1990s, the whole structure about who does what and where, and for how much, was transformed for the better.

David Plastow: January 1971-June 1980 (Sir David from 1986)

By today's standards, 1970s management was very autocratic, and, I guess, Rolls-Royce Motor Car Division more so than most. It was a legendary company, geographically isolated, on the outskirts of one of the most unlikely host towns. Within its boundaries the factory maintained a kind of British Empire set of standards and hierarchy. Due to its Merlin aero-engine background – and still wearing wartime camouflage paint – the site existed in something of a time warp (many of the cycles in the racks still had blackout-requirement white paint on their mudguards, for example). All the more surprising, then, to find a young, very switched on chap like David Plastow in charge of this slice of British anachronism.

Due to Rolls-Royce Aero experiencing problems with the RB211 engine, the Company, in 1971 was, well, bust. Many of the directors dealing with this awkward circumstance seemed 'old school'; John Hollings, the Chief Engineer, was particularly intimidating. About twice as tall as my boss, Fritz Feller, Hollings could, when required, project an aura of benign menace of Stalinesque proportions, when it was easy to imagine him using a large service revolver to dispatch a troublemaker. Tall, fair-haired David Plastow was, by comparison, much more subtle about getting what he wanted, possessing an easy charm and charisma that most prime ministers would envy. He called Fritz 'Fritzy,' much to our leader's mutual embarrassment and pleasure. Plastow was of the new generation of media-savvy industrialists; his PR advisor, one David Roscoe, concealed beneath a Cardinal Richelieu facade a great sense of fun and boyish enthusiasm. It took me years to figure out these people – at the time, pretty much running scared and completely out of my depth; just aware that we were privileged to be in the top corridor, frequently showing our work to these deities.

From his experience of selling many Silver Shadows, David Plastow understood the luxury car market, and re-launching the MPW two-door as Corniche was a brilliant move. Given that Camargue had been created entirely by Pininfarina, Plastow could easily have closed Crewe's Styling Department altogether, but luckily sensed the importance of an in-house resource. Like those who followed, he also appreciated the advantages of having an inner sanctum viewing and presentation area, and he it was who provided Styling with this key asset.

During the 1970s, factory attention focused on the fact that 97 per cent of all production was Rolls-Royce, although Plastow readily supported Styling's tentative forays into Bentley concept work, and his decision to launch Mulsanne in 1980, as part of the SZ family, was effectively the start of the Bentley revival. Grabbing the lifeline that was Vickers was evidence of a shrewd assessment of what was the best deal in town (leading a boarding party is a better analogy). In 1976, *The Guardian* newspaper named Plastow 'Young Business Man of the Year.'

Money was always too tight to mention, and like any medium-sized factory there were huge overheads and daily running costs. For instance, with a 3000-plus workforce and areas such as the comprehensive machine shop the electricity bill alone would have been enough to make anyone wince. Every time electricity consumption rose above a certain level, a series of klaxons would sound factory-wide, prompting workers to turn off something or other. The klaxons sounded one winter's afternoon, followed, seconds later, by David Plastow throwing open our office door. Casting wild glances around the room, he demanded, "Are these lights strictly necessary?" The

half dozen fluorescent tubes were hastily extinguished, leaving Crewe's futurists sitting in fading November light. "Gordon Bennett!" I thought "things must be tough!" Maybe being so close to the MD's office wasn't such a good idea, after all.

David Plastow stayed closely involved in Styling's activities, but generally believed that Fritz Feller understood the Rolls-Royce owner. Plastow never relied on a Styling Viewing Committee as such, but always ensured John Hollings and the other chief engineers, such as Macraith Fisher and Jock Knight, were present at these. After agreeing some new feature, he'd turn to them and ask, "So, who's going to do the work?" He probably imagined himself in the rôle of Rolls to Hollings' Royce.

All of the MDs experienced problems addressing the troops when they were assembled en masse for briefings, due to a strange dynamic, fairly typical of the British workforce in general, which ranged from excitement at the occasion to distrust and barely concealed hostility toward all management. General monthly briefings were conducted by local managers and, later, team leaders, though occasionally there was no alternative but to gather the entire workforce together for education and enlightenment sessions about the Company's present and future prospects. It was a kind of 'Meet the Directors' for the annual report and opportunity to ask questions.

The two Davids – Plastow and Roscoe – came up with a wizard wheeze to avoid any potential embarrassment at these presentations. Instead of Plastow attending in person, the assembled masses watched a large cinema screen on which our leader was interviewed by Brian Redhead. Redhead was a well known BBC TV and radio presenter, instantly recognized and liked. This tactic seemed a bit strange to me but, all respect to the idea as the audience seemed to accept it. I was at Crewe railway station on one occasion when Redhead appeared at the top of the stairs and roared out, to the world in general, "When is the next train to London?" He had a brilliant mind but media people do seem eventually to go slightly mad.

After leaving for Vickers headquarters in London, Sir David Plastow maintained his support and paternal interest in the car factory and its people – but he never wanted to hear the word 'Roller,' ever.

George Fenn: June 1980-mid-1983
Ideally, a managing director doesn't depart without the next incumbent having ridden shotgun for a while, and David Plastow had George Fenn shadowing him for some

time as George prepared to take over at Crewe as Chief Executive. The country and economy faced numerous problems during the period concerned: IRA mainland bombings; then the 1982 Falklands War, and ongoing industrial relation unease culminating in the miners' strike of 1984. Company sales had slumped by 1982, despite the relatively new four-door saloon. However, a glimmer of light was the turbocharged Mulsanne, identified by the simple but potent ploy of painting the radiator shell body colour.

Because of Fritz Feller's ongoing health issues, adding to George Fenn's problems was the fact that he often had to talk to a troglodyte like me about styling: presenting a Turbo wing badge and its proposed position to him, it was obvious that Mr Fenn had little faith in this RCA graduate. Still, despite all the trials and tribulations he had to deal with I don't recall any displays of bad temper, or even irritation from George Fenn: that sort of grace under pressure is no small achievement.

Mike Dunn asked me to do a framed rendering of the Silver Spirit for George's farewell presentation. Some years later George told me he still had it, although not in which room it hung ...

Richard Perry: mid-1983-October 1986

Everyone thought of Richard Perry as Dick, although it felt far too familiar to call him that. As George Fenn gradually handed over the reigns, Dick Perry took over full-time from running MPW in London. This now appears to have been part of a master plan by Vickers to keep the show on the road while a new regime had time to get to grips with multiple issues. Peter Ward arrived to take over Marketing, Mike Dunn Engineering, and John Stephenson to establish Product Planning. Also during this period Fritz Feller decided to retire, leaving me as Chief Stylist, so to speak.

Given the demands of running a factory in a harsh economic climate, aesthetics probably weren't too high on Dick Perry's list of concerns. Fortunately, we had just completed the SX concept car, so at least he had some evidence of intelligent life in Styling. It soon became obvious, however, that the only way of impressing an ex-Fleet Air Arm pilot would be to balance a pint of beer on my head while reciting all the verses of 'There's only one pub in town,' and as this wasn't really my forte, the future looked bleak. Dick was quite capable of good-old fashioned, motor industry raging anger. An engineer brought up from MPW a high-mounted stop lamp for Corniche to obtain sign-off at the Styling review. Admittedly, it wasn't

the prettiest of things, but Dick went absolutely ballistic, sparing the hapless presenter nothing. During the tirade I had to step away from the unfortunate recipient or risk scorch marks on my clothes!

Dick Perry had to deal with a rare, all-out strike by the hourly-paid workforce, which gave rise to a classic Dick Perry anecdote. Driving slowly through the large orderly picket every morning, he was regularly harangued by one Tony Jenkins, a very enthusiastic and effective shop steward. One evening, late, Dick ate the fieriest Indian meal he could stomach. Next morning, as Tony began his daily verbals, Dick wound down his window and, breathing the fiery fumes into Tony's face, thanked him for his comments, the pungent aroma shocking Tony into silence. Having heard this story from both sides, it appears to be true.

Most people who have served in the Forces possess a fairly black sense of humour. At a boardroom presentation on In-Car-Entertainment I argued against over-complicated controls as they could lead to fixed, puzzled, expressions in the morgue: the result of someone trying to master a stereo's graphic equalizer, say, whilst driving. This seemed to go down well and represented a turning point between Dick Perry and myself, as a shared sense of humour is a great bridge builder. Happily, the advent of the Turbo R also raised spirits. Ultimately, Dick Perry was the only managing director at Crewe who suggested Styling report directly to him, and it was also he who told me to work closer with John Heffernan and Ken Greenley on Corniche/Continental R.

For such a robust personality Dick was remarkably sensitive to the wants and needs of the workforce, replacing the segregated dining areas with one open-plan restaurant nicknamed 'Dick's Diner,' and run by a top catering firm. His masterstroke, after the debilitating strike, was ensuring every employee, regardless of status, got a company car ride: a huge undertaking with a couple of Rolls-Royces constantly employed giving joy rides. Most employees were hardly able to relate to the product they made, never previously experiencing the superb comfort of these legendary vehicles. The rides were particularly useful to the men and women involved with trimming the seats, as leather seat comfort is directly attributable to the skills of the machinist who tensions the surfaces. After the rides the men were given a company tie and the ladies a silk scarf. The exercise was a simple gesture but showed an appreciation of the workforce that was well received. I liked Dick Perry; not least because he'd been a development driver on the Austin A30, my first car. He was a rare example of a larger-than-life character you could enjoy working for.

Peter Ward: October 1986-December 1994

With Peter Ward taking the reins the Company was now led by a marketing man. Bright as a button, Ward had seized on Bentley as the way forward, and considered styling a key element of the product. Quite honestly, however, I never knew where I was with him. He once complained of being too busy to get a haircut (as if). He pretty much had me down as a backroom boy, and therefore not really marketable, saying he wanted "Ian Botham types." Despite this lack of personal synchronization, Styling's track record during his eight years was, if I may say so, remarkable, and we achieved –

• Continental R/Azure
• Java show car
• Numerous model year changes
• Numerous 'one-off,' specially-commissioned cars
• Two projects with BMW
• A second and larger Styling viewing area
• Four-door replacement family

At the end of the 1980s, annual production reached 3333 cars: very high for Crewe, and the Company managed to break even in 1993 in spite of a difficult trading background. Although Peter obviously enjoyed the car world, the running of any factory is a heavy burden, and being able to see opportunities and ways forward – but forced to wade through the heavy clay of manufacturing reality to reach them – can't have been easy for him.

There were lighter moments, of course. At one viewing we'd taken the bonnet off a Continental R, and lain it beside the vehicle being viewed. While addressing us, Peter walked back into the bonnet and, to keep his balance, was forced, arms windmilling, to step quickly right into the middle of this superbly finished piece of automotive perfection. Trying to make light of this highly embarrassing moment for him I blurted out, "Don't worry, it was knackered anyway." "It is now," was his reply.

Apart from all the usual Company activities, we were flirting with BMW, and there were pros and cons in such a co-operation. I was asked to be present in the Styling Studio while Peter took some BMW VIPs around the site, showing them renderings of P2000/P3000 (Arnage/Seraph) which could be candidates for some BMW systems. During a long, contemplative pause, I said, "A Rolls-Royce or Bentley will always be greater than the sum of its parts."

To my amazement, Peter gave me a surreptitious pat on the back: presumably, I'd said something right at last!

Regardless of personality differences, Peter Ward's grasp of the product could not be faulted. He was able to pick Bentley off the tree like ripe fruit, and everything we did for that marque worked. Rolls-Royce was a completely different matter. This marque was a conundrum, a Gordian knot, and it was very hard to revitalise the image of such a well established brand: the old King had to sit, immobile, on his throne while his younger brother, Prince Bentley, had all the fun. A Turbo R presentation of Peter's featured The Eagles track 'Life in the Fast Lane.' He may have felt less affinity with Rolls-Royce, but, given limited resources and Bentley's success and obvious potential, where would you have put your money? That's not to say the senior brand was ignored because Spirit/Spur had many reviews and updates. It was, of course, largely under Peter's watch that the P2000/P3000 family of Arnage and Seraph was designed, a programme ostensibly intended to first get Rolls-Royce right – which was what I was told to do, at least.

After working quite closely with someone for eight years it was a shock when Peter walked away one afternoon, apparently due to a commercial deal with BMW rather than Mercedes (it was generally believed that Peter favoured the latter company and Vickers the former). The first I knew of it was a headline in *The Evening Sentinel*, the Potteries' daily. It seems he did at least tuck the red tenth-scale model of the Continental R we'd organized for him underneath his arm as he left. Despite all of the pressures, Peter certainly enjoyed the styling aspect of the job with so many different and exciting projects.

Chris Woodwark: December 1994-March 1997

When I presented the new four-door to the Vickers Board on December 15, 1994, Rolls-Royce and Bentley Motors didn't have a managing director (or engineering director). However, unbeknownst to me, the next Chief Executive, Chris Woodwark, was drawn from the large gathering of Vickers bosses, and, out of the seven MDs I worked for over the years, was the only one to be parachuted into Crewe, because of Ward's sudden departure. Chris had previously been at Rover, and was another marketing man.

Not surprisingly, marketing men tend to understand marketing more than they do the nuts and bolts of a car, and one of the first things that Chris did was strengthen Marketing by adding a Brand wing to it, bringing in a number of people to study and create differentiation between the Rolls-Royce and Bentley marques.

Considering that Styling was already taking care of this aspect, I was somewhat bemused by this influx of specialist brand experts.

Having seen several MDs come and go, certain themes reoccur. The opening few months of the new MD's tenure are especially fraught as this is when he is most likely to make sweeping changes – 'Cabinet reshuffles' – and, inevitably, departures sometimes occur. Styling is a little sheltered from this potential firestorm unless the new MD hates something an individual's name is associated with, or you openly disagree with a new directive.

Production managers, eager to impress the new MD, would suggest instant cost-saving ideas, one of which concerned boot carpet, which was exactly the same quality, colour and binding as that used for the interior. Why not make all boot carpets black, and of a cheaper quality, was the suggestion, which always forced me into the rôle of party-pooper, because how could any stylist support such a downgrade?

Even worse than 'cheap' boot carpets, was the under-bonnet issue. Regardless of exterior paint colour, all cars had the engine bay carefully masked and sprayed low-gloss black, which no mass production car manufacturer bothered to do, leaving lumpy welds and ugly joint sealant clearly on view. I once arranged a comparison viewing, with those from Production who had suggested the idea, of two white cars – one with and one without black paint – to demonstrate the impracticality of this idea. At the viewing it was blindingly obvious that the white engine bay was that of a Ford or a Mercedes; the black-painted one could only be a Rolls-Royce or Bentley.

Unfortunately, whenever these old cost-savings 'initiatives' were resurrected it wasn't possible to simply state, "It won't work." When the new MD approached me with either suggestion I had to react as if this was the breakthrough we'd been waiting for and arrange yet another viewing.

When he arrived, Chris had very little room to manoeuvre regarding product. The four-door replacement could still be tweaked, but no one was suggesting we try and change the shape. He did have the early fillip of launching Azure, the Bentley Continental convertible, at Geneva in March 1995, but opportunities to style unique 'one-off' cars for special customers were reducing. Indeed, Chris had to ensure the tricky exclusivity issues associated with creating bespoke designs were organized to everyone's satisfaction. One of his main tasks was the ongoing job of converting the factory to an open-plan layout, and he

also had to suture the open wound to British pride caused by the recent decision to use BMW elements, including engines; the reason for his predecessor's departure. Chris was also a keen believer in all on the Crewe site wearing a Bentley 'uniform,' so everyone was issued with free, green-logoed sweaters, etc.

The engine issue – the switch from a British engine to German V8s and V12s – never went away. Styling had worked hard to dress the P2000/P3000 V8 and V12 engines and surrounds to achieve a credible Crewe product. At Styling's monthly viewing, Chris glanced at our two superb engine bay offerings and turned away, commenting that "… no one opens the bonnet anyway." As every road test I've ever seen has a photo of the engine bay, his comment may have been a reflection of how unsure he felt.

By the time that Chris came to Crewe, Styling's office accommodation had reached an all-time low. Following the glory days of Mahogany Row, we now occupied 'the bungalow,' a single-storey building at the front end of Third Avenue, while Engineering and Marketing enjoyed new or upgraded facilities. The upside was that security was excellent, as no one would waste torch batteries looking for secrets of the future in such an unlikely setting. Walking across the yard with Chris and my boss, Ian McKay, I invited Chris to visit the Company's Styling office, which, not surprisingly, he declined to do, having enough on his plate without worrying too much about Styling's circumstances. Due to his Rover experience he did, however, regard us as a core resource, and recognized that we needed better facilities, including an outside viewing area.

Monthly viewings in the Styling Studio/presentation area continued, and involved the directors, plus any other interested parties. I coordinated the people and exhibits, ran two dress rehearsals, and circulated the agenda and minutes, which was very time-consuming. Ian McKay was aware of my unease that what was structured to be decision-by-committee always ended up with the MD having the final say. I argued the case for cutting the number of attendees, but I guess everyone needed to feel involved.

During Prime Minister's Question Time, members of the Cabinet chat away behind the PM as he talks, and it would be much the same situation at these viewings. On one occasion when I was presenting an item, Chris was chatting away to Keith Sanders, the Marketing Director, so I stopped talking mid-sentence. After a while Chris noticed that his was the only voice that could be heard, and he stopped talking also, whereupon I resumed my presentation. This happened four times in total, until eventually Chris and Keith got the message, and the presentation continued in a more orderly fashion.

People are generally remembered for their interests and quirks: Chris was fond of quoting the concept of selling the idea of Christmas to turkeys. He moved on to Vickers Head Office.

Graham Morris: arrived March 1997, resigned July 1998, departed May 1999

The man who followed Chris Woodwark was from Liverpool and Audi, in that order. Graham Morris was another marketing man, and – like most people from Beatle City – was tough, though possessing a sense of humour. I'd come to appreciate, by the time that Graham took up the position, that running the Rolls-Royce and Bentley factory was extraordinarily difficult, not least because the Company's outward image and its actual day-to-day working life were so different: steep learning curve didn't begin to describe it.

Graham's tenure was especially eventful for a number of reasons –

- At the 'New MD addresses his managers' session, Graham's résumé included the information that at one company he'd worked for, he'd made his own father redundant. The implication being, if he could do that to his father ...
- Three months in, Graham was quoted as saying that all employees showed a lack of understanding of business in the world market, and that Company standards did not measure up to those of key competitors
- Six months in, Vickers decided to sell, Graham found out whilst on holiday
- Nine months in, Graham Morris launched the Rolls-Royce Silver Seraph
- Twelve months in, he launched the Bentley Arnage and BMW appeared to have bought the Company, though hadn't quite
- Sixteen months in, on July 3, 1998 VW bought the Company
- Sixteen months and three weeks in, on July 28, 1998, BMW/VW announced an agreement about splitting the two marques; Graham Morris resigned
- Despite having officially resigned, Graham continued at Crewe until Tony Gott formally became Chief Executive in May 1999

Not least of Graham's worries was a narrowly-averted shop floor strike on the eve of the Silver Seraph's UK launch at Crewe.

Marketing was to use the refurbished, open-plan factory as a key element of the launch. Graham had previously instructed factory managers to generally improve shop floor tidiness, and only allow refreshments in allocated areas. When a supervisor disciplined a chap who had a can of Coke on his bench, this got everyone's back up and a strike was threatened.

Marketing's Silver Seraph presentation to journalists, dealers, etc, occurred in a temporary theatre at the front of the factory shop floor. At the presentation's finale, it had been intended to theatrically fling open the back curtains to reveal a factory full of cars being happily worked on by staff, so imagine launch guests arriving at a picketed factory and being shown a strike-bound production line: an MD's nightmares don't get any worse. A desperate Graham Morris called a management meeting at the foot of the entrance hall stairs, and implored them to pull every string they knew to avert this possible strike action. At the eleventh hour things calmed down and visitors were unaware of the drama that had gone before.

As a footnote to the threatened 'Coke Strike,' coincidentally, a member of Styling kept an old, classic glass Coke bottle for aesthetic inspiration, just visible from the factory yard through a frosted glass window. Graham Morris made a rare visit to our office one day to order me to remove it. I don't suppose he ever drank Coke again, either ...

Apart from wrestling with everyday factory problems, Graham must have been, at best, bemused by the whole issue of 'special customer cars.' Not only was he trying to make sense of the economics of luxury car production, but also this significantly profitable element of production that was totally beyond anyone's business experience. (Examples of which are recounted in chapter 15.)

As well as the usual ongoing tasks, Styling's main projects during Graham Morris' reign were a stretched Silver Seraph, and Continental R and Corniche replacements. For the Seraph/Arnage launch, Marketing had wanted to 'split' the chief stylist's role between Rolls-Royce and Bentley, with me as Mr Rolls-Royce and someone else in the department as Mr Bentley. At this point, my neutral attitude towards Marketing took a negative turn. Whilst undoubtedly clever, its flexibility regarding reality was questionable, and Marketing would have been just as happy to bring in professional actors for these rôles.

Graham Morris' Bentley Arnage launch sidestepped my opposition by placing the emphasis on Engineering. This skewed philosophy continued, with Graham not allowing me to present both Rolls-Royce and Bentley projects to VW, even though I was directly responsible for the products in question.

Without a Mike Dunn-type chief engineer to inject some experience and practicality into Marketing's Disneyland, Styling viewings were definitely a touch fraught. The interface between fact and fantasy always make Marketing people irritable, but after one Continental R replacement (Bali) viewing on May 14, 1998, I almost left the Company, as it was all too apparent that the people running the show really didn't understand how cars were styled or designed. In the event, Bali was progressing quite well, and a few weeks later VW took over ownership of the Company anyway.

During Graham Morris' tenure our department finally got its new facilities – including an outside viewing area – despite even a small increase in the tiny head count being denied. Working for Graham Morris had not been without its moments, but like many people with a short fuse, the sun usually appeared again after any thunderstorm. His eventful employment included keeping a factory functioning as it was sold and its two iconic marques separated. Most regard his resignation as an honourable act in a troubled situation: that VW didn't want him to go – and that he continued to 'caretake' for some time – speaks volumes. I'll always remember him telling us that, as a boy, he'd delivered groceries to Beatle George Harrison.

Tony Gott: 1999-March 2002

Tony Gott worked his way up through Engineering, managing model year programmes, the exercise to get P1000 Java into production with BMW, and the later stages of Seraph/Arnage. Interested in watersports, he was, apparently, an efficient dinghy sailor.

VW was obviously going to be somewhat apprehensive about taking over the Crewe factory and its product. It appeared not to want to impose a German MD on proceedings initially, and certainly believed that an engineer should be in charge. Without going off-site, Tony Gott was the only person experienced enough to fit the bill, so it was hardly surprising that he was given the job.

Regardless of best intentions, it was pretty intimidating when the entire VW top management descended on Crewe for various meetings and viewings, and I sympathized with Tony having to deal with such a large group, the risk being that this powerful boarding party would swamp the good ship Rolls-Royce/Bentley.

Tony was an advocate of complete, cellular project teams, which meant, for instance, that he wanted a stylist allocated for the Bali team: in other words, engineering teams with their own styling element. I would continue as Chief Stylist, visiting my people in someone else's team. Apart from the fact that we didn't have the head count to do this, I wasn't aware of any other company that used a similar approach. Tony tried to sell me this idea a couple of times, but I was forced to point out the immediate flaws in the concept. We simply didn't have the breadth of experience or maturity to support, for instance, Bali, in the manner Tony had in mind.

Coinciding with Tony's reign we finally got an excellent new studio and viewing facility, but the plans showed no provision for a Chief Stylist's office. After talking to various people and being told this was Company policy, I made an appointment to see Tony – one of the few occasions during my career at Crewe that I'd formally asked to see the MD. The date was March 15, 1999. Tony told me that the absence of an office for me was academic, as he was bringing in a Director of Styling from VW.

Far from feeling shocked or stunned at this bombshell – as, no doubt, many would have been – I had developed a kind of semi-detached attitude to the organization during my time at Crewe, in an effort to protect my sanity, but during the interview Tony implied that my intellectual approach was a regrettable flaw. I expressed my view that Styling needed a significant increase in staffing, including an integrated Packaging and Design Engineering unit as a stand-alone function, rather than being absorbed into Engineering project teams.

Most people in this unenviable position would have resigned and walked away, but my overruling interest was how my new employer, VW, would tackle the job of styling. It, like all large automotive companies, knew how important this element was, and would have to pour resources into the Crewe site, and I was genuinely pleased that Rolls-Royce/Bentley would have a decent new facility and its own director. Never one for pathos, I'd nevertheless be lying if I said I didn't reflect that, after such a long struggle, the cherry on the cake was not to be mine.

Whether or not Tony found it easier working with the new Head of Styling, Design Director Dirk van Braeckel, than me I don't know. I carried on organizing the regular viewings for the MD and the Crewe Board of Directors, but sat it out when the VW Board came on-site. With Dr Piech present there was quite a different viewing dynamic.

At Silver Seraph's launch I explained my theory of Rolls-Royce being influenced by yacht aesthetics to Tony

Gott, and after Tony moved on to BMW's Goodwood Rolls-Royce factory in 2002, it was satisfying to detect yacht influences in the cars – although polished wooden rear decking was surprising, even to me!

Managing Directors – on reflection

Following Peter Ward's departure I spent a fair amount of time creating styling reference manuals of the differences between Rolls-Royce and Bentley exterior and interiors. Despite having to jump through hoops for new ringmasters, no one ever queried my styling strategy, and certainly no one on earth could have taken over this unique manufacturing establishment and overnight understood both marques.

Witnessing how seven managing directors and chief executives operated over thirty years at Crewe was a privilege and an education. While fronting such a prestigious company they had to accommodate daily issues ranging from the state of the drains to entertaining royalty, but I like to think that attending Styling Viewings was one of their more enjoyable tasks.

Departmental directors shouldn't be overlooked. These all tended to get on well with Styling, as one of the lighter aspects of their job. Brian Dickie was a Purchase Director from north of the border. A lover of Armani suits and Ferraris, he had the air (and hairstyle) often associated with professional footballers. One winter, he was complaining about the amount of anti-freeze his boat on Lake Windermere needed, whereupon a fellow director suggested he put the anti-freeze into the boat's engine rather than the lake ...

Brian could also dish it out. One of his senior buyers had a hygiene phobia. This was no laughing matter, as he was convinced the world was full of germs, and considered using airport public conveniences akin to voluntary euthanasia. One day, Brian came across an individual at the factory in full protective gear – respirator helmet, one-piece overalls, rubber boots and gloves, etc – and got him to turn up, unannounced, at the buyer's office, with clipboard and meter, to start 'testing.' One can only imagine the effect on our phobic friend ...

REPLACING THE SILVER SPIRIT
ONE BODY; TWO MISSIONS

Act 1 – A saloon for the new millennium

The Rolls-Royce Silver Shadow and Silver Spirit families remained in production for fifteen and eighteen years respectively, but what had Crewe Styling been doing in the eighteen years before Silver Seraph's 1998 launch?

Even as a new model is launched, all manufacturers begin the process of replacing it, and often chief stylists struggle to find something to say at a car's launch as their minds are already full of what they are currently working on (or possibly because the model was styled by a predecessor).

The Silver Spirit of 1980 (SZ) was the last of a line, utilising a platform and mechanics that been used once before, and an engine before that again. Spirit was sent down the slipway into stormy seas of oil crisis, new safety legislation, disparate world market requirements and social changes. There was no choice: the die was cast and the Company had to tough it out. The formula had worked before and, in the event, Spirit was the mainstay product for eighteen years: a style conceived as a Rolls-Royce was also able to double as a Bentley .

SX – the 'compact' Rolls-Royce

The 1983 SX 'small' Rolls-Royce exercise had been a brilliant opportunity, and had taught me a lot. Although involved with every aspect of SZ's external appearance, the basic shape of the body had been established before my arrival. With SX it was possible to develop a style from quarter-scale models through to a full-size clay and fibreglass replica – a first for the Crewe site. That the clay

was shaped by woodworkers wasn't ideal, but at least it helped reduce resistance to that material's use. The exercise was somewhat complicated by my boss, Fritz Feller, who regarded a smaller Rolls-Royce as "pointless."

People take things at face value; they see nothing more to styling than what meets the eye. There are never any prizes for a jolly good effort, even in adversity, if the end result is less than ideal. A very clever shape can be fashioned over an awkward package, but irritation can be the result if it doesn't look like a Ferrari. In the case of SX, it just wasn't big enough to be a Rolls-Royce; thus, Mike Dunn agreed to conserve Styling resource on the follow-up – SX/B – and let MGA at Coventry 'block-in' a shape around Engineering's layout.

The 1980s was a helter-skelter decade. In Styling, Fritz's failing health led to his retirement in 1984, and Ron Maddocks – our exceptional model-maker – took redundancy. The ascending star that was Bentley suddenly required lots of attention aesthetically, in particular the new Continental R; Rolls-Royce was rather left to tread water.

SXB – how to produce a proper new Rolls-Royce

When considering a replacement four-door it should be remembered that, in the last year of the 1980s, the Company sold 3333 cars, a contemporary record. This figure was achieved largely with a car that was ten years old, challenging conventional product life cycle thinking; also a reminder that the market for luxury goods is different. While the Company was contemplating a smaller, more

1990 montages of potential styles to replace the Silver Spirit family resulted in these two prime candidates. The 'Cloudesque' shape (left) was classic Rolls-Royce, but obviously retro and less than ideal for a Bentley variant. The proposal on the right, with strongly-shouldered falling waist line, led directly to the Silver Seraph/Arnage. The 'Cloudesque' was, in due course, built for limited order special commission. It was always important to picture these vehicles in their natural habitat, and here we have Nantwich's Rookery Hall as a backdrop. Typical American environments were also used.

efficient vehicle, the word from the marketplace was that it quite liked big luxury cars, thanks very much!

None of this helped the various MDs who took their responsibilities for these iconic marques very seriously, often stultifyingly so. Bentley was shaping up as the Golden Goose, but no one felt relaxed about Rolls-Royce: a difficult marque to analyse. Was it a celebration of man's achievements or the unacceptable face of capitalism: chariot of the gods – or something else? The usual British unease about overt displays of wealth was at odds with America, which considered the quest for success a wholesome pursuit. I'm not sure if Marketing ever got to grips with this conundrum. Apart from anything else we were able to sell the same body shape to two different sets of customer, simply by changing the radiator shell! I informed Marketing that what had been sold as a Bentley was, on many occasions, a stealth Rolls-Royce.

None of these issues had easy answers. However, it was necessary to establish the best size and weight for the next generation of four-door saloon. Demonstrating the 'Defenders of the Faith' mindset of the MD and the board, getting the Rolls-Royce right first was a given, after which we could make a Bentley from it. After ruminating for five years, by September 1988 the Company realised it had to get serious.

Are we sitting comfortably? – then we'll begin

The sensible way to design a Rolls-Royce is from the inside out, as typical occupants of these cars are used to creature comforts; they aren't choosing to be crushed into a sports car or bounced around in a people carrier. SZ's front seat compartment was about right, but four inches

(101.6mm) of extra rear legroom was needed. Given that overall vehicle size could become an issue, the question was, how best to maintain or reduce Silver Spirit's length while accommodating the Silver Spur long wheelbase (LWB) seating?

John Harding was one of the experienced design/draughtsman working on this Tardis trick, which was all rather complicated as steering wheel position and adjustable front and rear seats create endless permutations. Everyone agreed that the vehicle shouldn't be any lower, as a 'Command Position' was fundamental: apart from giving a feeling of superiority, the higher you sit the easier it is to place a vehicle on the road. Also, BMW believed that the average height of a person increased by 10mm every ten years!

George Ray, a development engineer, ensured adjustable seating bucks could be quickly built in order to assess and experience interior space: although computers continue to transform car design, simple mock-ups are indispensable. To really understand the Crewe-built Rolls-Royce and Bentley cars, it's not necessary to look much further than someone like George: a racing cyclist in his youth, determined tester of Silver Clouds at Oulton Park, and sometime member of the 'awkward squad.' With often limited resources and great expectations, George was one of the people who helped keep the legend alive, and even when semi-retired, was a source of knowledge for the VW Bentleys.

With a perfect seating package a given, boot space was always an SXB dilemma. A luxury five-seater can never have too much luggage space for cases and two sets of golf clubs, say, as the fleet of Rolls-Royces at the

Peninsula Hotel, Hong Kong, followed by vans carrying overflow luggage, demonstrated at the time. There has to be a compromise, though, because, even at Phantom size, rear passenger space is the overriding luxury car concern, and there's a fuel tank which must be taken into consideration, too. People say all cars look the same: not so, although it is true that, size-for-size, car packages are similar because so are interior requirements.

Rolls-Royce or Bentley?

As Bentley sales continued to increase during the 1980s, there was a growing intention that SXB Rolls-Royce and Bentley would share platforms but not bodies. My favoured scenario was to have Rolls-Royce standard and long-wheelbase bodies featuring two side windows and wide rear-quarter panel and long boot. Bentley would have one standard wheelbase, three side windows, slim rear quarter and short boot, which would separate the two marques into their natural zones.

Drawing Office scheme PL16576 of September 1988 demonstrated that the minimum length for SXB was 202 inches (5131mm) [SZ was 207.4 inches (5269mmm); LWB 211.4 inches (5369mm)]. The Bentley needed extra length at the front to protect the more peaked radiator. Engineering and Product Planning were drawing up a brief for SXB, and Styling, when possible, experimented with the proposed new platform. Bernard Preston, a long-serving Company man and GP14 dingy sailor, was our second Product Planning Director.

Due to the ongoing demarcation dispute between Styling and Experimental Woodshop personnel, we were limited, on-site, to scale work. The department was on the verge of losing Brian Hassall, our official modeller, but stylists enjoy working on scale models themselves. Brian had managed to model full-size seats and alloy wheels, etc, but in tense circumstances.

Stephen Everitt from Coventry University's Transport course, did some good work on SXB. (Stephen's father, Richard, produced Granada TV's popular *Lovejoy* series). Although Engineering assumed a vehicle 202 inches (5131mm) long, our best efforts with Bentley were 206 inches (5232mm); the extra mainly on the boot. It was difficult to see how a Manx-tailed Rolls-Royce version could ever look elegant, although the low nose and high, short tail of PL16576 was better for Bentley.

Despite Bentley sales growth no one was prepared to say other than that Rolls-Royce was the leading marque, but PL16576 wasn't going to provide a credible

Rolls-Royce. So, taking a leaf from Fritz Feller's canny approach, we demonstrated our 'open-mindedness' by requesting proposals from Peter Horbury of MGA and Mark Stehrenberger, strictly based on the tight PL16576 package. Mark, of America's West Coast, was supplying American and European magazines with fabulous renderings. In-house (apart from myself and Stephen Everitt) RCA and Coventry students, such as Lawrence Cutts and Eric Bellinger, were invited to explore Rolls-Royce's horizon.

Conveying the true size of SXB proposals without the aid of full-size replicas remained a concern. Photo montages were simple and effective, so we photographed a Cadillac or Mercedes on a typical American driveway, and montaged a photo of an SXB rendering or model alongside for comparison. These photos were shown to the board and sent to America for feedback: of course, the response was that impressive size was critical. Thus, we saved time and money by not building a replica of a non-starter. You could argue that all we had done was go up a blind alley, but lack of visual imagination is more common than you might think: many a chief stylist has gone red in the face as a result of the effort involved in trying to explain to the board that the dimensions in a brief are wrong. Hold up a comparison photo, however, and the job's in the bag.

Sir David Plastow at Vickers Head Office wanted a futuristic scale model of a Rolls-Royce. This simple request caused a below-stairs panic as our modeller had just departed to another department because of the staff versus works issue with the Experimental Woodshop. I was tempted to make the model on my kitchen table, but common sense prevailed and Stephen Everitt, working with Tim Hunton, later head of the Experimental Woodshop, did a great job. A picture of the model appeared in the press in the early 1990s, held by Sir David Plastow and Sir Colin Chandler; the accompanying article the first hint that the Company might be for sale.

In mid-1989 we made our first attempt at styling a Rolls-Royce on a computer. Intergraph's Alias was the magic new system: a spin-off from Cruise Missile topography mapping. We probably couldn't afford such exotic kit but accepted an extended trial anyway. We learnt a lot, and Alias became a key player in car styling. Apart from pure aesthetics, the ability to see the driver's view over the front wings, for instance, was very useful.

After many styling exercises, the SXB brief finally acknowledged that a Rolls-Royce which was smaller than SZ wasn't realistic for the foreseeable future. Attention began to focus instead on what constituted the aesthetic vocabulary of Crewe's motor cars.

For instance, despite practical advantages, there were no plastic rubbing strakes down the sides, or radiator shells made of plastic as seen on lesser marques such as Mercedes. By September 1989, with more realistic overall dimensions, Crewe started another loop of concept work, supplemented by Mark Stehrenberger, Heffernan and Greenley (at Anglo Swedish Design) and Peter Horbury (MGA).

A classic Rolls-Royce – the 'wedge running backward' conundrum

Briefing consultants forced me to reach some conclusions about Rolls-Royce and Bentley differentiation. There were many ways to develop Bentley, but with Rolls-Royce, the critical marque, there were more restrictions. Everyone regarded John Blatchley's Silver Cloud as the finest post-war Rolls-Royce; the Mulliner Park Ward two-door, of a similar period, was also highly rated. The trouble was the more I thought about it the more stark the challenge became. In the vital – but volatile – home market the image of ostentatious wealth, symbolized by the famous radiator shell, was something of an embarrassment. As one industrialist put it, "If you're closing factories, you can hardly drive through the gates in a new Rolls-Royce." Books have been written on the subject but Britain's attitude toward symbols of wealth varies considerably. John Lennon tapped into the zeitgeist with his psychedelic Phantom. It was all about the radiator shell: put a Bentley shell on an identical body and the car could slip under the wealth radar.

Apart from the Gordian knot of social mores, the body language of a Rolls-Royce belonged to a bygone age. In the car world the wedge had won, and wind-tunnels dictated a new commandment: 'Thou shalt have a low nose and a high tail.' The NSU Ro80 influenced a generation of stylists, and all three-box cars follow this dictate. The problem was the best Rolls-Royce styles were reverse wedges: high nose; low tail.

Yacht aesthetics and the Silver Cloud

At a viewing in the 1970s I'd compared the Camargue – its high radiator shell (bow) and tail (stern) almost dragging in the wake – to a motor launch under power. When analysing the body language of Silver Cloud, the nautical comparison was even easier, hence the concept of yacht aesthetics. Having drawn a diagram of the Silver Cloud as a boat, no one ever disagreed with this analogy. In the side view the radiator shell is vertical or sloping forward slightly, and very tall. The flowing front wings are like bow waves, and the curvaceous rear wings are secondary or wake waves. The tail/stern is low and slopes forward. The cabin is not dissimilar to yachts of the 1930s. Is it, then, really too fanciful to describe the Spirit of Ecstasy as a figurehead?

Subliminal or not this is the visual communication this supremely iconic Rolls-Royce conveys, and it was necessary to inject this DNA into a vehicle relevant to the new millennium, any lingering doubt about which was dispelled by a visit to America. Whilst addressing a gathering of Rolls-Royce enthusiasts, many owners, in turn, addressed me. They accepted Silver Shadows and Silver Spirits as fine machines, but wanted more of Silver Cloud's or Corniche's charisma, some kind of visual drama: 'the sweeping line.' So, no pressure there, then ...

SXB Rolls-Royce and Bentley saloons to have different bodies!

By the start of the 1990s, and issue 7 of PL16576, everyone realized that we had to get serious about this new saloon. Buoyed by recent record sales figures, Styling was given the go-ahead to find a replacement for our departed modeller. Attempting to fudge the demarcation issue we gave the position the title of Stylist/Modeller, and, after half a dozen interviews, were fortunate enough to employ James Dimbleby, an exceptional clay modeller who also sculpted the heads of people and horses (two of his horses could be seen adorning gate posts on the A40). He sold a lot of his work to Romany folk. Offering such a person the industry going rate troubled Personnel, but we managed to scrape enough together to tempt Jim to Crewe.

Well-filled coffers at the end of the 1980s prompted Peter Ward and his board to ask Styling to proceed with separate Rolls-Royce and Bentley saloon styles, and by mid-1990 I had signed Design Engineer Chris Burrow's brief for SXB's two bodyshells. To tackle this doubled workload, Styling consisted of Martin Bourne, Stephen Everitt, Jim Dimbleby, Ryan Lewis, and yours truly. We were also providing half-sponsorship to a student on the RCA Automotive Design Course. A brave/desperate plan to circumnavigate the stalemate on full-size styling work at Crewe was necessary. With Martin Bourne and Ryan Lewis concentrating on general interior tasks, Stephen, Jim and I worked on two quarter-scale models. Exploiting Jim's exceptional ability, we scale modelled two styles in-house and, using MGA's state-of-the-art, Mecoff computer-driven milling-cutter, converted them to full size. This was and still is a risky business unless you have lots of time for re-work (we didn't).

The SXB Rolls-Royce generated by the foregoing process was viewed in July 1990 by the following board members –

• Malcolm Hart – Sales and Marketing
• Howard Mosher – Sales and Marketing
• Bernard Tobin – Sales and Marketing
• Bernard Preston – Product Planning
• Peter Hill – Personnel
• Brian Dickie – Purchasing

– and the style was generally well received with a few general observations (known as 'builds' within the industry). Rolls-Royce was being styled from the inside-out, leading to a slightly fuller body. The sportier Bentley was styled from the outside-in, and was thus more 'shrink-wrapped.'

By October 1990, both painted clays had been viewed by Peter Ward and the full board. The clays showed that the SXB platform could carry the two famous marques along quite separate roads, and there were no fundamental criticisms of either proposal. This comparison of the two styles was of great personal interest to me and, in my opinion, the Bentley was ready to roll, whereas the Rolls-Royce lacked something ...

Skill can be taken for granted, but it was down to modeller Jim that this quick, effective and unique exercise was possible. Stephen Everitt decided to change departments at this stage: large studios can let young stylists play in the sandpit until they gain experience, whereas at Crewe I probably had to supervise people too closely for his liking.

Back to just one bodyshell

Other issues were surfacing. Peter Ward and Mike Dunn were in contact with BMW, which, apparently, had shown its own drawings for a Rolls-Royce. There were also ongoing debates about sourcing engines/drive trains, etc. The world was sliding into recession and sales were down, and the prospect of two SXB bodyshells rapidly receded. Sensing the drift, we put a dust sheet over the Bentley proposal and sat staring at the Rolls-Royce.

We again created photo montages of the SXB clay and new renderings, including an updated Silver Cloud against the backdrop of the local Rookery Hall. Undoubtedly, the 'Cloudesque'-style ticked all the boxes but, as Peter Ward ruefully said, he could sell 500 in the first year and that

would be that. Significantly, one of the proposals carried the styling feature that would become the basis for Seraph/Arnage. In a further twist we built the Cloudesque proposal for a special commission.

In June 1990 we had contact with my old RCA sponsor, Roy Axe, who had been Head of Rover Styling, but was now installed in a semi-independent studio in Warwickshire. Roy was allowed to cream off a hand-picked team from Rover with the brief to explore Britishness in design. This unit – Design Research Associates (DRA) – was first class. Our ex-Rover Commercial Director, Mike Donovan, knew about Roy's semi-secret facility, which had Mike Kemp as the commercial man, Graham Lewis for interiors, and Adrian Griffiths for exteriors. In September, we were shown an executive Rover saloon replica built by MGA from DRA's clay. DRA quoted nine months from start to finished replica. Roy had to clear any outside projects with his bosses.

Toward the end of 1990, we commissioned some Rolls-Royce sketches based on SXB engineering plans. A quarter-scale model leading to a full-size clay was required in the New Year. Although DRA worked to my styling brief, we wouldn't have called a halt to any promising deviations to this. At the end of November 1990, Peter Ward, Mike Dunn and my boss, Chris Cernes, visited DRA.

MGA, with Peter Horbury, was also in the loop for contributing solutions to my styling brief. Mark Stehrenberger was brought over from California for input. When checking how he spelt his name, he told me "M, a, r, k." Those Californian guys! I collected him from the picturesque local White Lion Hotel in a beautifully restored Silver Cloud, which impressed even this laid-back West Coast character, although I had no wish to influence his thinking, of course.

Closing in on the solution

While correlating outside studios, I worked in-house with Jim Dimbleby on a new, quarter-scale model. One of my renderings which had been montaged featured a very simple falling waistline. It looked like it was possible to retain some Silver Cloud DNA without the characteristic sculpted flared wings. Long periods considering what the Spirit of Ecstasy might grace reminded me of a person who had spent years studying the concert piano, who concluded it was a large black triangular object on three legs. My conclusion was that the cabin shouldn't be the widest part but inset from the wings, which form a strong shoulder running down the car, the front wings rising above the

Through the 1980s and into the '90s, the Company considered the best way forward for the four-door saloon.

Above, left: This formal solution was a scale model machined directly to full size, and a dedicated Rolls-Royce proposal only.

Above, right: This shape was intended to carry both marques while still attempting some Silver Cloud rear wing-type reference.

Below: June 1991. Crewe's Styling Viewing Area shows some of the ongoing effort to resolve the conundrum of how best to serve the ever-widening and separating marque values of Rolls-Royce and Bentley, whilst probably restricted to only one saloon bodyshell.

outer bonnet and falling toward the rear of the vehicle. The centre of the bonnet has to complement the rear of the radiator shell header tank. Behind the rear door the cabin should have no glass, and should semi-conceal rear seat occupants. The style should feature a short nose overhang and long tail. Separation of the car's wings from the main body would allow a strong reference to 'yacht aesthetics.' Meanwhile, the centre profile could reflect a more aerodynamic wedge influence.

Jim Dimbleby's scale model demonstrated that the foregoing formula worked, though, frustratingly, we still had to go off-site to build full-size clays for Peter and the board to view. Due to its previous success, we asked MGA at Coventry to scale-up our latest proposal. I had no idea how we'd get on with Roy Axe's SXB: although

a top professional organisation, DRA, hadn't previously worked as a consultancy. How would Roy regard this chap he hadn't given a job to after the RCA sponsorship when at Chrysler UK? Okay, it had been during an American firing cycle, but even so ...

Anyway, needs must when the devil drives, and soon I was again burning up M6 miles in regular visits to MGA and DRA. Styling was answering to Mike Dunn during this period; John Fowler, an experienced body engineer, had joined Mike from Rover. The ex-Rover people always seemed a bit aggressive/shell-shocked, but Cheshire air tended to calm them ... mostly.

By mid-1991 both consultancies had made good progress on the two clays, with DRA tending to favour a Cloudesque rear wing. Both proposals indicated viable solutions. Martin Bourne visited both studios as he was our last link with the Cloud's creator. Andrew Maiden, our aerodynamicist, kept abreast of things using scale models.

Although Jim had been able to work on the clay at MGA, he wasn't happy with the ongoing ban on such work at Crewe. If the recession hadn't prevented the sale of his Blackpool guesthouse, we might have held on to him, but we kept in touch, and his pivotal scale model remained on display in the Crewe reception display area for some years.

On June 26, 1991 the painted, dressed clays arrived at Crewe for Peter Ward and his board to pass judgement on. Peter and his Marketing Director, Malcolm Hart, were left to make the key comments, which were spot-on. The theme of the MGA clay featuring the falling, shouldered waist line worked okay, but the glass line was too high. The DRA clay tended toward the portly and attracted more 'builds.' On balance, however, DRA – with its Rover links – was a very solid setup, and it was decided to develop the DRA clay transferring MGA's falling waist line on to one side. Following this viewing, Mike Dunn proposed that Styling report to Mike Donovan.

The Company was being hit hard by the recession with lay-offs and periods of reduced pay. The powers-that-be were more nervous than ever about future market demand for a Rolls-Royce. It was decided that SXB(A), now at SZ LWB length, would have to be reduced, and DRA's excellent packaging man, Graham Lecornu, would feed information to Crewe's George Ray and Design Draughtsman Peter Tricklebank. I was bemused on one occasion to find Jonathan Ethrington cheerfully slicing a side elevation drawing of SXB(A) like a salami sausage to reduce its length. Jonathan was an engineering graduate, who, with his gaunt, slightly unkempt appearance and trademark ex-army greatcoat, put me in mind of a one-man representation of the retreat from Moscow. Still, he went on to become a chief engineer at a Norwegian electric car company. Rolls-Royce as an employer on your CV never hurt anyone.

Mid-September 1991, Peter Ward viewed our best efforts at DRA on the split clay: Cloudesque rear hip one side; simple falling waist line on the other. A Mercedes S Class was present for size comparison. I commented that after three attempts, regardless of our affection for it, the Cloudesque hip was struggling. The falling waist line side was approved to be balanced across. The concept of using SZ LWB length, SXB/A, was parked; let the 4 inch (101.6mm) salami slicing begin.

Whether or not DRA's Adrian Griffiths appreciated Hull's presence or simply realized he wasn't going away is not known. Working with consultants demands a fine balance, because, if they don't feel it's 'their' design, they can begin saluting with the wrong hand. However, it's your money, and your job is to get what you want and – hopefully – please your masters. We worked together on many projects subsequently so perhaps there was mutual benefit.

By October 1991 a major viewing of the SXB/A and SXB down-size proved we'd done the right thing. The larger car was considered overblown, with the slightly smaller version about right. With approval secured, we began work on a fibreglass, show-quality replica. SXB's overall length was now 208.2inches (5288mm); SZ 207.4(5268mm), with rear legroom target the same as that in SZ LWB. Working with DRA, interior styling began with front-end seating bucks.

Jekyll and Hyde

As 1991 became 1992 we gave consideration to Bentley SXB, which financial restrictions dictated should be based on the Rolls-Royce. We did, after all, have the new Bentley coupé, and Marketing wasn't complaining about SZ in Turbo R guise. When financial push comes to shove, pragmatism has the upper hand.

From Styling's viewpoint SXB didn't have the 'muscle' around the wheels of a real predator, but neither did it have the perpendicular architecture of earlier Roll-Royce cars. Although the party line had been "get the Rolls-Royce right first," SXB was always going to be something of a cross-dresser, and this body style could credibly carry the two different radiator shells, headlamps, outer sills, front and rear bumper/aprons, wheels and exhaust. Brightwork could be added or deleted.

The only large, expensive metal apart from the radiator shell that, ideally, should be different was the boot lid. Aerodynamically, the trailing edge of a booted car is super-critical. An applied spoiler or fence wasn't acceptable; therefore a new-style pressing was desirable to aid high-speed stability. A bonus in marque differentiation was the interior style; relatively low tooling costs meant significant changes could be achieved.

The Company continued to struggle with the economic situation. Most areas, including Styling, suffered often traumatic compulsory redundancies. However, the new star – Bentley – showed no signs of fading, which led Mike Donovan to ask, on June 19, 1992, the killer question:

if Rolls-Royce stayed as SXB, would a new Bentley saloon really look like SXB, too?

By the end of that month SXB had been quietly shunted into a siding, some 90 per cent right with convincing body language. This shape could be shared between the two marques, and we knew how to do the interiors. It was clear that Peter Ward and Mike Donovan felt we'd eventually figured out how to replace SZ; we just couldn't afford to build it.

There wasn't much time to dwell on this turn of events, however. I focused on face-lifts for SZ94 model year and SZ96, postponing any SXB decision. There were other interesting diversions due to BMW's interest and, significantly, one-off projects were emerging.

Act 2 – SXB reborn

With several one-off projects successfully completed during 1992 and 1993, things were looking up, and not only was Styling asked by Mike Donovan to embark on a Corniche replacement, but SXB was to be dusted off as well.

A refresher viewing of SXB was arranged for the end of January 1994, as things had moved on: Giugiaro had styled a four-door Bugatti, and a large Lagonda saloon had also been shown, which, although shorter than SXB in both cases, were highly relevant, and full-size photos of both were displayed in the Styling area. A two-year hiatus had allowed us to reassess the saloon.

Suddenly, it was all on for the 1998 model year. SXB was to be renamed P600, and Phil Harding – an experienced development engineer – would be Chief Engineer of the project. But where to do it? Although both marques shared a body, two exteriors and interiors were required, plus prove-out models, tooling check-outs, etc: in all, a huge amount of work.

Let battle commence

We'd had experience with nearly all of the non-attached UK and European studios, and several American ones as well, and all felt that this project had to be continued at Crewe because of the people involved and importance of Production input/reference. Luckily, a profound sea change had occurred at Crewe: realising we were all in the same boat, a new era of co-operation resulted as imagined or real partitions between departments largely disappeared. We were able to bring a team of clay modellers to Crewe for the first time, and installed a surface plate and measuring kit in the Styling Viewing Area in Third Avenue.

I had previously worked with Richard Hamblin's Omni

Design at Coventry on model year changes. He was ex-Ogle Design and Rover, and was very experienced in the disciplines necessary to drive a project like SXB through its paces. He was also used to my constant striving for perfection (ie irritating dictates and nagging whine). We would again use MGA for associated activities as, apart from parachuting in a cohesive functioning team, it made viewings much more convenient and got the small, young in-house team close to the action.

As a matter of courtesy I asked Richard Hamblin for his views on the existing SXB replica, expressing mine first, of course, to avoid any misunderstandings. He always regarded me with a degree of amusement, and was probably puzzled about how I'd retained my position for so long. Steady as a rock, Richard had once surprised me by going missing for a couple of days, later apologetically showing me a photo of the remains of his BMW 5 Series on the A5. It looked like the fire brigade had used cutters to get him out, but apparently a lorry had been responsible for the damage.

Phil Harding brought in Martin Vine, ex-Land Rover and steam enthusiast; a safe pair of hands for the hugely expensive body programme. Richard Hamblin agreed to coax Jim Dimbleby into leading the clay modelling, while Omni's Dick Bartlam would act as overall manager. On April 18, 1994, Omni was on-site to accept a clayed-up buck from MGA. Doubts regarding a Rolls-Royce for the new millennium persisted, but we were close to a solution. Even before we started, however, I was under pressure from MPW's 'Victorian iron foundry master' Jim Orr, not to ignore his specially-commissioned projects.

The final offering

After many false starts the moment of truth arrived, with three concerns remaining. Firstly, we owed it to posterity to have one last go at the Cloud/Corniche rear wing feature; secondly, if the simple falling waist line really was the solution, then the vehicle needed more shape because Silver Cloud barely had a straight line on it; thirdly, from motorway experience, it was apparent that there were more rear views than front views, whether queuing or holding station with others. The rear three-quarter view was especially important. Crewe's cars were associated with radiator shells, but a good suit isn't judged from the front only. I had pursued this aspect when working with Ken and John on the Continental R. The ploy was to achieve as much rear plan taper as possible, thus creating shape and reducing mass.

Concurrently, we worked on a 'Cloudesque' replica, based on an SZ platform, for a special customer. This was a Crewe-led team working at Futura's studio in the Midlands. By now we understood every twist and turn of the Cloud, and made a determined final attempt to get those evocative lines onto SXB. The result looked similar to the delightful MPW 2-door saloon of 1964, but had the appearance of a period piece rather than a fresh approach. After a brief discussion with Mike Donovan, we finally closed that book. Apart from anything else, the falling waist line on the clay's other side was becoming better and better: it was the answer.

We worked very well with Richard Hamblin's team. During May 1994, he managed to get some extra modelling equipment from Mike Gibbs' ADC setup at Luton, a sad, closing down sale of Wayne Cherry's old Vauxhall studios. Feasibility and packaging people remained thin on the ground at Crewe, and MGA staff had to be sub-contracted. P600 remained slightly longer than SZ but shorter than SZ LWB.

One might imagine that a period of quiet creativity ensued in this pleasant corner of Cheshire, but it was hardly that. By July 1994, our Chief Modeller, Jim Dimbleby, had walked away from us for the final time. Director viewings always put a lot of pressure on styling teams, and there had been a sudden flare-up amongst the modellers. Given time, Jim could have shaped the car on his own, but he didn't have this luxury.

Considering the disparate individuals involved in the SXB styling process, the entire thing could have been an unholy shambles. There was Peter Ward and Mike Donovan from the top corridor relying on me, Richard Hamblin and Dick Bartlam – and a lump of clay. The motivation, or terror, involved in shaping such a British icon ironed out any potential friction. Hats off to Peter Ward at this time, under a lot of pressure not only from daily factory issues and the specially-commissioned cars, but SXB still didn't have an engine!

Despite living over the shop I avoided hovering constantly round the SXB clay. Due to several other projects it wouldn't have been possible anyway, but it's easy to be too close, and not see the wood for the trees. The brain can dial out or compensate for imperfections – a well-known phenomenon – so artists occasionally look at their work in a mirror, as this can highlight errors of perspective and form. Similarly, looking at photographs of a styling mock-up before making decisions always helps, which is one reason why ever-present managers

ROLLS-ROYCE SILVER SERAPH - THE PURITY OF LINE

FLYING LADY

YACHT AESTHETICS

CLASSIC COACHBUILT LINES

1955 ROLLS-ROYCE SILVER CLOUD

EVOLVED 'RETRO' PROPOSAL

1998 ROLLS-ROYCE SILVER SERAPH

1-1-98   NUMBER   IN A LIMITED EDITION OF 250 PRINTS

'Yacht aesthetics.'

of open-plan studios is not an ideal situation. Working with many stylists who were my peers repeatedly proved the importance of a fresh eye. Richard Hamblin said, "I hate it when you walk round the clay for a while and say, 'What do you think about this bit?' because it always means there's something wrong."

An old RCA chum, Lawrence Martin, joined the clay gang, and Darren Day joined Crewe Styling from Coventry University. Harris Mann, a styling hero of mine, came in as part of the Omni team to help us on P600 Bentley. I'd always rated Harris' 1969 Zanda – British Leyland's concept car – very highly. In late July 1994 we were told that my boss, Mike Donovan, was leaving for BAE.

By October 1994 we had general sign-off for the P600 Rolls-Royce exterior from the Crewe Board and Vickers. Like SXB previously, we showed P600 in blue paint because

From the 1980s, the Company benefited from the work of some of the most talented clay sculptors. Shown here is Lawrence Martin, who trained at the Royal College of Art.

so many would wear that colour ultimately; universal styling silver would always flatter it anyway. Although P600 was based on SXB, every millimetre was changed: a good shape further refined is a stylist's dream. The front end received a new treatment. With approval granted, MGA could create a see-through fibreglass replica.

Strange days indeed – enter Mercedes

Some very strange things were occurring around us. We had previously been visited by Dr Wolfgang Reitzle of BMW, who had sensibly said that Rolls-Royce had to "pick up from the past," and that the only thing he knew about styling was that you had to try, try, and try again. For some months P600 had incorporated some BMW components, such as 7 Series headlamp reflectors, and interior elements such as air-conditioning units. It became increasingly likely that BMW V12 and V8 engines and gearboxes would be used: apparently, it would be too expensive to get Crewe's trusty V8 past forthcoming emission regulations.

Styling was then asked what the implications would be of putting P600 onto a Mercedes S Class platform! This wild card made us pause a bit; I suggested dropping a P600 fibreglass body onto an S Class underbody to see what needed modifying. Early drawings weren't promising, and a lose/lose situation seemed likely, compromising styling and mechanics. But it was obvious Vickers was preparing to let one of the German big boys get into the saddle.

Peter Ward and his directors regularly viewed P600 Rolls-Royce interiors, and Bentley exteriors and interiors. All eyes were now on the Bentley as this was where sale

volumes would be seen. We knew from earlier work that the shape responded well to Bentley's requirements. The composite bumper/aprons and sills were easy to change and, surprisingly, it was a case of reducing rather than injecting more steroids. As with Turbo R, the body-coloured radiator shell was a powerful differentiation to Rolls-Royce. Bentley alloy wheels could appear visually 'busier,' more 'frantic,' and were a good creative opportunity for the young in-house talent.

Attempts to sell a different boot lid for Bentley stalled. Only minor visual tweaks were necessary to influence top end aerodynamics, and Marketing preferred more visual bangs for its bucks elsewhere. Due to the use of BMW headlamp reflectors, the Bentley round headlamp signature was more subtle than ideal, although black masks did help. Given the brief, there were no reservations about having achieved a very credible Bentley saloon. It was signed off on December 9, 1994, along with the Rolls-Royce interior theme.

That Crewe now had two new offerings to represent its marques, coupled with year-end focus, seemed to trigger big changes. A tie-up with BMW was formally announced on December 19 that year by Vickers, and Peter Ward walked away after running Crewe for eight years (and spending three years previous to that as director of marketing). It's thought he favoured a deal with Mercedes, which immediately expressed its feelings of rejection by starting work on the Maybach. (*Autocar* later referred to these as "... big, brash, luxurious. No charm.")

Witley Park, Guildford

December 15, 1994 saw a gathering of Vickers management at Witley Park in Guildford, a country estate featuring lakes that had tunnels running underneath to Jules Verne-type observation chambers. I was sent there with the P600 Rolls-Royce replica, with thirty minutes to present it in.

An awful lot of people were there, with Sir Colin Chandler as the main man. As usual, thank goodness, pulling off the covers and revealing a show car overawed even the hardened cases. The presentation was reasonably well received and there were no awkward questions. Since Peter Ward's departure, there wasn't anyone on the bridge at Crewe, so yours truly was practically the only representative from the Cheshire Plains. In the audience, however, was Chris Woodwark, ex-Rover and Cosworth, already primed to take over at Crewe in early January 1995.

I had an interesting chat with a fellow acting as security at the presentation. Ex-SAS, he'd been waiting to 'attend to' anyone trying to photograph the car during the night. He was interested to know my father had been in the Airborne, but less so concerning my parachute jump: he'd made hundreds, including one with his leg in plaster! Following the presentation, Vickers hierarchy withdrew to a sumptuous dining hall, whilst I had a snack with the staff in the kitchen. Sir Colin's chauffeur was a useful insight to life as a full-time Turbo R jockey: he felt that VIPs weren't interested in whistles and bells in a vehicle, and just wanted it to be comfortable, easy to drive, and fast when required.

Chris Woodwark takes the helm

Many 'big men' involved in finding a replacement for SZ had been and gone during the preceding years: Dick Perry, Mike Dunn, Malcolm Hart, Howard Mosher, Mike Donovan, Peter Ward, and others.

Chris Woodwark immediately had to face a hundred and one issues, not least being the plan to build P600 bodyshells at Crewe. While attending Styling viewings with the Product Policy Committee, he seemed to accept what we were doing, and, in this respect, it probably helped that he knew Richard Hamblin from Rover days, although there was never much camaraderie amongst the old boys of that particular school.

A huge amount of effort was going into detail work, which included softening the Rolls-Royce radiator shell that would be assembled from pressings rather than flat sheet. Parallel activities included checking the hardwood tooling master model being machined in Wolverhampton from digitized information from the clay. By May 1995, P600 became P2000/P3000 for Bentley and Rolls-Royce respectively.

Omni's Mark Butler was working at Crewe on interiors, some of the details of which gave rise to a little creative debate between us, although, ultimately, using the factory's craftsmanship approach was paramount. Getting two separate interior styles approved by the Product Policy Committee and accepted by Production as doable was a challenge. The famous Crewe wood veneers were a major issue; developing new, complex shapes required more stable metal substrates instead of wood. Although sympathising with practical problems more than most, the Company still had to raise its game.

The Magic Matrix

We needed something special for Bentley radiator shells, which had traditionally borrowed Rolls-Royce vanes.

Driven by Marketing, we had previously used woven-wire mesh for the 'entry model' Bentley Eight. Although evocative of Cricklewood days, I was no fan of this as it was also used by Jaguar and on kit cars. On holiday, a visit to the National Motor Museum at Beaulieu included analysis of radiator matrix construction, and it was apparent that the most effective had a three-dimensional element: from most angles you couldn't see through them.

We came up with the scalloped grid that has become a Bentley staple, and early proof of its effectiveness was when two visiting Pininfarina employees subjected it to intense study. Expensive to shape out of laser-cut stainless steel, the engineers who figured out how to make it have my enduring gratitude. Later, the Chrysler 300 used the Bentley grid, as did Jaguar from 2008.

It's not over, even when the fat lady sings

Project sign-off/style approval meant negotiations then began with lots more people, such as in Manufacturing, all intent on showing you the error of your ways; this is why it pays to be nice to them in peacetime.

By December 1995, Martin Vine was anxious to sign off the master model stack, a block of very stable material, machined from digitized data, which had to faithfully represent what the board had approved in the replica. Up until this point, the financial gun wasn't loaded: now it was, and cutting metal press tools put all Company chips on the table. Richard Hamblin's support at this stage was invaluable. The P3000 launch was pencilled-in for the Frankfurt Motor Show of 1997.

Purchase was offered a bargain rate slot with a toolmaker for the large roof panel. The problem was that, by March 1996, the master tooling model hadn't been signed off. As the savings were so attractive, work began anyway. So I'm standing looking at a dodgy run-out on a roof channel, having to say "but we can't accept that," whilst a massive milling cutter in a far-off land is faithfully reproducing this area in a huge block of press tool steel. Somehow, surfacing fixes for these glitches caught up with the final cutter path, but that's living dangerously. Who needs to go base jumping when you can style motor cars?

The devil is in the detail

Phil Harding's team had many engineers responsible for particular exterior and interior items. Unlike previous projects, most of the pieces were new and, practically, only the body pressings were shared between the marques. A street market developed around my desk as various people came and went bearing prototype parts, usually with some reworks necessary. A group I regarded as 'The Stalkers' – Mike Lewis, Colin Brandon, Derek Gardner, Alan Bishop and others – took care of interior elements such as steering wheels, seat controls, column stalks, etc. All of the components came from different suppliers, and, apart from having to function superbly, required identical black finish and graining. Lighting had a similar group of specialists with its own requirements, and Alan Bishop was another regular visitor. They may have resented my constant moaning and criticism, but it prevented them from being savaged at future board viewings when timings were desperately tight.

Phil Harding, P2000/P3000 Chief Engineer, left the Company to work for one of our consultants. Although Phil was a chassis development disciple, he managed to oversee a complex new car project, and accommodated the weird and wonderful world of styling with barely a snarl or grimace. By May 1996, Tony Gott, who had been involved in explorative work with German companies, became P2000/P3000's Chief Engineer.

Tony was a follower of the independent project team philosophy. Since 1970, Styling had organized Product Policy Committee viewings for all projects. Tony, attending the first Styling viewing in his new role, declared the withdrawal of P2000/P3000 items, and stated he would arrange his own viewings. The big advantage of our established system was that the directors first met in the boardroom to discuss issues, and then reconvened in the studio. Assembling this critical mass at other times was practically impossible. Following a late policy decision to further soften the Rolls-Royce shell, Tony publicly demanded to know why this wasn't on display? My efforts to relieve the situation didn't seem to help, although asking if he understood body language confused him sufficiently to allow the moment to pass. The pressure that engineers are under to deliver on time and under budget is immense, but differences are best aired off-line.

Of course, the Company situation at this time was not conducive to soothing the nerves. The P1000 (Java) project in Germany had not been easy, and massive effort was being expended on customer special projects. The increasing tie-up with BMW was fundamental; the factory and its layout were under continuous shake-up. Also, a large part of Engineering had never before been involved with a new Rolls-Royce or Bentley. Oh, and we had a new Managing Director ...

In February 1996 we decided that the Omni team could leave our studio; I would continue to visit them at Coventry for P2000/P3000 and special customer projects (we worked well together for several years). Crewe projects had affected the entire Midlands automotive support industry and, at one point, Richard Hamblin had to warn off Geoff Mathews Design's Chief Modeller, from trying to poach his modellers in the Crewe dining area!

In July 1996, I attended the funeral of former Chief Engineer John Hollings, who, no doubt, would have been bemused by the maelstrom at Crewe compared to the previous gentlemen's club it had been.

'That' radiator shell

Chris Woodwark remained nervous about the perceived 'arrogance' of the traditional Rolls-Royce radiator shell, and soon after he took the baton from Peter Ward, I was called into his office and shown a newspaper article. It was written by a female journalist who, experiencing a previously-owned Silver Shadow, was called a 'rich bitch' by someone on a garage forecourt. A previous, tongue-in-cheek, suggestion of mine was that, during economic downturns, we should offer a 'recession' version of the car, which would be finished in Tarmac grey, with cat's eyes painted down the centre line to maintain a low profile ...

In SXB we had strived to create a shape in the round (see Java), so that, instead of the classic architectural elevations of front/side/rear, the eye was rewarded by moving smoothly round the vehicle in a continuous motion. The objective was to reduce 'visual' weight and any suggestion of arrogance. The famous radiator shell was not flaunted but formed part of the whole.

What had been nominally approved was a 'softer' version of the famous Greek temple; also the Spirit of Ecstasy was slightly smaller. Nevertheless, Chris asked us to revisit this iconic element to see what more could be done, an exercise that proved highly enjoyable, with several exciting and viable proposals resulting. Apart from combining formal Greek architecture with more organic influences, it was also possible to introduce elements of body colour. We even put The Spirit of Ecstasy in a lit, mirrored box, flush with the radiator shutters. It was a rather bizarre viewing because everything we'd proposed was approved – but not until some time in the future.

When it came to the crunch, however, Chris ruefully admitted we'd done enough previous to this.

By September 1996, Martin Vine, Richard Hamblin and myself were going over the body surfaces with a fine tooth comb, and very expensive computers. As someone once said, if you're spending all that money, you may as well get it right.

Time to address the engines, and consider a diet
October found us wrestling with dressing the BMW V8 and V12 engines for Crewe. Traditionally, behind-the-scenes at Crewe looked like a ship's engine room, reminiscent of the period of Isambard Kingdom Brunel, and requiring just a wipe with an oily rag. Apart from marque lettering and warning labels, there was little input from Styling (the old brigade would have laughed at the very idea). Styling's 'Turbo' on the air box had once been pretty daring; now we were claying-up the entire top of the engine bay.

Magazine road tests usually have a picture of the engine bay, which manufacturers strive to convey as immaculate, rather than the hot, dirty and possibly rusty reality. Bugatti got it right with its proudly-displayed and beautifully-designed functional components. Modern engines, though, are usually buried beneath pumps, turbos, sensors, servos, air cleaners, wires, hoses and warning labels: the higher a vehicle's specification, the greater the clutter. P2000/P3000's answer was to cover up as much as possible and ensure that BMW components weren't too apparent. To assist in this respect we decided on a two-colour policy – black and silver – avoiding the 'colours of the rainbow' plastic-clip syndrome.

An eleventh hour programme to reduce the car's weight was led by Rob Oldaker, Product Development Director and later Rover's Chief Engineer. Such exercises are difficult as weight-saving should be dialled-in at conception, as with aircraft. Styling people, as custodians of the visual and tactile interface with the car, can appear unsympathetic to such initiatives – what's the point in changing to plastic door handles if four men are required to lift a front sub-frame assembly? Actually, we may have agreed to take a few piles per square metre out of the boot carpets ...

Graham Morris gets behind the wheel for the closing laps
At the Geneva Motor Show, March 1997, I met Graham Morris, who had just taken over as Chief Executive at Crewe, when Chris Woodwark moved to Vickers HQ.

By April that year, we knew that P3000 was going to have the ethereal name of Silver Seraph, and the Company's chromed and enamelled brass nameplates were a work of art, with a quality that simply wasn't seen anywhere else in the industry. Keith Harper, ex-Manager

of Technical Publications, worked with us on these as always, lovingly adjusting letters and spaces. When future archaeologists are sifting through our detritus, they'll wonder what kind of people were these who put so much care into a badge

Apart from pursuing the limousine version, efforts were being made to improve rear legroom in the standard car. This was sorted out but the solution was not in time for initial production. Seat trimming and angles are critical, and are linked to an occupant's H-point (the position of their pelvis when seated in the car). H-points – like a car's 0-datum (the master line on a graph background that is drawn through a car's sill area, and upon which a 250mm (10 inch) grid is based covering the entire vehicle) – are the foundation stones of any vehicle. They baffle those who don't understand them, and obsess packaging experts who do.

Due to Crewe craftsmanship and manufacturing processes it's impossible to simply turn over a style to Engineering; every part has to be followed through to manufacture. In addition, just when you can see light at the end of the tunnel, someone discovers that the USA, Canada and Australia require seatbelt mounts for child seats on the rear parcel shelf! Then, the word 'airbag' has to appear adjacent to the actual device, and seats have to have an airbag flag. However, there's nothing to be gained by questioning legislative logic.

On September 10, 1997 a Design Condition Silver Seraph was viewed by the board. Previous to this, everything was prototype status but Design Condition is off-tools, and constitutes the product offer. At such a viewing it's important not to be lost in love and wonder, and instead try to pick fault. Sales people are good at this as it's a natural reversal of their usual role. Martin Vine still found time to refine such items as visible seat-slider nuts and wiper parking, etc.

Early December found me in a studio with a film crew gathered around Silver Seraph and P2000. The idea was to make a promotional feature, with a designer walking around the cars, describing their design philosophy, and the differences between the two marques. No thespian, by any means, for me it was an education; thankfully, the director was very patient.

The sound man told me never to assume that the mike was off, as President Bush, Prime Minister Blair and also Gordon Brown had all done. Filming seemed to go reasonably well but Marketing fell out with the agency and the footage was lost to posterity.

The launch

Unveiling a new Rolls-Royce is an occasion; this one especially because of the 18-year gap since the last launch, and the rumoured takeover. Of all that could be claimed about the Seraph's styling, the following was my pitch –

• Solidness without heaviness
• Authority without arrogance
• Elegance without effort
• Presence without pomp

One journalist said he wished he'd come up with this description – praise indeed. PR Director Richard Charlesworth used my yacht aesthetics rendering as a limited edition print to allow chosen journalists to understand and appreciate the vehicle's aesthetic premise in advance of the viewing.

The launch in January 1998 was at Ackergill Tower, a castle at the top of Scotland, and Richard, as Master of Ceremonies, did a magnificent job. Five days were set aside for different nationality journalists – UK, USA, Japan, Germany, and others. These be-kilted scribes were served the local firewater, and encouraged to dance Scottish reels round a beach bonfire to squeeze-box accompaniment, and earlier the Royal Ballet's Prima Ballerina, Deborah Bull as the Spirit of Ecstasy, performed a more refined dance around the Seraph.

My birthday fell on the first day of the launch (January 5), which made everything seem rather surreal. I managed to purloin a Seraph later in the week and took it for a magical first drive. In my opinion, though, car launches should be left to PR types and actors, which later was the case at factory launches.

As a survivor of a thousand Styling viewings I suggested to Marketing that its plan for an unveiling with people milling around was not a good idea. Add in a liquid buffet and you'd need mounted police to control proceedings. And so it came to pass at Wentworth Golf Club on March 10 that year, when I went through the motions of explaining the wonders of the new car as the audience jostled to be first behind the wheel. Still, the string ensemble's rendition of the evocative Harry Lime theme cheered me up.

The main London launch at the Dorchester Hotel ten days later was better, the invited VIPs kept at bay by a rotating turntable with a Seraph and a flitting Deborah Bull. An apparently very knowledgeable person there explained to me that the Silver Seraph had a feminine front and a masculine rear; I assured him that this was because angels are hermaphrodites.

Following the press launches the Silver Seraph was publicly revealed at the Geneva Motor Show later that year. The image of the delightful Deborah's Spirit of Ecstasy and the silver Silver Seraph was captured by every camera in the motoring world. (Deborah went on to become author, TV presenter, creative director of the Royal Opera House and a governor of the BBC.)

The Bentley Arnage was launched in April 1998 at Le Mans. Styling had spent as much time on it as it had Seraph, but it was going to be an Engineering-focused event. Victims (passengers) enjoyed being flung around by F1 driver Nigel Mansell. Richard Charlesworth took along a large sepia painting of a Bentley four-and-a-half litre daubed by me some years before. Styling was now deeply immersed in the new Corniche and a Bentley coupé.

Due to the delicate situation regarding co-operation with BMW, the Company was keen to involve the Rolls-Royce Enthusiasts Club with Seraph. Marketing asked me to be present at the Club's weekend rally at Cottesbrook Park, Northampton, on June 7, 1998. Set up with an easel and the yacht aesthetics diagram, it was great to talk to so many true believers and, as ever, their knowledge and attitude of their role as temporary custodians of these classic vehicles was impressive. They seemed to regard the Seraph's style as something of a re-birth. Graham Morris and Keith Sanders walked past without stopping, deep in conversation.

Post-launch

Early 1998 was a fantastic time at Crewe as the factory had undergone a major overhaul, and there were new Rolls-Royce and Bentley saloons. Vickers had a mouthwatering package with which to tempt those shopping for a couple of unique marques. To top it all, a new, stand-alone Styling facility with an outside viewing area was under way.

Feelings were mixed about technical aspects of the new saloons. Having BMW V8 and V12 engines meant we were using the latest technology, but what about British engineering? The revvy German V8 couldn't really better the Turbo R's stump-pulling torque, although, to me, the V12 did seem intrinsically Rolls-Royce. Away from the world of showbiz, Styling resource was being lapped up. Seraph and Arnage required support, still, in the form of various degrees of stretch and a small backlight option. The style allowed for stretching, anything from 6 inches (152.4mm). No arguing with that (in fact, standard cars

One bodyshell, two personas:

Rolls-Royce Silver Seraph launch at Ackergill Tower in Scotland, January 1998, with directors and support team.

soon gained two inches (50.8mm) by a little rear seat packaging work that could have been done at birth).

In early January 1999 we had a visit from Tony Brooker, a knowledgeable Seraph owner, who thought the car looked great and was simply keen to help us make it even better. His main request was an additional 4 inches (101.6mm) of rear legroom. (Subsequent cars had a late re-packaging modification which increased rear legroom by 2 inches (50.8mm): anything more would have required a longer wheelbase.)

The muscular doppelganger Bentley Arnage. Launched at Le Mans in April 1998, it's demonstrated here with a degree of élan by Nigel Mansell, OBE.

The Park Ward Rolls-Royce Touring Saloon launched in 2000 was ten inches (254mm) longer than Silver-Seraph. By adding eight inches (203mm) to rear doors and two inches (50.8mm) to front doors, very elegant proportions were achieved, further enhanced by stainless steel sill finishers which support and emphasize Seraph's falling, shouldered waist line. Rear occupants enjoyed exceptional legroom, additional air-conditioning and controls, and ample space for any features they cared to specify.

Styling's marque differentiation work stipulated that Bentley should get four, separate round headlamps as soon as possible, and this was achieved in due course.

Conclusion

This bodyshell remained in production from 1998 to 2009, latterly as a Bentley only. Aesthetically, the styling theme of the Silver Seraph/Arnage, with its falling waist line, is not found wanting. Ten years later a motoring journal described the shape as "well proportioned and pretty." A quote in an April 1998 *Sunday Times* article entitled 'Cool Britannia' described Rolls-Royce as an inimitable example of style that would remain so. The side elevation of the Seraph's general statement is maintained on Goodwood's Rolls-Royce Phantom and Ghost, the convertible bearing overt reference to yacht aesthetics.

In December 2002, the World's Most Beautiful Automobile Competition in Italy elected the Bentley T as the most beautiful luxury car, "A limousine with an extraordinary image, a car that maintains the formal philosophy of the brand and underlines the quality of the body and equipment with the best and typical British refinement."

A spin-off from the P2000/P3000 styling programme was that it ended Crewe's embargo on clay modelling at the factory, which really changed everything. The new owners took over a world-class styling facility.

At the Silver Seraph Geneva launch I was introduced to Stan Mott, a brilliant cartoonist whose work mainly appeared in the American motoring press. One cartoon depicted St Peter showing a newcomer around heaven. An outrageous, open 'hot rod' is hurtling past, the figure at the wheel has long flowing white hair and beard, and is accompanied by angels blowing long, golden trumpets.
"What made you think that God wouldn't like cars?" St Peter asks the newcomer.

THE DRAMA OF
THE 1990s
A GOLDEN DECADE OF BESPOKE COACHBUILDING

Rolls-Royce and Bentley history is not without its share of drama. The birth, marriage and separation of the two marques is well documented, except for a period that ranks as extraordinary, and is the least understood or acknowledged. Quite simply, the 1990s witnessed an unparalleled increase in activity at Crewe, when the Company raised its game to meet a demand that probably enabled the two marques to survive into the new millennium.

The background – coachbuilding

While, with the demise of the separate chassis, the automotive industry moved away from coachbuilt bodies, one-off or limited production designs continued, usually commissioned by film stars and the like who could indulge their desire to own a totally unique car.

Rolls-Royce and Bentley Motors tended to leave this work to specialists – Crewe and MPW in London had their hands full making production cars. Customers were offered a comprehensive bespoke service, but one-off monocoque bodies were a different matter altogether.

Estate versions of SY existed, but it wasn't until the launch of the 1980 SZ, particularly turbocharged versions, that the bespoke body business began to pick up. UK firms, particularly Hoopers and Jankel, produced heavily modified saloons and limousines, with the latter even creating a sports car around the Turbo R power plant. Crewe was reasonably friendly with the people concerned with this work, although, apart from Jankel's limousine work, it generally was kept at arm's length. Fritz Feller and

I were dining with Giorgetto Giugiaro when he suggested that Ital Design obtain a Turbo R platform, in response to which Fritz's 'firewall' slid smoothly into place to block the request.

Resource issues aside, why should R-RMC put its name to any products other than mainstream ones unless the overheads per unit could be absorbed by the asking price, which would necessitate exceptionally wealthy patrons.

In the rarefied atmosphere of personalized yachts and jets, a 'standard' Rolls-Royce or Bentley appears small beer. It's not easy to imagine the mindset of extremely wealthy people, but enthusiasts can identify with the wish to establish a dream car collection, and the last MPW Phantom went straight into such a collection. An American I showed around the factory, who carried his wealth with a deal of humour and grace, had fifteen red Ferraris, and was buying a red Continental R to join them. His everyday car was a Mercedes coupé with a sheet of plywood over the rear seats for his Alsatian. Sir David Plastow once quipped that the choice of some individuals was between a Rolls-Royce or a swimming pool for their horses. Rich people are different, but all car enthusiasts speak the same language.

A new dawn – the Bentley Continental R effect

Despite the excellent sales situation at the end of the 1980s, the early 1990s brought lay-offs at Crewe, a downturn driven by the general economy rather than deficiency of product. A fillip was needed, and the timely appearance of the

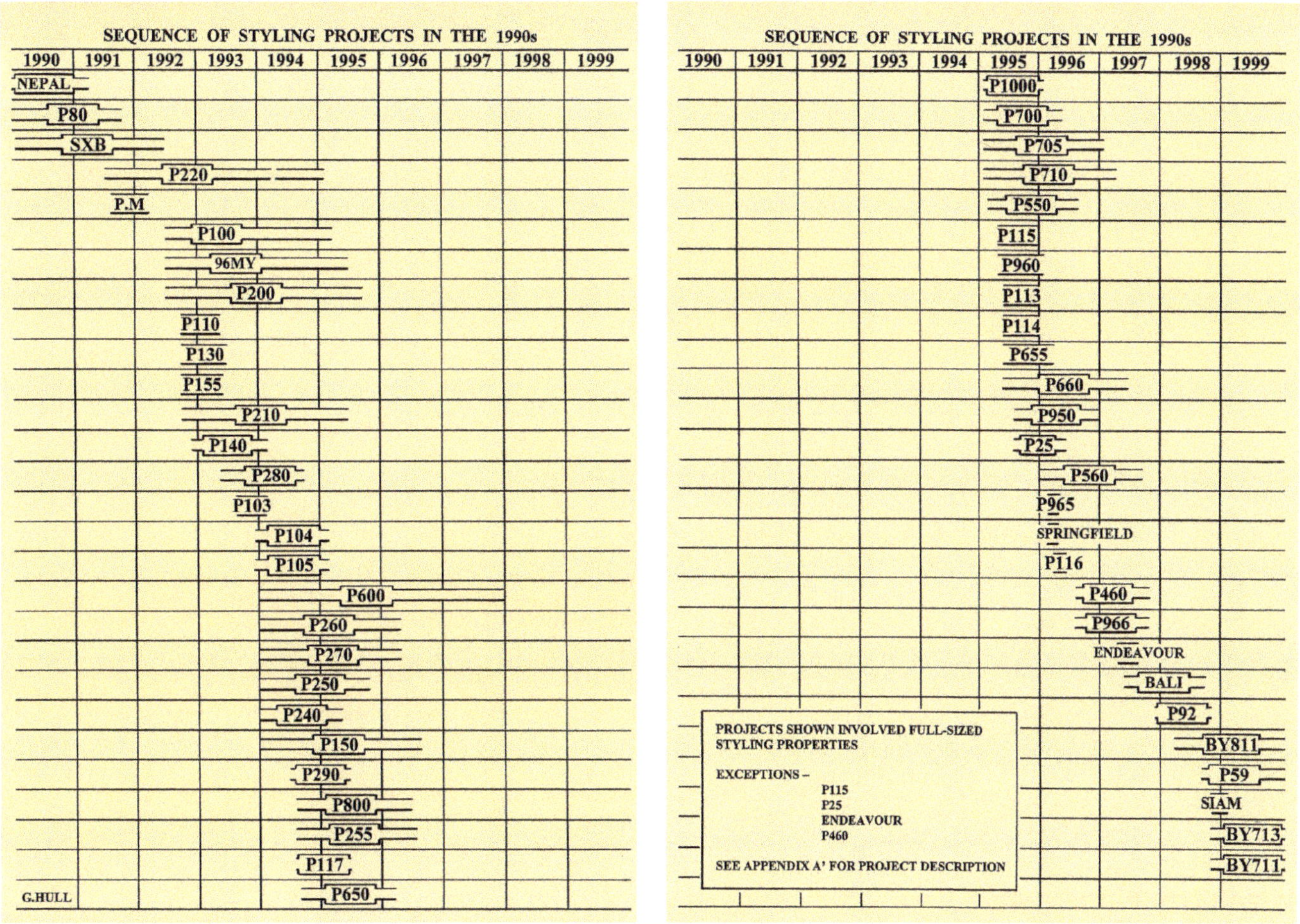

SEQUENCE OF STYLING PROJECTS IN THE 1990s

1990	1991	1992	1993	1994	1995	1996	1997	1998	1999

Left chart projects: NEPAL, P80, SXB, P220, P.M, P100, 96MY, P200, P110, P130, P155, P210, P140, P280, P103, P104, P105, P600, P260, P270, P250, P240, P150, P290, P800, P255, P117, G.HULL, P650

SEQUENCE OF STYLING PROJECTS IN THE 1990s

1990	1991	1992	1993	1994	1995	1996	1997	1998	1999

Right chart projects: P1000, P700, P705, P710, P550, P115, P960, P113, P114, P655, P660, P950, P25, P560, P965, SPRINGFIELD, P116, P460, P966, ENDEAVOUR, BALI, P92, BY811, P59, SIAM, BY713, BY711

PROJECTS SHOWN INVOLVED FULL-SIZED STYLING PROPERTIES

EXCEPTIONS –
P115
P25
ENDEAVOUR
P460

SEE APPENDIX 'A' FOR PROJECT DESCRIPTION

The span of Styling projects in the 1990s which required full-size 'properties' (clays/replicas/prototypes).

Bentley Continental R at the 1991 Geneva Motor Show was a godsend to Peter Ward. The theatrical arrival of the Vermilion show car was such a revelation that, as mentioned previously, the Sultan of Brunei immediately asked to buy it, not the least deterred by the fact that this was the only example and not for sale. This unusual situation demonstrated how the revitalized Bentley marque was sparking the imagination of certain individuals: the Company had struck gold!

As the stunning Continental R was essentially old wine in a new bottle, it was possible that special customers would be prepared to pay for other new bottles of Crewe's heady brew. Rumours began to circulate that Pininfarina, the most respected coachbuilder in the world, was working on one-off versions of Crewe product. Given there were other 'underground' conversions of SZs to estate cars, convertibles and limousines, etc, the involvement of Pininfarina was obviously of interest.

Crewe Styling had more than enough work servicing mainstream product to worry about more speculative projects, although we had previously been involved with a customer who wanted an SZ estate on their yacht! Despite our best efforts to avoid participation, in June 1992 the floor began to move under our feet: actually, it felt more like an express escalator, which only slowed some years later.

Into overdrive

The focus at Crewe had been to engineer the best car in the world. The SZ and associated rebirth of Bentley in the 1980s coincided with changing market forces, and engineering worthiness was no longer enough. Significantly, Chief Engineer Mike Dunn left in 1992, and was not replaced for several years.

Matthew Waterhouse, a deceptively able engineer from the development wing of R-RMC, was a leading light in the Daimler Dart Owner's Club, but otherwise seemed okay. Bowling into the office one day, he began to talk about ten special limousines for the Sultan of Brunei. This wasn't all that unusual as the Touring Limousine was proving a success, and similar quantities of saloons had previously been supplied to the Peninsula Hotel in Hong Kong.

The same week I had a conversation with Barry Threadgold, who managed the interesting/challenging Experimental Garage, and was now the manager of Project Contan, the convertible version of Continental R, which Pininfarina was going to design and build six examples of. Convertibles are difficult to design and engineer and, although the hood to body interface looked pretty good on renderings, the Italians would have to work for their money. The good thing from a styling viewpoint was that Italian engineers had sound aesthetic sense (not always a characteristic of this rôle). This union with the Italians would prove very useful, and become part of a much bigger picture.

By the end of June 1992, Pininfarina was also commissioned by a special customer to create a new-shape Phantom, and during July, Crewe gave MPW Touring Limousine information to the Italians, apparently for use as the basis of this new vehicle (P200). In addition, someone – without Crewe's involvement – had built to order a not terribly sophisticated Bentley Turbo R convertible, and there were also rumours of an estate and four-door hatchback. A higher performance Continental R – Sufacon – was under way at Crewe.

Given the dire straits of the economy in general, and R-RMC in particular, the apparently new opportunities to generate funds became increasingly attractive to the board. Styling, previously considered something of a necessary evil, began to be considered as a source of income, and therefore regarded in a new light. Amongst speculative proposals from various sources, Nick Shakespeare of Descartes Design offered us a large-scale model of a new Rolls-Royce Phantom styled on traditional lines. Not dissimilar to our own thoughts, this was another piece in the growing jigsaw of opportunity.

Despite the workload at Crewe, Peter Ward said I should become more directly involved with Project Contan in Italy. The laws of geometry governing hood packaging restrict styling opportunity, whereas work in the UK on SZ family updates and SXB was more rewarding. However, I provided what input I could to the exterior and interior of Contan in Italy, and it was then returned to Crewe to resolve the tricky waist brightwork.

Iron Orr in Blackpool

Mike Donovan arrived from Rover in early 1991, soon becoming responsible for new projects. Mike Dunn had never been too relaxed about 'owning' Styling, and, in any case, had his hands full with the demands of the ever-faster turbocharged cars. Mike Donovan took over the SXB new saloon programme in June 1991, and Styling a month later.

Following on the heels of Mike Donovan, also from Rover, was Jim Orr. These two had been prime movers in the game-changing Land Rover Discovery project, facing and resolving issues not dissimilar to those currently affecting R-RMC and SXB. Mike was a very civilized, quick-witted chap; Jim was also quick-witted. It soon emerged that Jim, a mentally and physically powerful Scot, was Mike's enforcer. He spent his weekends killing pheasants, and would hang large numbers of these harmless creatures amongst his team's anoraks and raincoats as a Monday morning gift. By September 1991, however, I was trying to avoid Jim, who stalked the corridors menacingly, apparently intent on strangling anyone he perceived to be obstructing his special MPW projects.

Jim's ability to work out the complex networks of interlocked activities involved in car design – the various disciplines of underbody, body, electrical, etc; not to mention the 'known/unknowns' of Styling – was awesome. A real bulldozer, he was cleverer than me, and handy with a shotgun. At our first meeting I had to ask him to take his feet off my desk. Fortunately, in company with most Englishmen, I like the Scots, and also those with character, which was just as well, because, as it turned out, Jim was a key element in the Company's survival during the troubled 1990s.

It always amused me that specially-commissioned vehicles and associated activities were code named Blackpool. How such exotic endeavours were made to wear a kiss-me-quick hat was a joke no one tired of: a top corridor throwaway label that had somehow stuck, no doubt.

As the number of projects increased with both mainstream and special customer orders, the entire structure of Crewe Engineering had to change, but no one could have foreseen just how big and fast the change would be. With Mike Dunn gone, Donovan and Orr organized Crewe-based project teams to control all activities.

Apart from on-going updates and model year changes to production cars, in the six months to the end of 1992 the following projects were coming across Styling's desk –

General world market –
- Contan (Continental R convertible)
- Medium-Sized Bentley (MSB)
- Corniche replacement
- SXB (Four-door replacement)

Customer-commissioned or speculative –
- Non-standard Touring Limousines
- Phantom VII (P200 Phantom Royale)
- Uprated Continental R (Sufacon)
- 4-door estates
- 2-door estates
- Phantom (P210)
- Folding hardtop Continental R (P155)
- Hoscars (Head of State cars)
- 4-door Continental R

Getting a quart out of a pint pot

Crewe Styling in the 1990s was approximately the same size as it had been for SY and SZ. Mike Donovan – desperate to cut payroll – stated that the department couldn't expand. In fact, one member had to be lost during Mike Dunn's time in office and another under Mike Donovan! We also kept losing our model-maker because the issue of staff versus hourly paid hadn't been resolved, although, from 1994, contract clay modellers were allowed on-site. Previously, the Company had been able to compensate for any lack of resource by extending the time-line, but current events no longer allowed this.

Because yours truly had successfully worked off-site with design and prototype houses on elements of Turbo R and Continental R, it was assumed this could continue. Certainly, Crewe Engineering didn't have enough spare people to tackle the increased workload on-site. Using our contacts, a number of consultants, mainly UK Midlands-based, were lined up, the only international input being Pininfarina, initially.

Commercial integrity was taken very seriously. When purchasing a Savile Row suit, it's reasonable to expect it to be made by a Savile Row tailor, and therefore Peter Ward had to ensure that Crewe personnel were closely involved in any off-site work. The only time R-RMC walked on thin ice in this respect was with the earliest Jankel limousines, and that was unintentional. Separately, Ward, Donovan and Orr all told me to get close to any aesthetic work that was going on, wherever it may be. All three men visited each project at various stages to ensure we were getting what we wanted. Jim Orr was a constant 'heavy' presence,

particularly with regard to project costs. The consultants relied on me for 'everyday' input, and on Ward, Donovan and me for actual sign-off.

This degree of top management involvement threw up another unforeseen human resource issue. Whereas the purchasers of production vehicles wouldn't normally expect the personal attention of the Company's managing director, royalty and the super-super wealthy usually did. Displaying a split personality, on-site, Peter Ward was the tough factory boss, but his natural role – and where he felt most comfortable – was that of salesman, and he was able to establish good personal relationships with these important clients, at times waiting around in hotels – albeit luxury ones – to be summoned into their presence. In a moment of rare candour Peter told me he had had to get used to early Sunday morning phone calls at home from one deity or another asking his opinion on colour, or whether or not to have chrome wheels, etc.

The other half of the elite tag selling team was smooth operator Nigel Cornelius, he of the Harley Street consultant image. If Jim Orr built the special order vehicles, Peter and Nigel secured the vital commissions for him to do so.

Initial requests for unique vehicles tended to be influenced by the Continental R, and one early example had a Continental R front end melded to an SZ Touring Limousine! The Company soon came to appreciate that certain individuals weren't at all fazed by the price of 'one-off' vehicles, which had to take into account Styling, Development, Tooling and Manufacture costings. Such vehicles represented a return to the coachbuilder's art of the 1920s and 1930s, but based on much more sophisticated technology. In addition, the unit price fell as the number of each design ordered increased, so why not take half a dozen of each, sir?

The styling process of Blackpool cars

A fundamental issue was buyer and seller reaching agreement on style. Earlier requests in 1992 for stretched, convertible or estate versions of production cars appeared straightforward enough, but assumptions – as in "I assumed the gun wasn't loaded" – are best avoided. The only way to preclude misunderstanding is to provide a written specification with a very accurate rendering of the proposal.

Generally, car renderings, unless done after the event, are not very accurate, and are intended to be used in-house as part of ongoing style development. We now had to offer renderings of styles that we knew would work. A tailor can't go back to a customer and say, "I'm sorry, sir, but that suit we showed you? Well, we couldn't make it after all, but never mind, here's another style," and neither could we do this with a customer's chosen car design. By early 1993, Peter Ward was asking Jim Orr to provide him with presentation books he could show the client.

Typically, the books showed –

• Touring Limousines
• Continental R-based convertibles (additional to Azure)
• Sufacon
• Sufacon Estate
• Phantom Royale
• 36-inch stretch limousines

– and contained a technical description and specification, rendered views of the style and, if available, a record of work-in-progress such as full-size clay and vehicle build. The renderings were super-critical, and, whether generated in-house or by consultants, had full Crewe input to ensure the correct DNA and character of a Rolls-Royce or Bentley. Once the drawings were approved, the car's style was set in concrete!

A few months into the process of a special build, Peter and Nigel began to better understand a client's requirements, which allowed more speculative design proposals to be included in the presentation books. A stretched Continental R 4 door Sedan with raised roof was one such example.

Although the appearance and packaging of these various vehicles encompassed much of the proposed vehicle's unique appeal, mechanical elements were also enhanced, with more powerful engines and brakes, limited slip differentials, 4x4 proposals, etc. By the end of 1993, the general forward plan or work-in-progress on customer 'one-offs' looked like this –

• P104 & P105 – rebodied Continental R convertibles
• P260 & P270 – rebodied Continental Rs
• P250 – sports car
• P240 – Cloudesque Phantom Limousine
• P150 – Super Sports (folding roof)
• P200 – Phantom VII, Royale
• P210 – Phantom Majestic
• P140 – Continental R Sedan
• P190 – Grand Prix

P104 and P105 were two different styles based on the yet-to-be-launched Continental R convertible. Although conceived by Pininfarina, they soon came under Crewe's sign-off umbrella, and I therefore found myself making frequent trips to Italy to ensure Bentley DNA was properly inseminated. It says a lot for the mutual respect between our companies that this process was workable. I avoided being deposited at high speed on an autostrada, in any case.

Consultancies

Everyone in the motor industry uses consultancies, whether for engineering or styling: even the giants will collaborate with their suppliers, who will advise on specialist areas such as airbags, fuel-injection, catalytic converters, etc. Off-site styling support is a little more complicated, as different companies have varying skill sets and agendas. Some of the ones we used to a greater or lesser extent during this period could be classified as follows –

Styling concepts –
Mark Stehrenberger
Tom Kellogg
Peter Stevens
Styling concepts and clay modelling –
DRA
Omni Design
Krafthouse
Styling concepts, clay modelling, model-making, replicas and prototyping –
MGA
Styling International (Geoff Mathews) (Howtal Whiting)
Descartes (Motor Panels, Abbey Panels)
IAD
ASC/Metalcrafters (USA)
Pininfarina (Italy)
Bertone (Italy)
Ital Design (Italy)
Heurliez (France)
Clay modelling, model-making and replicas –
Futura
Model-making –
Dave Evans

This list is not exhaustive, and certain changes occurred as company structure altered. In addition, there was continuous interaction with CAD-based engineering consultancies and pattern makers.

The first experience R-RMC had with styling consultants was the complete exterior and interior of Pininfarina's Camargue in the late 1960s. My first interaction with consultants was with John Heffernan and Ken Greenley on the exteriors of a Corniche proposal and the Continental R. As they were primarily selling their styling expertise, my input was a little contentious. Those companies linked to model-making, and prototyping in particular, were much more relaxed about styling

P560 'Highlander' (Tornado): a specially-commissioned, four-door coupé

P250 'Grand Prix 190': a specially-commissioned, two-seater Bentley coupé of 1994/5. It had an aluminium structure with advanced composite clamshell bonnet. The L410-V8 was rearward biased with rearward biased four-wheel drive. (See Appendix for styling body development.)

authorship: indeed, specialist model and replica maker Futura requested and relied on external styling supervision.

When using consultants, we tried to regard them as an extension of the Company studio, just as, say, GM did, which had many different studios in America and around the world. The consultants knew I wasn't playing one studio against another, inept at politics as I was, and whether or not they were irritated by my regular visits I don't know. However, they realized that having me involved on a weekly basis meant that matters progressed smoothly when Crewe's big guns turned up for major viewings.

Probably because of my earlier experience with Heffernan and Greenley, and the subsequent success of the Continental R, getting on with consultants seemed to be one of my Unique Selling Points. Peter Horbury of MGA – later Ford and then Volvo – thought I should be more assertive: ie kicking open the studio door and demanding tea and biscuits. Roy Axe described my job as

"nice work if you can get it," and Graham Morris – as a back-handed compliment, I hope – said he'd never known stylists get along with one another.

During the intense activity of the Blackpool era, there weren't any real disagreements or stand-offs with consultants, and any issues that did exist tended to come from Crewe project managers, and were linked to time or money pressures. It was my job to achieve as good a solution as possible (strangely, if a car isn't looking so great, the overall project manager is never in the firing line). An exasperated Crewe project manager said to me after one fraught session round a clay, "Anyway, Peter Ward and Mike Donovan are the Chief Stylists," whereupon I told him not to overlook Jim Orr. As it happened, Peter and Mike always supported me if it came to the crunch. Years of firing shotguns had blunted Jim's aesthetic sensitivity somewhat, but he, too, seemed to regard my approach as generally reasonable.

The juggling act

The number of simultaneous projects being run by individual engineering teams presented Jim Orr with colossal logistical problems, which, if a committee had been trying to sort, would still be unresolved. It needed a bulldozer like Jim to pull the levers and relentlessly create circumstances capable of driving the Blackpool/special customer opportunities to completion. Recruiting staff mainly from the Midlands meant that one of the problems was getting folk to relocate to Crewe, and many – including Jim – started out making long, daily commutes. To help persuade people to join the ranks, an MPW project drawing office was set up in the North Midlands as a halfway house.

To ensure that Rolls-Royce and Bentley culture wasn't watered down, the most experienced Crewe engineers were either running teams or evenly distributed between them. As there was only the one home-grown chief stylist, Jim had to ensure that the teams got me involved. As he resented people working on anything other than his MPW projects, this caused the occasional contretemps.

Blackpool viewings

The only real Achilles heel of Jim's complex project network was coordinating the work-in-progress timetables and sign-off viewings, which, despite the best of intentions, proved impossible. Even if each car programme hit every target, getting chief executives to attend project viewing windows just wasn't practicable. The fact that all of the teams delivered the goods demonstrated the capability of individuals unhampered by committees.

Although Jim Orr couldn't bully Peter Ward or even most of the directors, I was fair game for his tactics, which fluctuated between barely suppressed violence to his equally unnerving version of Scottish charm. After one session in my office where he explained how I was failing to support his endeavours, he departed, singing that old temperance anthem 'Come and join us, come and join us.' On another occasion he phoned me at Crewe, to say, angrily, that he was standing in a studio in the Midlands looking at a large lump of clay, and where was I? Attempting to humour him and win approval I took to wearing a tartan scarf whenever possible, although, due to inter-clan rivalry, this was a risky ploy.

In fairness, no one could have worked harder than Jim Orr, as he made plate spinners look like somnambulates. Refusing to acknowledge distance as an obstacle, he would board a Boeing 747 in shirtsleeves, carrying just a document folder, and on one occasion found himself on a transatlantic mission without even his passport.

Of course, mine was a dream job: often visiting four different projects in the Midlands on the same day, or flying to America, Italy, Germany or France and, at each destination, helping these fantastic dream machines to take shape. It is impossible to exaggerate the atmosphere and excitement of the mid-1990s for those involved in Crewe's Blackpool adventure.

The E-word – Exclusivity

Of the ninety-six Company project codes that existed in the 1990s, eighty or so had Styling involvement to a greater or lesser degree. Of these eighty, over twenty were unique vehicles, with styles that included coupés, convertibles and estate versions of a host style, which were unavailable to the general public. Over half-a-dozen more Styling projects had code names only (ie Bali).

Production cars with major styling modifications, such as estates and limousines, were also not for general consumption, and other projects included the Anniversary Corniche package, and a very large number of renderings for individual customer specifications (the latter exploiting the extensive MPW palette). Styling's general workload in this extraordinary period had 'stabilized' into the following modules –
• Future new production
• Model year changes
• Special order 'Blackpool' status
• Dealer limited editions
• Bespoke customer specifications

A growing complication in this mix of production and commissioned vehicles was exclusivity. For instance, if a customer paid for the conversion of a Continental R to an estate, could the Company build a similar vehicle for someone else? This awkward question wouldn't go away, and was particularly pertinent by the late 1990s due to the growing number of permutations and variations of exterior and interior styles.

There was huge pressure to generate funds in the short term, but selling the family silver to pay the rent became an ever-present spectre, and those in Styling were up to our necks in the issue. Customers might not be too precious about a mechanical upgrade, but if visual exclusivity was the prime motivation, the style had better be theirs alone.

Confidentiality in the automotive industry is of paramount importance, and especially so with most special commissions. Normally, secrecy ceases when a

SILVER WRAITH

1989. Similar retro styles were built to commission in the 1990s.

1998. 'Endeavour': futuristic computer exercise with body-coloured radiator shell, and illuminated Spirit of Ecstasy in mirrored glass compartment. An open-and-slide rear door was proposed. An animated film and scale model were made.

style is released in a blaze of popping cameras, but many of Crewe's 1990s creations were never promoted, either before or after hand over. Security was so tight that only a handful of people at Crewe, and none off-site, had an overview of all the work. Part of my job, therefore, was to guide the design contribution to ensure that contributors didn't get too close to another project's unique specification.

As well as achieving exclusivity of a car's exterior shape, areas such as alloy wheels and interiors became more challenging as time passed. The facia or dashboard of a Rolls-Royce or Bentley is an extremely complex and sophisticated technological area; described as the most expensive real estate in the world. Although clients were buying into the ambience and charm of Crewe's famous instrument boards, they still expected a unique creation on their particular car, and by unique they didn't mean merely different: each facia had to be a beautiful fusion of style and practicality worthy of the marque's heritage.

By the second half of the decade the Company's saloon and coupé had been in production for fifteen and five years respectively, and some of the larger dealers in London and America began to request their own limited editions. A change in visual appearance was the obvious first option, which meant that anything that didn't affect structural body pressings was a candidate for modification.

Previously developed for a Blackpool car was a 'Desperate Dan'-type chin-dam air-intake, which looked aggressive, allowing the engine to gulp more air, and it helped aerodynamics. The powers-that-be decided to use

this style – a decent period of time after its original use on a customer special – on a dealer limited edition. A nice rendering of this by our Darren Day appeared in *Autocar*, which was brought to the attention of the original customer. Walking into a London showroom, he saw 'his' air dam/ air-intake on another's car and was not best pleased.

By now, Peter Ward had sailed off into the sunset to run Cunard, and Chris Woodwark, his replacement, lost about a stone in weight smoothing ruffled feathers, whilst Styling had to very rapidly develop an alternative solution for the dealer. It had been a close call but did remind the Company how important aesthetics were. Needless to say, plans to use, say, P260's facia on a mainstream product were hastily reviewed. 1997 found Styling having to create reference books – which became essential reading – on everything from wheels to seat patterns to guard against duplication and near-misses.

Amongst the special-edition 'standard' cars, the 1996 P116 Talamo Continental R stands out. Ordered by an Italian dealer, it had a special front apron and polished alloy vented bonnet. There were no rear seats, but the interior had large areas of quilted leather, overlapping machined swirls of engine turning on facias and doors, and much more. Produced in-house, I thought the car a little extreme, but the formula was successfully echoed by the rather more subtle 2009 Bentley Supersport.

GH.10

A speculative programme for a mid-engined, two-seater Bentley of 1996/8, intended for special commission, small batch manufacture. It incorporated variable geometry aerodynamics and adjustable ride height/attitude. Although not taken to prototype stage, the version depicted indicates the way that the Engineering and Styling programme was heading. Ease of ingress and egress was a special consideration.

GH.10

Big Boys' Toys

The Crewe factory had always had a reputation for creating motor cars of great longevity, in terms of both mileage and body style. The re-birth of Bentley and advent of the Continental R and the Java show car changed decades-old public perception, and the hidden world of Blackpool projects would have surprised even the most worldly-wise observer.

Whilst the variations on Rolls-Royce and Bentley themes were fascinating, it was their conceptual span that was truly breathtaking –

- Convertibles
- Hardtops
- Coupés
- Folding roofs
- Raised roof limousines
- Head of State cars
- Classic/retro/replica
- Sports saloons
- 4x4 recreational
- 4x4 sports cars
- Estates
- Mid-engine (concept only)

All projects followed the same design discipline of rendering, clay mock-up, vehicle build and development. The clay sequence followed normal industry practice (three typical exterior clay Blackpool programmes are shown in the Appendix).

Technically, the most intriguing project was, perhaps, P250, a 4-wheel-drive, two-seater coupé, which had a unique aluminium chassis with a very highly tuned Crewe V8 moved as far rearward as possible. The project was entrusted to Peter Hill, one of the most experienced development engineers. A keen motorcyclist and vintage car buff, Peter sported a bow tie and infectious laugh. He was one of the few engineers trusted to talk to journalists

and celebrities; if L J K Setright or Stirling Moss was around, Peter was always wheeled out.

British development engineers such as Peter seem to be able to set up a car in such a way that they achieve a personality that others lack. Driving several raw prototypes around the former RAF Bruntingthorpe airfield was a nerve-racking experience when you consider how man-hours were tied up in each one, but also demonstrated how refined the final cars became. It was all down to Peter and his colleagues.

Shaken and stirred – the James Bond touch

P250 led to one of the most memorable events relating to Blackpool projects. Keith Sanders, our Marketing Director, requested my presence at MIRA Road Research Laboratory on the evening of March 26, 1997, to meet a chap who looked after the car collection of a special customer and, it would seem, inspect and put them through the paces before taking delivery. He was there with a legal representative to approve the P250 and P800 4x4 Dominator. These two projects, coupled with the P700 family, had drawn the Company into a whole new world of car design, linked by DNA but not chassis, to Crewe product. I was there to show sketches which floated the idea of a new, customer unique brand: ie a totally bespoke marque.

This was Graham Morris', Chris Woodwark's replacement, first contact with the secret world of extreme car enthusiasts. Morris, Sanders and I waited in the dark in the middle of a field as the lights of a helicopter approached. After a brief greeting the customer's personal 'taster' jumped into P250 and blasted off round the unlit handling track, the classic bellow of an unleashed V8 echoing back to us in the darkness, traction control apparent on every bend as the furious engine note broke up under electronic restraint. A traumatised Mr Morris looked at me and said, "Well, I'm not going to drive it like that."

We waited while this Stig-like character debriefed the engineers, and then had a quick look at P800. He confirmed that the latest sketched proposals I showed him of a unique brand were not so far off the mark. However, the impression was that this particular special customer probably now had enough vehicles to be going on with.

In hindsight, the most novel aspect of the night's work was Keith Sanders' proposal of offering certain selected individuals access to what was, in effect, a new British luxury brand.

A question of taste

It's said that when money comes in the door, taste goes out the window, and certainly I had tended to believe that wealth was no barrier to vulgarity. A reporter famously said of Elvis Presley's house, Gracelands, "If bad taste were gunpowder you wouldn't want to smoke in there." Of course, there is new money and there is old money; Alan Clarke remarked of a fellow MP, "He's the sort of chap who has to buy his own furniture." (Clarke inherited the family castle).

R-RMC always strove to offer its customers refined elegance. Unless someone was really determined to have an outrageous paint or fabric, they would be gently steered in other directions. Often, shocking colours or embellishments were intended purely to grab attention rather than an expression of innate bad taste (John Lennon's Phantom, for example).

One of the special projects which proved the inherent good taste of the client was P705, the middle of the trio of convertible/coupé/estate, based on the Java show car of 1994. This was a major undertaking using a much smaller package than the Crewe norm. Although sharing some exterior and interior elements, the three-vehicle designs were quite separate. Working at MGA, we decided to tackle the hardest first – the P700 convertible – then P710 estate, leaving the 'easy' coupé to last.

Of course, as is usually the case, the 'easiest' turned out to be the hardest. Coupés have only one mission in

life: to look stunning, and for the first and only time we began to receive negative feedback via Nigel Cornelius that progress photos weren't going down too well with the customer. Our 'Honest John' packaging approach of accommodating four large people in a smaller vehicle tended to make the rear roof look 'humped' and the overall shape appear dumpy. This criticism impressed me because anyone just wanting something different would have okayed the design.

In most companies, due to the associated engineering issues that were inevitable with a major project direction change, the plug would have been pulled on this awkward coupé variant: drawings would have been rolled up, CAD discs stored, and clay recycled. But we were made of sterner stuff and, by the way, the project was effectively pre-sold; no one was going to tell the man he couldn't have his car. So, rolling up my sleeves, and saying with a grin "I'll sort this out," I reached for the phone and proceeded to harangue the chief modeller! No, actually, Geoff Mathews and I had spent a long time figuring out how to get this device right. We had to tell Nigel that rear occupant accommodation would be reduced, thus allowing the roof to be slimmer. We used larger wheels and moved the rear ones back. The vehicle was re-skinned, but still Java in origin, and very pretty, too. Apparently, it was always intended to carry only children in the back, anyway.

My bête noire concerning taste was chromed wheels, which came from America, the land of chrome. Most alloy wheels are styled to be finished in silver paint, and chroming results in a chaotic confusion of mirrored reflections. We styled Rolls-Royce wheels with stainless steel discs to reflect effortless motion; Bentley wheels were intended to be jerky and frantic. Chrome usually destroys design intent and creates a jumble of ricocheting light, whether a car is still or in motion. Of course, you can try and avoid this at conception, but chroming wheels designed to be painted is just plain wrong. End of rant.

What was heartening about designing vehicles for special customers was that, without exception, and regardless of country of origin, they all bought in to the Company's philosophy. None of the unique exteriors and interiors strayed outside of marque ethos, and any one of the projects could have appeared on Motor Show stands without being at odds with the creed established by Sir Henry Royce or W O Bentley.

The one that got away – mid-engine

At the end of July 1996, a meeting with Nigel Cornelius and

myself was held in Keith Sander's office. Keith, reasonably pragmatic for a marketing man, wanted to know if a new platform could be created for Blackpool-type projects. Certainly, the dimensions of the L410 engine/gearbox and air-conditioning unit tended to dominate packaging and proportions, and I pointed out that, as P250 had the engine moved rearward, it was virtually mid-engine: why not go the whole hog?

There were three possible scenarios –
• Genuine Le Mans-type racer
• 110 per cent scale two-seater
• Four-seater

The second option seemed the best bet as Le Mans cars require a soaped shoehorn to enable ingress and egress, and 110 per cent scale would make it more user-friendly. Keith and Nigel seemed to go along with this thinking. Mathew Waterhouse and MPW's Midland office were involved in alternative layouts, and I was asked to issue a styling brief. This stipulated an overtly mid-engined theme with an evolved Bentley radiator shell: something along the lines of sanitized Le Mans racer meets Ferrari Testarossa, projecting dominant power and avoiding a stripped-out interior.

It was felt that any enthusiast would find Bentley's interpretation of a mid-engine theme intriguing and, hopefully, irresistible. Also, as it was unlikely to be a production line prospect, it was ideally suited to private collections without sacrificing the Company's crown jewels. We supplemented Crewe Styling by employing extra studios, approaching DRA, Geoff Mathews Design (GMD), and another RCA 'old boy,' Peter (McLaren F1) Stevens.

Early 2D viewings with Nigel Cornelius, Jim Orr, and key MPW people prompted no obvious frontrunner, although the specification for what was now called ME did, however, begin to gel: top speed would be 203mph (Jim) 210mph (Nigel), with adjustable aerodynamics for stability and cooling, and variable ride height. Easy access and exit were essential.

November 1996 saw credible early sketches of a mid-engined Bentley. Because DRA had arguably the best artists, all of the most promising elements of styling contributions received were fed to them. This, coupled with their competence at getting tricky 2D surfaces to work in 3D, resulted in a superb, practical, realistically rendered proposal.

For any child of the 1960s the mid-engine layout has a magic potency, and to see a Bentley proposal emerge

for this charismatic design was truly exciting. However, despite my best efforts to campaign for Project ME, it remained on the back burner, because, it seemed, the powers-that-be regarded such devices as being of fringe interest. That may be so, but isn't that what's called niche? Regardless, by August 1997, Project ME merited a P460 code, and I suggested we made a scale model and/or computer animation. Matthew Waterhouse was very much on-board, and that year we made a last few tweaks to the renderings and P460 was named Sabre. Aircraft-style, head-up displays (where instrument read-outs are projected onto the screen) were being investigated, and targeted top speed was a realistic 185mph.

The project's potential was so strong I could taste it, but it remained one of those teasing "what might have beens." A victim of circumstance, there was too much going on; the Blackpool era was slowing down, and then VW and BMW were dividing up the Company. P460's final flicker was when Tony Gott, made acting Chief Executive at the end of 1998, showed the renderings to *Autocar* as an example of what we could achieve. One can imagine my mixed emotions when one of VW's first acts was to show the world the Hunaudières, its own interpretation of a mid-engine Bentley.

The 1990s and Blackpool reflections
The events which occurred at Crewe during the 1990s were so unlikely that if woven into a novel they would be dismissed as ridiculous or gross exaggeration.

After best-ever sales figures at the end of the previous decade, yet another dip in the helter-skelter that was the economy occurred, forcing cycles of redundancies and short-time working. In the face of these problems the Continental R of 1991 provided a big boost for the Company. Customers began commissioning many unique designs, and the 1994 Java concept surprised and influenced the car world. Desperately short of money, Crewe managed to launch a new four-door saloon in 1998 which, in Bentley form, was produced for eleven years. The factory was re-fitted and upgraded, and a replacement for the iconic Rolls-Royce Corniche was launched, together with a stretched Seraph; the Company was also working on a replacement for Continental R. During this hectic period, four different MDs came and went, and by the end of the decade, BMW owned Rolls-Royce and VW owned Bentley.

The impact of special customer orders during the Blackpool era was profound, securing funds that the traditional market hadn't been able to. For such a small organization to meet this challenging opportunity must be unique in motoring history. If it had occurred a few years earlier I doubt whether R-RMC's personnel and infrastructure would have been flexible enough to cope. By the 1990s, attitude had changed for the better: swim together or sink together; even so, pressure on existing structures and individuals was colossal.

Jim Orr's MPW became a firm within a firm, the host firm carrying on with Engineering/Production/Marketing functions as normal. Jim's swashbuckling approach used its facilities as required, as well as many other off-site Company contacts. The ad hoc nature of Jim's fluid, ever-changing network of teams that were necessary to complete the projects inevitably caused friction, not least with Styling, which answered to Ian McKay of Marketing for production car matters. On the other hand, Jim had no doubt that our first duty was to support his teams. Ian was wise never to go grouse-shooting with Jim. As it was, Ian's and Jim's worlds didn't collide because they inhabited different galaxies.

Nigel Cornelius required just one or two individuals such as Paul Cartwright to handle Blackpool sales. This caused muttering within the ranks as Chris Woodwark's new band of Branders was mainly sidelined.

The 1990s thrust Styling into the Company's consciousness because Engineering's traditional evolution was suddenly revved-up, and the projects needed lots of design input quickly. Whilst the board still wouldn't increase Styling staffing, those few involved had a fantastic opportunity, as not only could they contribute to these wonderful projects, but could also see how some of the best talent in the world operated. It was also possible to rapidly get up to speed with very sophisticated CAD design. On top of that, department members could see that all aesthetic efforts were controlled by Crewe.

Jim Orr was such a force of nature that his immediate team was pretty much run ragged. Chris Skade, a youngish chap, had the joy of helping with Jim's financial matters. Chris trained in martial arts but to my knowledge never used them at work. The following indicates how Chris coped.

I asked Chris, as he pounded a calculator, where Jim was.

"He's gone for his annual medical."

"Any idea when he'll be back?"

"Hard to say, it will start on-site with the Company doctor but they'll probably transfer to the psychiatric wing at Leighton Hospital."

Like all of us there, Chris had a genuine respect and affection for the amazing Jim.

CORNICHE
THE RIVIERA TOUCH

How to replace an icon

The Corniche of 1971 was a cleverly re-launched Mulliner Park Ward two-door of 1966/7 origin, penned under John Blatchley's regime, with Bill Allen as key stylist. It was a classic that wouldn't be replaced until the next millennium.

A source of concern with Corniche by the 1980s was that it featured so many styling cues from the 1965 SY Silver Shadow, and none from the 1980 SZ Silver Spirit. Although this vehicle was a 1960s period piece, the first-generation federal bumpers it carried latterly woefully lacked the charm of the original chrome ones. An SZ convertible mock-up displayed none of Corniche's charisma.

When Dick Perry took over R-RMC in 1984, he was keen to help MPW Willesden, London, and energized the ongoing search for a new, two-door convertible. Some preliminary renderings and quarter-scale models based on an SZ platform were made in-house at Crewe, but, because of the ever-increasing Bentley work, this was on an 'as and when possible' basis.

John Heffernan and Ken Greenley had worked alone on Bentley P90 at IAD Worthing on the south coast, and following this exercise, continued at this genteel seaside resort looking at a Corniche replacement. John Stephenson, our first Product Planning Director, was an ex-colleague of John's and Ken's from Vauxhall days, and he suggested I also used the IAD facilities to make an alternative quarter-scale model. It was impractical to closely supervise the work in Worthing so I gave one of

Bill Allen joined the Company as a stylist in 1935, and retired in 1977. He worked closely with John Blatchley on cars such as the Silver Cloud and Silver Shadow, and laid down the theme and lines of the Silver Shadow two-door, later named Corniche. Bill was a master of the traditional coachbuilder's design skills of sketching, draughting, and model-making. Before the advent of full-size clay mock-ups, Bill's generation could draw 2D body lines and sections that would generate, computer-like, resolved 3D surfaces and intersections. It was a privilege to work alongside such a skilled person; his dedication and professionalism helped ensure aesthetic integrity – a unique aspect of the Company's heritage.

1996, and the last of the line. Bill Allen with the final, 1960s-designed Corniche. Bill was laid to rest on the day of the 2000 Corniche launch.

1984. The search for the elusive new Rolls-Royce convertible continued. This rendering was the extreme end of a trilogy, proposing classic Corniche forms with a more organic flourish and Silver Spirit-type headlamps.

1986. When funds became available the style chosen for a full-size clay bypassed any Corniche influence in preference of a modernistic, extruded look. The sketches (above & below) show the approach that was taken to achieve more shape in a Mk11 follow-up clay, which proved successful. The style then switched marques and was developed into the Bentley Continental R Coupé. Bentley's time had come, and Rolls-Royce would have to wait until the year 2000 for a new Convertible.

IAD's modellers a rendering, and asked him to do the best he could.

Having just taken over as Chief Stylist from Fritz Feller, this wasn't the best of arrangements, given the issues at Crewe. When time permitted, members of the in-house team – Brian Hassall, Stephan Everitt, Ryan Lewis and Norman Webster – continued looking at ideas for the convertible, including hood mechanisms. The hood was a major issue: should they use the existing 'pram' type or a more sophisticated/expensive design that disappeared completely when lowered? Norman was brilliant with the hinges and links for this.

During a snowy February in 1986 I put one of our models into the Company's Renault Espace and took it to MPW, Willesden. On arrival I reversed into a snow-obscured rose garden and, with a lurch, the Renault was suddenly sitting on its belly. With determined forward/reverse gear rocking it clawed its way out in clouds of steam, almost tearing off the front apron in the process. The incident seemed symbolic of Styling's situation at the time ... John Lake, the bearded engineer running MPW's effort, was left to wonder what to tell the gardener come the thaw.

Dick Perry decided to develop John's and Ken's model, which was also rendered full-size. The two were set up in a temporary studio at MPW to undertake full-size Corniche clay work. Dick Perry probably wanted Willesden to own this project, which also avoided the unresolved issues about full-size clay modelling at Crewe.

Replacing an icon – take one

Replacing Corniche was never going to be easy. The venerable convertible's sculptured style meant it still sold quite well, particularly in America. All home-based efforts assumed a continuation of Corniche's character, though not retro or mainstream European style. John's and Ken's proposal was a more 'modern' offering that eschewed all of Corniche's 'Coke bottle' wing forms, and adopted an extruded constant side section. The speed and quality of their team of professional clay modellers showed just what Crewe was missing out on.

I had to tell Chief Engineer Mike Dunn, my boss, and Dick Perry, Mike's boss, that the proposal made at MPW lacked the brio of a Corniche replacement. We had comparison photographs taken and shown to all interested parties, including the Americans. At a Product Policy Committee viewing of photos at Crewe on March 8, 1986, I was asked to work more closely with John and Ken.

Replacing an icon – take two
The second phase was much more promising, to the extent that I suggested converting the car into a Bentley Coupé. Thus, Rolls-Royce lost its potential new convertible in April 1987. Several unofficial SZ soft-tops were built in America, simply by cutting off the roof and fashioning a hood: not a great idea.

Corniche was a hard act to follow, and everyone felt more confident about Bentley's place in the world as a result of the new model. Work did continue on a replacement but with back burner status. One tactic we tried was to photograph a rendering and enlarge it to 17 feet long (5.2 metres), mount it on plywood, and make a cut-out, which we took up to the Rolls-Royce sports field off Minshull New Road. With modeller Brian Hassall behind it posing as a driver, the illusion was quite effective (later, we would have used a computer to achieve the same result).

Replacing an icon – take three
Six years would pass before the dust was blown off the 'Corniche replacement' file, previous to which we had worked with Pininfarina on Azure, the Continental R convertible, and were involved with two Azure-based specials with the Italians. Mike Donovan, by then my boss, was obviously sensitive to the lack of any real progress on the Rolls-Royce front, and asked me what we could do about a new convertible. As usual, money and resources were tight. Corniche, like the Porsche 911, had never really gone out of fashion, and so I suggested why not 'do a Porsche' and build a Corniche replica on the Azure – 'old style, new mechanics.'? So it came to pass that a small team was set up at Crewe for P103.

Peter Tricklebank, probably Crewe's most experienced body design/draughtsman, laid out Corniche lines over Azure. Could we also incorporate the planned '96 model year SZ's revised front and rear bumper/aprons, and smaller radiator shell, etc? It seemed possible.

As Styling's Martin Bourne, now freelancing, had worked with Corniche's original creators, I asked him to be the man on the spot. We used MGA's clay modelling studios at Coventry as a base. Corniche was, by now, digitized, so it was possible to rough-machine the basic form, albeit a little wider, on to Azure's platform. After pushing and pulling around the clay, Martin achieved a very credible effort: the old, classic lines interfaced with Azure's hood remarkably well. The clay was fully dressed and looked good in silver. In addition, a great improvement was made by using the latest bumper systems to replace the federal versions Corniche had been forced to wear (aesthetically marginal, even in body colour). It all looked very promising so we also styled a hardtop as a possible option.

P103 was well received when viewed at Crewe on January 24, 1994. It was a 'definite maybe' moment, giving a high visual return for minimum expenditure and low risk. In the event the sheer weight of other more obviously viable projects overwhelmed this retro offering. Something of a missed opportunity, yes, though it was no coincidence that, at this time, we used the same formula to style and manufacture some Silver Cloud replicas based on our latest platforms. Crewe was never short of ideas, just money.

Replacing an icon – take four
The Bentley Azure was very successful, and became the recognized Company convertible (Corniche gracefully motoring towards its final sunset in 1996). There followed a long gap, during which the Silver Seraph was fully resolved. It was naturally assumed there would be a demand for a convertible version, and at a Graham Morris policy meeting on September 18, 1997, Styling was asked to embark on a new Corniche programme. Two scenarios were to be explored –
• Evolutionary
• Radical

Michael May of Brand was taking the minutes and I asked him to record that, this time round, Styling needed up-front Engineering support, for the benefit of Graham Morris, who'd previously pointed out to me that it was no good styling things that couldn't be made.

Michael contributed Brand input to the new P92 brief: as with our previous P103 exercise, the idea was to

1980s Corniche, film-set-style. A rendering of a Corniche proposal was enlarged to full size, glued onto a sheet of plywood, and then photographed on the Rolls-Royce sports ground at Minshull New Road. Could a contemporary style replace the iconic 1966 original?

Ninety years of Rolls-Royce convertibles.

Clay model of P103 Corniche proposal, January 14, 1994. Corniche lines were applied to the Bentley Azure platform and cabin, and 1996 model year front and rear Silver Spirit elements also employed.
L-R: Martin Bourne, author, Jim Potter, Ken Hartley, Ron Saunders.

use Azure as the starting point but dress it with as much Silver Seraph hardware as possible. This approach went against my purity of style ethos but, pragmatically, it made sense. All we had to do was come up with the additional stylistic flourish that a Corniche customer would expect – and at a time when not only were in-house resources fully occupied, but we were working off-site as well.

Resolutely maintaining an old Crewe tradition, Graham Morris wouldn't allow any increase in Styling staff. Needing to stay in daily contact with this particular project, I brought one of our consultant's people, Jonathan Gould of Geoff Mathews Design (GMD), on site. Even though I'd earmarked a CAD-generated styling exercise theme (Project Endeavour) to influence Corniche, it was still necessary to render a number of proposals to give the board a feeling of choice.

Front and rear ends would be as the Seraph, with different side sculpting below an Azure hood. Of course, simply putting a Rolls-Royce radiator shell onto an Azure was shamelessly also offered as a choice, and the MPW Midland Design Office would work the engineering feasibility issues.

In early December that year Graham Morris gave the go ahead for P92, styled as per the renderings we'd recommended: a theme based on an elongated S-shaped falling waist line running from nose to tail, supplemented by soft rear haunches. Programme timing was very tight, so, if possible, Seraph or even Arnage facia and console would be used. MPW's Paul Smith, a keen motorcyclist, would lead the engineering effort.

Not least of P92's issues was that the project occurred in the middle of the Seraph and Arnage launches, but by February 1998 work on P92 was under way with GMD. (Geoff Mathews had moved from the Midlands to Essex when Hawtal Whiting sold its Midlands site.) On P92's full-size tape layouts and clay we experimented with different side sections, but the final solution was an easy choice. What wasn't so easy was marrying Seraph's front headlamps, etc, to Azure's platform. One of the reasons I worked with Geoff was his engineering background before he enlisted at the RCA, otherwise known as 'the fun palace.'

The previous month P92 had been given the code name Borrego, and by mid-April we had the board's approval of the general style. That same month I had to miss an important boardroom discussion on a new Crewe Styling area as I was in Essex working on P92 (an irony that wasn't lost on the board, apparently), checking highlights on the painted Dynoc clay. This was a critical outside viewing, and early that Sunday morning was the only time we could risk it in the built-up area there.

A convertible, with hood stowed, flaunts its interior wares in all their glory, and P92 had to live up to Crewe's world-class reputation. Much can be agreed in the boardroom about rationalization and carry-over from other family members, but the Stylist is still expected to pull a little extra out of the bag. We made sure that Michael May of Brand was aware of all the day-to-day Styling development, so that he understood the working process. In the end, everyone was happy.

Replacing an icon – take five

Taking control from May 7, 1998, VW knew about P92 Borrego, and by mid-September that year, wanted to retain the style, even though unsure about using the Azure platform. Understandably, it was thought more logical to use the more recent Seraph platform, albeit still with the Azure hood, and Crewe's L410 engine rather than BMW's V12. A VW platform was also considered.

Ken Scott, a tall, undertaker-like Scot, had been a Blackpool team leader, and was to manage the latest exercise – code named Siam – which wasn't as straightforward as it sounds. Seraph had a 50mm longer wheelbase, and was wider than Azure. We had ten weeks to prove the styling and engineering of this new hybrid. There was still no spare in-house resource, so we worked with TWR (home of the Arrows F1 team) in Oxfordshire, telling its Ian Callum, later Jaguar Design Chief, that we wanted a 'Chinese copy' of P92. Not the most stimulating brief.

TWR started off by building Borrego/Siam body surfaces on an Alias computer, and a full-size clay was then machined from this data. This simple transfer across exercise turned out to be a real challenge, however, as areas of Seraph's underbody – especially at the base of the windscreen – caused problems. Moving a body surface even a few millimetres initiates a knock-on effect, which can virtually re-surface the whole car. Interior styling was much easier, however, as Seraph's facia, etc, fitted.

Despite a lot of hard work, Siam threatened to be the rather plain sister. I'd arranged for the P92 Borrego prove-out body to be in TWR's studio, as Ian had an exceptional chief modeller who could see the issues as well as any stylist. However, one session was spent pointing out the blindingly obvious to this chap by means of a flip chart. Shortly afterwards, he came across Ian and I discussing the interior, "Are you still here?" he snarled in passing. Ian apologized, saying the chap was having a bad reaction to a vaccination: we both knew, though, that certain talented people need a lot of slack.

In the middle of all that was going on, Graham Morris decreed that the entire Crewe factory had to attend Jack Black MindStore positive-thinking seminars, which espoused a cult-like, motivational take on life. Although I never achieved the hoped-for self-levitation, it was all good stuff.

Don White now became Siam Chief Engineer as 'the undertaker' was diverted to look at P92 on a VW platform. Don was another very experienced Blackpool project man, who impressed me by having an early carbon fibre bicycle.

The Corniche of 2000 was the last new Rolls-Royce motor car to come about at the Crewe factory, after numerous exercises had explored how to replace the iconic 1960s model. The solution was a melding of the Azure platform with visual elements of Seraph, and more pronounced side feature and 'hips.' Sporting 17 inch wheels, the largest that Rolls-Royce, Crewe achieved, the classic fine whitewall increases wheel size visually. Due to ongoing engineering debate, the same body style was modelled on to both Bentley Azure and Arnage platforms. With a back-to-back comparison, the Azure platform-based option was the winner.

Being a Rolls-Royce, interior ambiance was traditionally relaxed. The gear change lever resumed its location on the steering column, whilst sculptured rear side panels accommodated the hood mechanism. Rear occupants sat within the width of the stowed windscreen header rail.

The TWR Siam was a well-finished, superbly-painted effort which carried all of P92 Borrego's styling features and had more interior room. The two versions looked like sisters: one was well turned out and sensible-looking, but most who saw them would want to go out with the other one!

On December 14 that year VW's viewing committee came to Crewe. Amongst other projects Dr Piech wanted to see the two convertibles. It was not at all clear whether VW would prefer the prettier of the two, or the one that was better in the kitchen, and it fell to me to step forward and explain the differences. After a couple of sentences it became obvious that Dr Piech had paid help in his kitchen. Turned out his wife liked the new P92 Corniche as well.

Replacing an icon – take six

The new convertible had one last prima donna moment before taking to the stage. Although used to late engineering requirements, in November 1999 we had to re-style the front apron air intake just weeks before the January 2000 launch! Not enough air was reaching the intercoolers, and there was no alternative but to make the aperture wider. Considering the time spent refining such details, including vanes and additional lamps, modifications like this are hugely frustrating, and last minute by any standards. It's probably true that the air intake of any powerful car on the road isn't as originally conceived, because, even with computer flow modelling, prototype testing is the only way to guarantee correct air volume.

The convertible of 2000 was VW's first mayor product decision for the Company and the last new Rolls-Royce design to be built at Crewe. The only outstanding issue after this long saga was what to call it; there was only one name it could have, of course: Corniche.

The Company bought an early Renault Espace to study the possible use of composite panels on SXB. I liked driving it, being a fan of the Beetle-based Brubaker Box MPV. The Espace had a terrible life, mercilessly thrashed as Experimental Garage's hack. Approaching the end of its tough career it packed up on me at busy traffic lights. To avoid being shunted clear by the huge truck behind, I drove round the corner on the starter motor. My passenger was future MD, Tony Gott.

Alan Dutton, then manager of Experimental Garage, brought me back from the Midlands in the department's venerable, high-mileage Corniche. Alan, apparently behind schedule for a social engagement, fairly stormed up the M6: when required, these Grand Dame convertibles could hitch up their skirts, shrug off the years, and really go.

I attended Bill Allen's funeral in Crewe on the very day of the Corniche's launch in America: it seemed a strange coincidence. His widow, Barbara, had placed a framed photo on Bill's coffin of him standing proudly by the last Mk IV Corniche.

About this time there was a 25 year long service dinner; I put my presentation cheque towards a traditional English pendulum chimer. At its 15-year service I discovered it had a German mechanism ...

STYLING VIEWINGS
THE CRITICAL MASS

Presentation, presentation, presentation

The Chief Executive and Board of Directors routinely met in the boardroom in the top corridor, Mahogany Row, to discuss all aspects of the company. Nervous managers, usually with a well-thumbed folder, were often asked to attend to explain something, or even themselves, in a situation where it was possible to enter the room as head of a department, but leave knowing you now had more time to spend with the family ...

Numerous sessions in the boardroom caused me to dislike the experience. There was often the whiff of adrenaline in the air, and any loose remark either hung horribly in the chilled silence that followed, or was pounced on with predator-like intensity. Newcomers arriving early to the big table would desperately try to decide where the MD might sit. I found it best to sit on the same side as the MD and one person away; never in the direct line of fire. Chris Woodwark adroitly remarked at one meeting that his Purchasing Director was studying his shoes and that I had my eye on the door handle. All due respect, therefore, to Peter Cable, a seen-it-all lifer who loudly described a refreshment break as reminiscent of a chimpanzees' tea party.

So boardroom meetings were very high-pressure, high-risk gatherings. Relatively few people ever got to see all of the directors together here, which is why the Product Policy Committee Styling viewings – at times the only regular interface between the board and the people creating the car – were rather unique at the Crewe factory.

These viewings started in a small way in the 1970s, but over the next thirty years became a major element of the Company's product development process.

Birth of the Styling viewing process

In the early 1970s, Fritz Feller, in theory answering to Chief Engineer John Hollings, only jumped through a hoop for MD David Plastow. John Hollings' main concern was maintaining Rolls-Royce's engineering ethos of steady development: introducing rack and pinion steering, for instance, on the SY Silver Shadow. Hollings was openly suspicious of Fritz, regarding him as too clever by half, and considered Styling to be a rather distasteful necessity at best. David Plastow, on the other hand, was a natural salesman who understood the marketplace and liked Fritz.

Although members of the board attended Styling work-in-progress sessions, Fritz knew he only had to deal with Plastow and Hollings. The key topic of early viewing meetings was primarily a re-skinned SY. I think Hollings regarded the body as just a way to protect passengers from the elements, and stop the hardware going rusty, and it was down to Plastow to say yea or nay to aesthetics. Fritz loved the limelight, and listening to him talk through the issues was very entertaining, Hollings glowering in the background as Plastow chuckled at Fritz being his charming best.

An example of Fritz's grasp of human nature was his 'percentage gain' ploy. A diagram of SY showed available items with which to visually upgrade the car: new wheel trims, mirrors, and chrome strips, etc. For a boardroom presentation Fritz got me to arrow the proposed changes, with so-called associated percentage gains: wheel trims 26 per cent, bright strip 14 per cent, mirrors 11 per cent, and so on. It was pure hokum but Fritz, with a wink, said "They'll love it!" And they did, of course, happily choosing items and adding up little lists of percentage 'gains.'

Despite the somewhat primitive circumstances of Crewe Styling resource we achieved a high standard of presentation. Time and again at college I'd witnessed the power of good presentation: it's not the be-all and end-all, but you can lose everything if you don't show something in its best light. Against the worthy but somewhat dowdy backdrop of a factory, Styling presentations shone brightly. David Plastow was quick to spot this and rewarded us with a permanent, well-dressed viewing area, a pivotal facility that was maintained, at different locations, from then on.

The institution matures

From my perspective Crewe's Plastow years were the best for Styling viewings, when we had only to convince or be instructed by the head of the Company, who just needed his chief engineer to state whether or not something could be made. Perhaps it wasn't the most sophisticated system, but it worked, and was not too dissimilar to VW's system of years later. Obviously, the MD had to carry his board with him, but seldom at any one time were there more than one or two people at the top of the Company with the requisite 'magic spark.'

Inevitably, Styling viewings became more structured as numbers of attendees grew. The MD had to formally ask his marketing people whether they could sell the car or items viewed, and the engineering director had to get confirmation from Body Engineering that it could tool the job; can Manufacturing build it or Purchase source the new lamps, etc? Once you begin to get a gathering of key players such as these, many more are drawn to the action. Personnel and Finance were soon regulars. If you weren't at the Styling viewings you weren't really on the Captain's table.

This situation ebbed and flowed, relative to the amount of styling work that was going on. By the time Dick Perry took over from George Fenn during 1983, we had a Product Policy Committee. Largely due to the re-birth of Bentley, this committee met monthly, initially in the boardroom and reconvening in the Styling viewing area. Whereas before we were targeting one key decision-maker, the MD, Styling, now led by yours truly, had a much more pro-active

board. Peter Ward, Marketing, John Stephenson, Product Planning, and Mike Dunn, Engineering: all expected to be heard as part of the management team. This had the effect of prompting other directors to up their game, as they also wanted to be a force to be reckoned with.

In Fritz's era there existed a gentleman's agreement about viewing decisions. Key points would be recorded but the structure was not intrusive. Out of my depth when having to marshal the assembled Crewe high-fliers, I began writing everything down meticulously. A large number of directors and associates rapidly descend into chaos when in an open space with many interesting exhibits, so a system was developed whereby papers describing viewing exhibits were circulated. Usually, I presented the items, and also logged comments and decisions, which were duly circulated, along with any required action. This made it easy to confirm who said what, although I admit to attributing more weight to the comments of certain individuals, and especially those of the MD!

Some drawings could be shown in the boardroom, but, generally, we tried to bundle all the work together as part of the monthly Styling viewing opportunity. Viewings were very popular, and it was never difficult to achieve a full house every time. The dates were in everyone's diary, and it gave the directors a real chance to influence the product that was going out the factory gates.

Part of the fabric of the place

The MD and his board became used to regularly visiting the House of Styling Delights, soon taking the area for granted by assuming that the toy cupboard was always well-stocked, neat and tidy. That the area was primarily a workplace was a fact that often escaped them, and after a good lunch, they could suddenly decide to have their own private viewing without telling anyone. After one lunch in particular, they descended en masse to find their view of the latest full-size mock-up obscured by screens. Moving a screen they discovered someone from the Experimental Woodshop carrying out a puncture repair of a bicycle tyre in the water-filled Dynoc tank. What a missed photo opportunity: a group of suits surrounding a mortified chap wrestling with a much patched inner tube!

The influence of Styling presentations was out of all proportion to the size of the department, and although it took a lot of effort to service this institution, it was worth it. During Peter Ward's years this aspect of Styling's activity became very well organized. Having lost the Chief Engineer, Mike Dunn, in 1992, Styling presentations to the

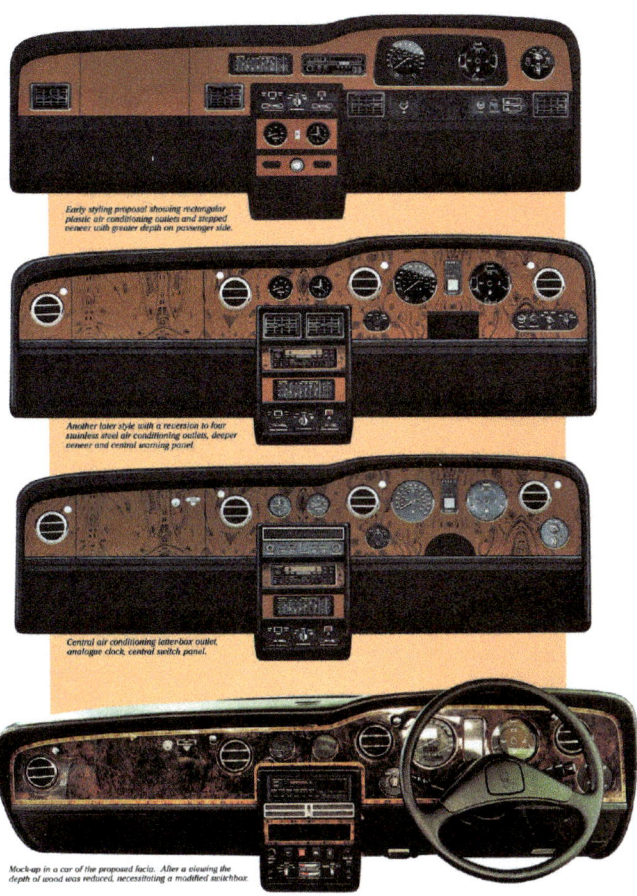

Early styling proposal showing rectangular plastic air conditioning outlets and stepped veneer with greater depth on passenger side.

Another later style with a reversion to four stainless steel air conditioning outlets, deeper veneer and central warning panel.

Central air conditioning letter-box outlet, analogue clock, central switch panel.

Mock-up in a car of the proposed fascia. After a viewing the depth of wood was reduced, necessitating a modified switchbox.

Product Policy Committee began to acquire a life of their own. As there was no engineering director, more and more engineering issues had to be addressed at the viewings, which caused a new and quite worrying phenomenon.

Young, inexperienced engineers who had, perhaps, never spoken to a company director, let alone the MD, were suddenly confronted by the entire board. Design students were used to presenting and selling their work, but engineers generally weren't trained to do this, and so their response ranged from paralysed, rabbit-caught-in-the-headlight, star-struck nervousness, to a stroppy 'take-it-or-leave-it-because-you-lot-don't-understand-practical-things-anyway' attitude.

The system

It wasn't in Styling's interest to upset the viewing committee so we began to hold rehearsals, as a result of which the system evolved into a carefully layered sequence –

- Trawl the various disciplines involved in any styling-related activity that required presentation to the board
- Assemble a rough-cut agenda, with some interrogation of potential presenters

Original viewing area writ large in Company magazine *Queste*. SZ wears contemporary regulation USA headlamps.

Dashboard mock-ups for viewing (top), plus Styling pre-positioning on digital readouts.

Putting on the Style –

Establish if we were presenting for –

- Work-in-progress, information/feedback
- Concept approval
- Production approval
- Have a trial viewing with any exhibits, statements, general costing
- Full Product Policy Committee Styling Review

During the trial runs/rehearsals I tried to involve someone from upper middle management, who was well-versed in boardroom dynamics, such as my boss, Ian McKay of Marketing, or someone from Product Planning/Brand, or a senior engineer. We then played devil's advocate, trying to destroy the credibility of what was on view.

To test the Styling/Design brief, we would question what it was the presenter was actually asking for.

Model year changes were always contentious, as the costs had to be understood and justified. The only reasons for any product expenditure were –

- Sell more units
- Stop sales sliding
- Remedy some deficiency

The truth was that although chief executives understood these business facts of life, many engineers didn't. As viewings involved the presentation of engineering product to marketing-biased MDs, frustration and exasperation were always just half a sentence away, and it was often necessary to remind inexperienced presenters that if they didn't know all of the answers they'd be torn to pieces.

A stylist also had to be prepared. A new air bag steering wheel will be immediately judged on its appearance, but like anything on a car it's based on numerous engineering factors. Explaining why something looks the way it does can be quite involved, but this was no time for arrogance or, conversely, to be cowed if challenged.

Every line a laugh

The pre-viewing filtration system worked well, and viewings became a good way to progress projects. During viewings there was always a macho atmosphere amongst the directors, the MD asserting his authority with the occasional put-down that tended to encourage others to join in. Every viewing had it moments; the following give a taste –

- David Plastow listened to my long, erudite (I thought) explanation concerning legal requirements that affected Continental R's rear number plate, then simply said "Bullshit!"
- John Carpenter, Marketing, compared a beautifully-made bas-relief of the Spirit of Ecstasy intended for the Shadow rear quarter with the Playboy Club logo
- Peter Ward described a complicated alloy wheel mock-up as looking like a drunken spider
- A proposed new paint colour reminded Malcolm Hart, Marketing, of a baby's soiled nappy
- Christine Gaskell, Personnel, compared some headlamps to Mr Magoo
- Doug Dickson, Manufacturing, compared a new clock face to something that might be seen in a gypsy caravan
- Graham Morris, hearing of the difficulties of making the new Bentley radiator matrix, likened its creation to your numbers coming up on the lottery – when you hadn't bought a ticket

But the most cutting comment must have been when Chris Woodwark declared that he was bored!

Any stylist working in the automotive world will have anecdotes about viewings. Bill Mitchell of GM was famous for his one-liners, describing one proposed exterior style as being like something from a fire sale.

Viewings in retrospect

In a perverse way I enjoyed the viewings, which were a good shop window for our department, and eventually became resigned to the fact that there were always too many people present. In the latter part of the 1990s, in an effort at crowd control, we arranged rows of chairs, and tried to display most exhibits on tables at the front.

The biggest challenge were interior items, which had to be viewed in situ. Once four directors got themselves settled into those luxurious seats, it was the devil's own job to get them out again, as they sat comfortably whilst their colleagues and fellow directors, department heads, senior engineers, purchase buyers, etc, had to crane their necks in an effort to hear what was being said. Some would then drift away to look at something else, and suddenly you'd lost control of the critical mass. So frustrated did I become trying to retain control of the crowd that I often felt like shouting, "Everyone born in wedlock, over here please!"

I always had to resist the temptation to get personal when it came to taste, but I found that those with questionable judgement invariably had the most ostentatious gold buckles on their shoes, prompting me to wonder how long since some had had plaster ducks on their wall, or the Malaysian lady with the turquoise face.

Certain engineering managers came to resent Styling's viewing event, which became more of an issue in the closing years of the 1990s when some of the younger, ex-Blackpool managers didn't appreciate the necessary sequence of events.

Styling was due to advise of progress on the Continental R replacement, requiring Engineering to explain the platform and packaging parameters, which were fluid, to say the least. At the pre-viewing, the project manager and his right-hand man attended apparently as observers only, and I had to ask them how they intended to present the elusive packaging parameters that Styling was expected to accommodate. The two simply stared at me, saying nothing, and, after a moment's reflection, I walked away, leaving them standing there. It was a very sad moment, because exasperation had got the better of me.

Tony Gott, at one stage, declared he would organize his own viewings. Nothing came of this, however, and when he became Chief Executive, Tony seemed to accept that the established monthly gathering was effective. Under VW, the system continued much as before for the Crewe-based structure. The separate viewings for visiting, high-level VW board members at Crewe were run along remarkably similar lines. Interestingly, Dr Piech preferred to personally attend pre-viewings, obviously in no doubt about the importance of these events.

"Everything can be measured and what gets measured gets managed." – McKinsey & Co (government advisor)
On the other hand –
"Not everything that can be counted counts, and not everything that counts can be counted." – Albert Einstein

BENTLEY BALI
THE ONE THAT GOT AWAY

Since 1997 the Company had worked on ways to create a new Bentley two-door, finally achieving fruition with the Continental GT of 2003. This may seem a relatively long gestation period, but the period was not without landmark or incident.

Brand gets a grip

During 1997 Chris Woodwark's Brand team reached certain conclusions about the Company's product. It had established, for example, that two separate marques were involved, both represented by large vehicles with distinctive radiator shells ... The team also concluded that not sharing the 1991 Bentley Continental R's body style with Rolls-Royce had been a good idea. Growing in confidence, Brand now suggested that a replacement for Continental R might be another good idea.

In fairness to this largely misunderstood band of branders, they had not had much opportunity to exert any influence, as the Silver Seraph and Arnage programmes had reached a critical mass by the time Chris Woodwark took the controls. The department also had virtually no say in the many customer special commissions, as those elements of Marketing that dealt with individual orders didn't request Brand input. P966, the Continental R Sedanca, was Brand's first baby.

Arriving in early 1997, Graham Morris, our new Chief Executive was – like Chris Woodwark before him – a marketing man who expected Brand to be a key player in the formulation of the Company's Product Plan: an all-encompassing map of how to take the business forward which Graham Morris would submit to Vickers. Such plans don't appear overnight, of course, but to keep the kettle boiling Brand, quite reasonably, assumed that a premium Bentley would be involved in it.

One of the department's number, Michael May, a rather owlish Oxbridge type, was emerging as a brander on a mission. If big is good, then bigger is better, and he regarded visual acreage as a prime component of future product.

Following this simple philosophy, it was decided there would be a premium Rolls-Royce offering, code named China, over and above the Silver Seraph; to balance the scales, a premium Bentley two-door above Arnage, code named Bali. (Premium doesn't necessarily mean bigger, but in the emerging Product Plan this was absolutely the case for Rolls-Royce, and nothing to be ashamed of for Bentley.)

Being naturally cautious, I was inclined to shy away from this philosophy, and post-Silver Spirit styling activity tended to play down the fact that these vehicles were over seventeen feet (5.2 metres) long, weighing in at two-and-a-quarter tons (2286kg). Reducing visual weight was fundamental because economic climates change faster than you can tool-up a motor car. It's possible to elongate a vehicle when times are good, but difficult to shorten it in the event of an economic downturn. In addition, big, two-door coupés are a tricky proposition; the Continental R being an exception rather than the rule.

Rules of engagement

By July 1997 the Board of Directors had bought into the basic brief for Bali, a two-door replacement for Continental R. Brand briefs can be similar to a child's letter to Father Christmas, and just as wishful. Brand wanted an 'aesthetic' coupé based on a P2000 (Arnage), with that vehicle's interior space, and a 'clever' roof (folding panels of some kind, not fabric, leaving the cabin sides fixed).

Other Brand wish-list items were –

- All-new skin, aluminium closures, composite bumpers and sills
- P2000 radiator matrix, but consider new ideas for radiator shell
- Large air intakes
- Twilight chrome
- Good aerodynamics
- Twin exhaust
  Styling's thoughts in response –
- Check boot space requirements – Samsonite cases, golf clubs x2?
- 'Clever' roof has to be stowed in boot
- Low-lip boot opening, as P2000?
- If based on P2000, wipers still not recessed
- Aerodynamics – variable geometry spoilers, etc?
- 18 inch wheels?
- Frameless drop-glass?

Viewing structure, timing and 'deliverables' (items that would be delivered) hadn't been established other than that Styling would submit three approaches: evolutionary; middle of the road; radical. Mike Booth would be Chief Engineer and Project Leader. (Mike was a relative newcomer to the Company who enjoyed taking Aston Martins for a spin.)

A question of size

My immediate reaction to the design brief was, "Do they realize just how big this coupé is?" The successful Medium-Sized Bentley (MSB) Java exercise of 1994 suggested that a vehicle smaller than P2000 could be built in considerable number. The opportunities (challenges) this much bigger device presented set my alarm bells ringing. In August our new Chief Executive, Graham Morris, asked to see all Java and P1000 work regarding the MSB approach, despite all the pressures of the pending new saloon.

Graham Morris was an unknown quantity, and the Crewe water could have a funny effect on people. The previously frustrated branders now had the opportunity to sink their teeth into a project. In addition, Engineering still

hadn't stabilized the feasibility and packaging functions, each project working independently, which again would result in Styling being forced to proceed, with Engineering playing catch-up.

In July 1997, I suggested to Mike Booth that a short-wheelbase P2000 might be a good starting point for Bali: after all, Continental T was six inches (152.4mm) shorter than the new saloon. Mike couldn't comment as his team hadn't even embarked on a first-look 'brown-paper' exercise at that time! Luckily, due to factory-wide efforts leading up to the Seraph/Arnage launch, and possible Company sale, Styling was under no great pressure to deliver Bali, although it was no doubt considered a good idea to have an active project on the slipway to show potential buyers of the Company.

Regardless of personal reservations about the brief, Bali was, nevertheless, a good opportunity to have most of the Styling department sketch ideas for this top-of-the-range Bentley, and so Simon Loasby, Darren Day and Robin Page were turned loose on the project. As it was Mike Booth's budget, we also approached Richard Hamlin's Omni Design, Roy Axe's DRA, and the American DZN studio.

Styling's own package drawings of Continental R and P2000 confirmed my worst fears about the potential size of Bali. A further complication was that, when it came to big Bentley coupés and heritage, the 1950s R-Type Continental of Ivan Evernden's watch was the obvious benchmark. Apart from stylized wing shapes, its most obvious feature was the fastback.

When visiting my parents I used to study an R-Type near the Great Barn (a beautifully preserved c1280 barn adjacent to the moated Manor House Farm, former site of a Norman motte-and-bailey castle, c1070) at Ruislip, in the London borough of Hillingdon. It is an outstanding, aristocratic motor car, but perhaps connoisseurs will forgive me for preferring the 1938 Embiricos Bentley. Whatever, a vehicle of that shape doesn't have great rear passenger accommodation, and even less boot space. To get a similar fastback roof style round a P2000 would result in something gargantuan, as well as suggest a pastiche or retro look, something the Continental R had successfully avoided. Despite all of the foregoing, however, the R-Type fastback was something we were expected to explore.

The process

Apart from casting a wide net for styling contributions we were also working with Hawtal Whiting on a packaging and seating buck, for which computers were used, including a state-of-the-art Alias computer station hired for use in Crewe's studio. Full-sized tape lines were employed and scale models made. I encouraged Robin Page to pursue interior styling issues as he was acquiring the maturity this demanding aspect requires.

Although engineering packaging and feasibility was hardly robust by January 20, 1998, Styling had enough of its own drawings to explain the implications of Brand's brief. We presented the work to Graham Morris, Keith Sanders, Tony Gott (now a chief engineer), and Ian McKay, boss of Styling and Brand.

Explaining that the Styling themes were only a starting point, we stressed that the shapes and proportions were based round a very questionable package, particularly for rear occupants. I rattled off lots of comparisons, demonstrating how much longer Bali was inclined to be compared to P2000 and Continental R, as the proposals were several inches larger in every direction (millimetres confused my audience). My pitch was aimed at re-writing the brief.

The directors acknowledged that size was an issue, and also that rear occupants would have to accept some restrictions compared to the four-door. Whilst sympathising with Brand's wish to accommodate five basketball players, there has to be a compromise with coupés. It was agreed to accommodate six feet two inch (1880mm) front occupants and six feet (1829mm) in the rear. It was lucky that we didn't have any very tall directors as they assume that if they can sit comfortably, all is right with the world. An in-house Darren Day-style was chosen to develop in clay. It had a more rounded front with sloping radiator shell and long tail – generally in-line with Styling's Design Strategy Paper.

Having achieved size concessions, we were now, in effect, re-skinning Continental R; the Company needed a new platform and package, which wasn't part of the Company plan – I seemed destined to be the bearer of bad tidings. Andy Hemmings, from the Midland's Design Office, was working on Bali packaging (Andy, a real enthusiast, had the lowest profile tyres ever on his Golf GTi). We asked him to investigate a raft of issues which needed answers. Hawtal Whiting's seating buck included large door apertures because large cars are expected to have easy ingress and egress. Darren was working his quarter-scale model with the usual Styling 'builds.'

During March 1998 VW visited Crewe and was shown Styling activities, including work on Bali. The same month, Tony Gott indicated that Styling should be in his portfolio. In April, a full-size clay was copy milled from Darren's scale model at Howtal Whiting, whose interior mock-up was also available. As expected, when the clay was seen outdoors, a long list of tweaks/major surgery became obvious. Due to the prevailing project team philosophy, the entire Mike Booth team arrived to witness the bloody reality of clay hacking, with a very apparent "Make up your mind, and we'll engineer it" attitude, causing thoughts of chicken-and-egg to spring to mind.

May 7 that year witnessed Styling having a long session with Brand over Bentley, including MSB. Brand was quite adamant that Java had been too small and not feasible, despite its BMW underpinnings, but it was hard not to imagine that anyone buying the Company might wonder why we hadn't pursued this, or something similar.

The following day it was announced that VW would be buying Rolls-Royce and Bentley.

A fraught viewing

A week later, on May 14, 1998, we bought the Bali clay to Crewe, dressed in Dynoc film, for its first product policy viewing. As feared, the board hadn't appreciated just how big this fastback style, applied over what amounted to a saloon package, would be, and, in addition, seemed to have little experience of the styling process (which is why many chief stylists won't show anything other than Motor Show-quality replicas to directors).

Due to the shambolic nature of the viewing, I attempted to get a consensus on general builds, which turned out to be a bad move as Graham Morris informed me that he and his board would have a private discussion round the mock-up. I walked off-stage to the sound of my own footsteps: thank you and goodnight ...

The viewing, following a difficult build-up, was so frustrating that, in the evening I took all my diaries off-site in preparation for leaving the Company, the only time in thirty years that I seriously considered resigning and taking the long walk.

The following day there was a de-briefing by Ian McKay, with the obvious conclusion that the board didn't understand the work-in-progress nature of viewings. There was agreement that the back end of this big fastback didn't look right and, with this in mind, there would be a concession on the boot capacity requirement. Apparently, Ian made the point that I had suggested going full-size much earlier in the programme to help communicate to the board the brief's size.

Maybe security reported seeing me pushing a

wheelbarrow full of diaries out the main gate that night, because shortly afterward there was another session with Graham Morris, who told me that he felt his requirements for Bali hadn't been listened to on previous viewings. All I could tell him was that we had to get the proportions right before working on details, though trying to explain the futility of perfecting tail-lamps if the back of the car was in the wrong place seemed pointless! The upshot was that we were asked to make Bali more conservative, and that aping the R-Type Continental was no longer necessary: if boot space proved a problem we could omit one of the golf bags.

After carefully studying photos of Bali, I asked for 32 'adjustments' to be made. Despite everything, we weren't that far away from a very handsome motor car, after all.

Regardless of the risk of impromptu viewings, it seemed logical to keep the Bali clay on-site for the ongoing work. Usually, it's best to stay arm's length from daily clay development, but Bali was fulfilling its threat of being a hot potato.

Fourteen months into the project Engineering had to move the fuel tank forward four inches (101.6mm), moving rear occupants the same amount in turn, to accommodate long-specified, rigid Samsonite suitcases (politely known, technically, as a late tear-up). The Company desperately needed an advanced unit of engineering sharpshooters to help Styling, and communicate to top management the nuts-and-bolts issues up-front. Individual project teams were often relying on different consultants unfamiliar with Company product, a fundamental issue that was not ever addressed until VW took ownership.

The devil again turns up in the detail

A personal aversion were windscreen wipers, and Styling had made a big effort with Seraph/Arnage to conceal these, much to the consternation of the very excited engineer given the task, who heatedly declared it to be impossible due to a carry-over air-conditioning unit.

The wiper situation with Bali would be same-old-same-old, as I pointedly explained to the board. Many months later we presented Bali with other marques such as a Mercedes, etc, for comparison, whereupon Christine Gaskell suggested we should have concealed wipers, like the Mercedes did. At the earliest opportunity I found a quiet corner where I could repeatedly bang my head against the wall! Christine was our Personnel Director, and first full-time female member of the board, which can't have been easy in macho-land. Originally, Christine had sported

a distinctive red hairstyle, reminiscent of Wendolene, the character who played the owner of the wool shop in a *Wallace and Gromit* film.

The final phase

Because our outside viewing area was not finished, usually we had to go into work on weekend mornings and screen off part of Third Avenue by the Road Test department, whereupon a group of clay modellers would haul the substantial weight of Bentley-shaped modelling clay out into the daylight.

We arranged a viewing for the board shortly before VW took over. This viewing was much more successful: apart from anything else, the board could now appreciate the tactics that Styling used to progress the theme. We had developed a notched fastback which broke up the previous lumpen appearance, although a long list of refinements were still required. Some good work had been done on the interior mock-up by Robin Page, using as much as possible from P2000/3000.

On Saturday, July 6, 1998, Dr Piech addressed the Company managers to explain VW's plans. An MSB would be pursued, coupled with an increase in production, and competing again at Le Mans was a real possibility.

A few days later Styling put on a presentation of all projects for VW, in what was to be the new studios. Graham Morris and Keith Sanders pursued their strategy of having me present Rolls-Royce projects only (did other companies prevent their Chief Stylist from presenting their designs at this level, I wondered?). The individual chosen to present Bali began by showing Dr Piech a rather extreme, non-representative rear view rendering, which prompted Dr Piech to immediately express his view that Bentley was all about the front end, and did not need an aggressive tail, therefore. By the time the actual car was unveiled – demonstrating its much more subtle rear style treatment – the verdict had been passed. As it happened, Dr Piech thought Bali's front end was aggressive enough, and the only 'build' was to make the tail less aggressive: Piech wanted a soft tail, with twin exhaust pipes, referring to the R-Type Continental as an example! When I mentioned the requirement of accommodating a stack of Samsonite suitcases, Dr Piech smiled the smile of someone quite capable of buying the Samsonite company in order to re-shape the cases!

A lot happened over the next few days. We received more formal feedback from the viewing: clay development work would continue on Bali. VW liked the Bentley

continued page 140

Proposed Bentley Continental R replacement, Project Bali, as viewed on June 25, 1998.

G.H.11

PROJECT BALI

March 1982 witnessed the launch of the turbocharged V8. Styling ventured under the bonnet with the author's simplistic cast Turbo lettering and surround. 1998's Bali proposal would have used essentially the same legendary engine. Mulsanne got the rocket to the launch pad in 1980, but this power plant ensured Bentley's true lift-off.

TURBO

Project Bali. Proposed Bentley Continental R replacement. Painted clay viewed in screened-off Third Avenue at factory, June 25, 1998, demonstrating how different styles can share a similar package to the original Rolls-Royce Silver Shadow.

radiator shell sitting between four round headlamps; apparently, Dr Piech felt that the Styling department was doing good work. The de-brief came from Tony Gott, who, in line with VW policy, would now have Styling report to him as Chief Engineer.

On July 28, 1998, it was announced that BMW had acquired the rights to Rolls-Royce. Due to this separation of the two marques, Graham Morris resigned.

Bali – its place in the overall scheme of things

To suggest that Graham Morris' resignation at the end of July was the eye of the storm may seem odd, but in Bali World it was, and everyone was waiting for the other shoe to drop. Brand's slightly eccentric Product Plan for a new family of increasingly larger motor cars never seemed quite of this world. VW was no doubt considering engine and platform strategy: Project Leader Mike Booth went on to greener pastures, and Ken Scott – still reminiscent of a Scottish funeral director – took over Bali.

With Crewe directors working on numerous drafts of a new Product Plan, it was decided, presumably by VW, to refresh Continental R and put Bali on hold until 2003. Styling was able to demonstrate again by full-size tape lines and computer that the R-Type's fastback style wasn't viable. The full-sized clay's rear end was refined to obviate any tendency toward aggressiveness. Interior work continued, and it was again obvious that this area of expertise was of great interest to both VW and BMW.

The new Product Plan's main thrust was based on MSB, which Dr Piech more accurately named Medium Priced Bentley. VW's D1 platform would lend itself to a smaller vehicle than Bali. It was obvious that Bali was ticking the marque's boxes, but would this style theme suit a new platform? Despite effectively mothballing Bali in September, clay work did continue until late 1998, still tweaking that super-sensitive rear end.

Considering the hiatus with Project Bali, Styling could be proud of the eventual outcome. It was a noble beast, worthy of its place in Bentley's lineage, and demonstrating the philosophy expressed in the Design Strategy Paper requested by Graham Morris. Using the P2000 platform had proved impractical without basic modification.

The role of Brand at Crewe pre-VW remained something of a puzzle, its discipline apparently more relevant to a conglomerate with several marques and model sub-divisions, all sharing platforms but needing to communicate separate identities.

An element of the Bali project was experience; it gave the young Styling team on-the-job training. Darren Day, Simon Loasby and Robin Page had come to Crewe straight from college. In a larger company there would have been a structured system where young stylists could be mentored and observe how older generations operated, so goodness knows what they thought of my approach.

Apart from being somewhat older, I'd been involved in the American studio culture originally, and then had years at Crewe. It's impossible for novices to empathise with the mindset of Rolls-Royce and Bentley customers; even if they could, negotiating the obstacles before a product reaches the market needs realism, pragmatism and grim determination – attributes not usually common in young stylists. At Crewe, Darren was able to experience the ups and downs of grappling with full-scale clays; Simon could learn to pursue the many administrative tasks that projects require, and Robin could begin to develop a feel for the demanding world of interiors, all of which stood them in good stead for the future.

Bali was a distinct phase in Bentley design; also the last project before globalisation of the Company's ownership. Inevitably, it demonstrated the strengths and weaknesses of the automotive industry in late 20th century Britain.

"You need not find all the answers, but you ought to get the questions in the right order" – Lord Donald Soper

VW/BENTLEY
BMW/ROLLS-ROYCE
THE GREAT DIVIDE

All change at Crewe

The sale of any great British institution to a foreign buyer is a notable event, and very little was more notable than Rolls-Royce – the epitome of British motor engineering – being sold to a German company. The circumstance of Volkswagen's eleventh hour outbidding of BMW (which subsequently wrestled ownership of Rolls-Royce from VW) is the stuff of novels, and everyone was surprised when Vickers led out the blushing bride to meet her unexpected VW suitor on May 7, 1998: the 'People's Car' meets the 'Aristocrat's Car' ... surreal!

Truth to tell, Rolls-Royce and Bentley deserved better than what late twentieth century British industry could supply: noteworthy about the Crewe cars is the fact that they remained superb vehicles, despite endemic under-investment in British manufacturing. VW's first action was a cash injection of 500 million pounds for this venerable British company. Goodness knows how much BMW invested, once it had acquired Rolls-Royce: apart from coming up with new models, it had to build a new factory as well! Both marques then benefited from VW and BMW Research & Development resources and production expertise which, coupled with pressure brought to bear on suppliers, constituted an awesome package, enabling both new guardians to produce the most technically advanced examples of Rolls-Royce and Bentley cars to date.

The view from Styling's Ivory Tower

We already had experience of working with stylists from America, Italy, France, Sweden and Germany, to which would be added Brazilian and Belgian contributions. Despite different cultural backgrounds, talent is universal and design international.

Whilst having high regard for the American approach, witnessed in Chrysler and GM studios, the Germans, in particular, always intrigued me. They seemed to possess an affinity with anything mechanical that was all-consuming: to any enthusiast the gull-wing Mercedes, NSU Ro80 and Porsche 911 have to be in or near the top ten list of desirable/noteworthy cars. Despite experiencing – and enjoying – such diverse machinery as a Messerschmitt, Steyr-Puch and Ro80, I wasn't sure, however, whether German vehicles possessed charisma in the same way as, say, Jaguar, Aston Martin and Crewe cars did.

Whilst the Company sale process was fascinating/extraordinary to outsiders, to those immersed in ongoing projects it was less so: until, that is, the Rolls-Royce and Bentley Siamese twins were separated. Although the two marques demanded more resource than Crewe could provide, they naturally complemented each other, representing two faces of the same coin.

I visited BMW at Munich in the early 1990s, whose Carl-Peter Forster (who, some believe, wondered about the possibility of eventually heading-up Rolls-Royce) commissioned a Rolls-Royce/Bentley interior as a one-off in a BMW 8 Series. A group of BMW VIPs came to Crewe Styling studio to view the car and take it back to Germany. Bernd Pischetsrieder, BMW's MD, visited Crewe in 1995 after the Bentley Java concept car had been shown at Geneva. He was very interested in Java, and also an early Rolls-Royce Silver Spirit replacement proposal that I showed him. Chris Bangle, BMW Director of Design, also soon journeyed to see us, and we began an exercise in Munich to reproduce Java around the forthcoming 5 Series platform.

Whilst searching for engines and other hardware, Crewe had talked to BMW and Mercedes, and Styling was involved as the aesthetics of the four-door replacement would be affected. It appears our MD, Peter Ward, opted for a Mercedes tie-up but was overruled by Vickers. On Peter's subsequent immediate resignation, BMW became the prime candidate as the source of major components.

Munich was particularly interested in Crewe interiors philosophy and craftsmanship, and was obviously looking for closer ties. (Pischetsrieder opened the bidding for the Company, and eventually counter-attacked VW, splitting Rolls-Royce from Bentley.)

Into the bear-pit?

Peter Ward's departure at the end of 1994 was a pivotal event. In one way the game was up; in another a much bigger game with potent stakes was just beginning. The German motor industry was fiercely competitive, especially internally, with Mercedes, BMW and VW regarding themselves and each other as the only manufacturers truly worthy of their Teutonic steel. Porsche, perhaps due to its niche approach, was an outsider (until, of course, it set its sights on VW). The Japanese raised overall vehicle quality standards, but you didn't hear the Germans talking about them with the same competitiveness that they talked about each other. A BMW engineer was telling me what percentage of each vehicle could be recycled, and I asked what they did with recycled material. "We sell it to Mercedes," he replied. When Vickers turned its back on Mercedes, the latter immediately got serious about the Maybach in retaliation. Given this fierce competitiveness, it was inevitable that Crewe's commercial deal with BMW would stir up a hornet's nest.

Here there be giants

With the Silver Seraph launched and Arnage waiting in the wings, VW visited Crewe. Given that the new four-door and refreshed factory were, in part, a Vickers sales promotion, the visit was hardly surprising. VW people had discussions with Graham Morris, and were then taken into the Styling studio to see work being done on Bali.

However, on March 30, 1998, just a couple of weeks later, it was announced that BMW had 'bought' the Company, which made a further announcement on May 8 the same year that a sale to VW had been agreed "in principle" completely bemusing. Nevertheless, the deal with VW was formalized on July 3, 1998.

Previously under the impression that I'd be working with BMW's Chris Bangle, VW's styling infrastructure was a complete unknown. Also 'VW' was actually Volkswagen, Audi, Seat and Skoda; a completely different kettle of cars, bestridden by the colossus Dr Piech.

Initial feedback was that VW wanted to increase production numbers with a model based on a medium-size Bentley. Regardless of general intent, it was obviously going to take time for Crewe to synchronize with Wolfsburg; I knew the Germans well enough to realize they regarded Rolls-Royce and Bentley as rather 'precious.' Styling's ability with interiors would be something VW would be especially protective about. The styling resources of large automotive companies are wonderful: product appearance is so important that no stone can be left unturned in this respect. However, this doesn't necessarily mean that quality of output is proportionally greater than that of a smaller resource. In addition, of course, larger concerns often have many more different types and sizes of vehicles to work with, including commercial machines, and the personnel required to take care of it all is multi-layered in skill, age and experience.

Apart from a similar objective – create great-looking vehicles, be they BMW/VW or Rolls-Royce/Bentley – the culture and circumstances of the two companies couldn't have been more different. Someone working their way through the ranks in German studios would not be able to comprehend how the Crewe team operated or survived (often, neither could I!). But Styling's small world-view was as nothing compared to the bigger picture.

On July 7 that year, BMW, which had had its corporate nose put badly out of joint by VW's triumph, threatened to withdraw the supply of components for Seraph/Arnage (Rolls-Royce or Bentley standing on bricks would lack a certain je ne sais quoi, n'est-ce pas?) Three weeks later BMW announced that it had obtained the rights to Rolls-Royce motor cars, and would build them away from Bentley/Crewe from 2002. Standing in the studio discussing some detail or other, my first thought when I received this piece of information was, "Good grief, this really will put the cat amongst the pigeons!" Two days later Graham Morris resigned: splitting the marques broke his promise to the workforce that the two would always stay together.

Could Crewe Styling survive?

While the big boys played hard ball over our heads, we in Styling stoically carried on working, reporting to Chief Engineer Tony Gott.

Despite all of the background drama, the challenging, everyday workload kept us occupied: there was no point worrying about events beyond our control. The Company's aesthetic heritage had to be one of the jewels in Crewe's crown, and perhaps VW really would let us get on with it. My main concern was our immediate ruling class, currently wrestling with three separate issues. Firstly, how to handle the pending loss of Rolls-Royce; secondly, there was no agreed Five Year Product Plan; thirdly, the inadequacies in engineering structure compared to Wolfsburg. The elephant in the room, however, was could Crewe hierarchy retain control with VW holding the reins?

Styling was an unwilling key player in this unsettled environment because we were joining industry mainstream, where styling was very much in the foreground. Additionally, due to group-shared platforms, styling body language provided vital differentiation.

It had always been my intention to keep a low profile, thus avoiding the politics and games that top players appear to enjoy. But from September 1998 I had to attend a series of meetings with Tony Gott, Chief Engineer and potential next MD (Graham Morris was still walking the deck, despite having resigned). There seemed to be two current topics, over and above pure aesthetics: the effect on the Product Plan now that it was to be based on VW's philosophy of shared platforms, and how Graham Hull fitted into Tony's proposed structure for Design.

Could Crewe Engineering survive?

A big problem over the years at Crewe had been that there seemed little evidence of a completely integrated Design/Engineering infrastructure. Whilst development skills were second to none, actual ground-up car design was not a company forte, and the lack of a packaging/feasibility department was a massive blind spot. It wasn't until VW's Dr Ulrich Hackenberg appointed an ex-Rover packaging engineer to establish a team at Crewe that the issue was properly addressed and, because of this, I was not a huge fan of the engineering management system. While respecting individuals as capable and well-qualified, they were certainly not ideally suited to be responsible for Styling. As

Tony Gott was now my immediate boss, and was shaping up to be my ultimate boss, I had deep forebodings about the fact that he seemed keen to restructure us to support Engineering, when, in my experience, it was Engineering which required restructuring to support Styling!

Tony was talking about a new concept centre, with stylists in separate engineering project teams, which seemed to negate the new, almost-ready Styling facility. It was envisaged that yours truly would have a floating, aesthetic overview, but with particular people in my team allowed to get some cars 'under their belt.' This approach might have worked within a large styling concern with many studios, but it really wasn't the obvious tactic at Crewe. A large slice of already limited resources could be apportioned to pursue full-size clays, possibly only on the strength of someone getting, say, a gear knob into production.

Despite several sessions with Tony, which prompted me to produce diagrams illustrating various scenarios, it seemed I wasn't getting my point across. Apart from anything else, I was arguing in favour of VW's (and everyone else's) proposed structure for the styling discipline! It seemed obvious that our new studio and viewing facility would provide an ideal opportunity to establish a group of stylists, packaging engineers and modellers, as all other car manufacturers did, but, for some reason, Crewe Engineering didn't agree with this. The rather unsatisfactory discussions continued as something of a side show, at the same time as we were having various meetings with – and receiving feedback from – VW. The replacement for Continental R – Bali – now a reasonably resolved clay, was mothballed to allow a new VW platform strategy to be studied for the Product Plan.

VW styling personnel paid us visits in numbers usually greater than those in our entire department (VW styling teams ran into hundreds, spread across the various brands), and chatting with them told us more than any formal briefings did. Projects were driven through VW PSK (Produkt Strategie Komitee) gatherings, which were much like our Product Policy Committee Styling Viewings. Senior VW management tended only to view fully finished mock-ups. I met Director of Design Hartmut Warkuss on numerous occasions, who, unlike most of their top people, apparently spoke virtually no English. He was a pilot and owned a vintage biplane.

Visits to Wolfsburg were amazing; the sheer size of the plant – which is really a city – was overwhelming. The fact that the entire entity depended on the success of the

Golf, etc, really drove home the importance of styling and engineering design. I couldn't help a bemused smile when shown the colour and trim facilities, with over a dozen specialists: at Crewe this aspect, involving a larger range than, say Audi, was taken care of by me within Styling as a sideline.

VW obviously wanted to use Crewe's talents, but I'm not sure if its people could get their heads around just how small the home team was. Hartmut Warkuss wanted to exchange three exterior stylists between Crewe and Wolfsburg, but, as we barely had three exterior stylists in total, let alone to spare, this was impossible. We settled on swapping VW's Crispin Marshfield for our Richard Stevens; thus, the young Coventry undergraduate was given the opportunity of a lifetime.

I was dispatched to Lamborghini to advise on a new interior for the Diablo (Dr Piech wanted his own personalized example), and whilst there was quietly asked for my candid opinion on the prototype Diablo replacement, Canto L147 (which was subsequently aborted). In addition, Ital Design had been commissioned to produce a Bugatti four-door and, again, I was sent to steer Giugiaro regarding interior design. It felt a bit like telling a concert pianist what keys to press, but he seemed relaxed, listening to my input. Ital had better reference photo albums on Crewe interiors than we did!

Plenty to be getting on with

Styling's worklist appeared to be from Dr Piech, who doubtless had mixed views about allowing his sedan chair to be carried over Crewe Engineering's somewhat unknown bridge –

• Medium-Size Bentley (MSB) (based on a VW platform)
• Continental R face-lift
• P2000 F1 (minimum change route to accept Crewe's L410 V8)
• P2000 F2 (new lamps, composite panels, etc)
• P92 (Corniche) (Borrego style to be applied to a P3000 or VW platform)
• Production upgrades such as side air-bags
• New 'British' interior for a VW four-door saloon
• Rolls-Royce upgrades and 'hygiene'
• P2000/P3000 Limousine

VW allowed us to process these projects by whatever method we thought best. Engineering set up separate project teams using on-site and off-site resources as necessary. The MPW cellular teams which proved so effective in the frantic merry-go-round of Blackpool projects were now

being absorbed into mainstream engineering. But the missing vital ingredient at the centre was iron man Jim Orr, and so some less experienced team leaders began doing their own thing.

Another change was that top management wanted to summon-up the mystic powers of Brand, so 'branders' were attached to various projects to help us understand our tasks, despite the fact they had no approved Product Plan. Lack of knowledge about how a VW platform might interface with Crewe product was an immediate problem, and once again we were desperate for in-house packaging experts.

It seemed sensible to do as much as possible of MSB on-site, using the existing old studio; with Darren Day, Simon Loasby and Crispin Marshfield working on three scale models. Young stylists can be full of hubris, pumped-up on heroic lunchtime discussion, and scale models are a good opportunity for them to let off steam with maximum freedom. It's important, however, for the Executive to have the wit to let the Chief Stylist run his own show.

Interior work, including that for a VW saloon, would ideally be contained on-site. For overflow tasks we worked with consultants and, as before, I acted as the regularly-visiting Crewe 'conscience.' With work proceeding with Ian Callum at TWR on the lookalike Borrego convertible (Siam), we also asked him to do a MSB quarter-scale, but I avoided any direct input other than briefing. Heurliez also made a model from our selection of VW sketches. We eventually decided to do the VW interior mock-up at DRA. We were also engaged in sorting out Styling's new facility, including the outside viewing area, for which, working with Mike Brookes, I had long been trying to buy some land from Crewe and Nantwich Council.

We were still involved with the tail end of the Blackpool projects, which entailed working with ex-Land Rover Discovery man Dave Evans, who was supervising scale model construction for owners of 'one-off' specials. Our studio wall was covered in exterior and interior photos of this extraordinary collection of vehicles, which must have amazed VW (I could hardly believe it myself), though what it made of the Blackpool era remained a mystery.

BY713 (MSB) and P2000 Arnage F1 and F2

MSB was now coded BY713, but whether it would be a two- or four-door, folding hardtop or fastback was not established. By December, a local 'packaging group' was in operation interfacing with Wolfsburg, which included Mike Smith and our Crewe veteran George Ray. Styling was desperate for any information about how the VW platforms compared to our products, although five on- and off-site theme scale models were created nevertheless. Thus, a reasonable 'car park' could be mustered for the 1998 year end viewing.

Mid-December brought a major event when VW's PSK visited Crewe to see our various projects, including Corniche replacement clays (VW suggested considering a Bentley version, as Rolls-Royce probably wouldn't sell in Germany!) A very well-finished, large 'BY713' Bentley four-door replica was brought over from Wolfsburg: apparently a Passat on steroids, but Styling wasn't expected to comment, just told "You show us what you can do." I bravely pointed out that the car was standing on twenty-inch wheels, and we were struggling to get tyres for eighteen-inch versions!

Luckily, we'd prepared full-size line comparison drawings showing just how large these BY713 proposals were compared to P2000, which surprised VW and the Crewe board alike, as curtailing P2000 wasn't on the agenda. This little demonstration proved that Crewe Styling could operate at even this rarefied altitude.

Wolfsburg had a dedicated 24/7 factory for styling mock-ups, which could produce a clay replica in about three weeks: the time and effort we expended creating similar replicas at a variety of different establishments was irrelevant, as VW took such quality for granted.

Our collection of quarter-scale BY713 MSB models interested everyone, and flushed out useful feedback: this front is good, that rear is worth developing, maybe this side section, and so on. One side of a Heurliez model was particularly favoured. We'd stayed in touch with this company after a Blackpool project, and had been sent a mass of sketches: it looked like we'd chosen the right one to model, which was just as well as some French desperado had driven eleven hours through the night to get it to the viewing.

The long wheelbase P3000 was signed off, its ability to be easily stretched built-in at conception. P2000 A2 face-lift sketches got the go ahead for mock-up, including the four separate round headlamp treatment. Again, I pushed the point about needing larger tyres, and Dr Piech asked Dr Martin Winterkorn to pursue this matter.

The very next day Tony Gott became acting Chief Executive, and we managed to get Darren Day and Robin Page upgraded with company cars, too.

In January 1999, as Tony was acting MD, Rob Oldaker became Engineering Director, Dereck Best (an ex-boss of mine, returning from a long illness) was Manager:

Engineering Resource and Mike Morris Crewe's interface with VW. In practice, Styling had to interface with about ten Crewe Engineering managers 'empowered' to deliver projects independently, some of whom were ex-Blackpool; others from engine design, etc. In addition, Tony seemed to want Ken Scott (of Scottish undertaker similarity) to run a concept centre.

Our BY713 scale model work proceeded on five themes, despite having no firm Product Plan or platform. As ever, it was assumed that, as long as Styling was creating something, all was well. So far, the full-size Bali clay with visual reference to front and rear wing features was still the strongest influence. Although Heurliez demonstrated a nice alternative side-section, it was not considered truly 'Bentley.'

Work continued on BY811/ F1 – the L410-engined, refreshed P2000 – and BY811/ F2, the latter with its four separate, round headlamps. Brand's Julian Hadrill (refreshingly sensible and engineering trained, and in the process of restoring some obscure car), was working with us on current production modifications.

F1 was the minimum route whereby to get Crewe's legendary L410 V8 under P2000's bonnet, courtesy of VW cash. Dr Piech held the admirable belief that engine appearance mattered, and Styling had to lay down the law about not simply sweeping everything under a carpet of plastic covers, enabling the 'oily bits' to show evidence of intelligent life. Stalwart Dave Preece of MPW was also dedicated to making engines look good. We restricted under-bonnet colours to black and silver.

There was no common understanding between engine designers and stylists; tidying up F1's L410 was tough. It then took many months to influence Cosworth and Crewe engineers over the bigger changes for the F2 twin turbo.

The revitalized L410 was greedy for air, and P2000's front intake – which had satisfied BMW's V8 – couldn't deliver. An engineering manager refused the funds necessary for clay modelling a revised front apron to resolve this problem: he'd never been involved with Styling before, and decided the problem could be resolved on a computer screen immediately before digital release for tooling. I had to explain that, regardless of my irritating desire to make things look good, there had to be a mock-up for board approval. The same chap reacted to my request to clay model the top of the engine bay with a mixture of fear and loathing.

The lack of packaging/feasibility continued to frustrate. For instance, we wanted to use the latest VW

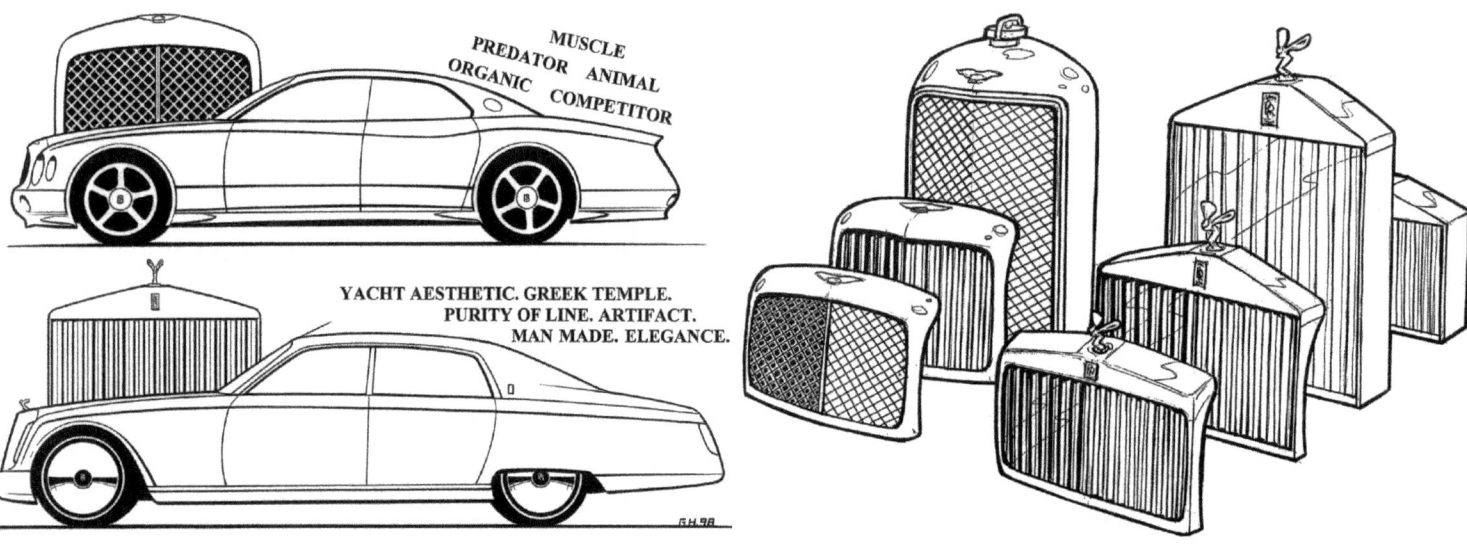

MUSCLE
PREDATOR ANIMAL
ORGANIC COMPETITOR

YACHT AESTHETIC. GREEK TEMPLE.
PURITY OF LINE. ARTIFACT.
MAN MADE. ELEGANCE.

1998 Styling presentation to VW included the visual differentiation philosophy between the two complementary, but separate, marques. 'Frantic' versus 'Serene' wheel styles were a potent and achievable cue.

1980s and 1990s Styling Strategy Papers for the MD and board included a reminder of the large and varied historic interpretations of the two classic radiator shells. Bill Allen had foreseen the next millennium's Rolls-Royce 'Parthenon' evolution in the 1940s.

projector headlamps on current cars, but the packaging of radiators, pumps, etc, threatened to extend the entire front end. This was potentially a massive re-work requiring an entire new front end, and engineering feedback wasn't readily available. Fortunately, we had ex-Lucas lighting wizard Nike Tyso, who helped with other changes as well (Dr Piech didn't like the 'Old English Marmalade' colour of P2000/P3000's front side lamp lens).

Apart from needing VW platform information, track, wheelbase, influence of fuel tank on seating, and so on, parts bin suitability was also critical. I'd warned against using an Audi mirror because journalists would accuse us of being part bin vultures. Unfortunately, we did and they did.

Lashed to the helm

By the end of January 1999, Styling's bearings were running hot, if not smoking. Due to the 3D work being accommodated in-house, we were employing about a dozen contract clay modellers, but we had no proper system to take care of the wants and needs of such a band of free spirits. Security complained as some modellers pointedly refused to open their bags for spot checks at the gate; modellers also felt harassed and persecuted about factory access for their cars. Another department's manager complained about modellers congregating round the office coffee machine and smoking.

Ordinarily, workshop or studio managers would structure and guide such a team, but there was no one at Crewe to do this, or sanction the employment of someone who could. We also lacked full-time cleaner support (clay is messy stuff), and our old studio was hopelessly overcrowded, and being run down due to the pending move. To cap it all, a large steam pipe burst, filling the studio with an impenetrable fog of very hot steam that soaked everything, jettisoning lagging and necessitating an asbestos safety check. Then the roof began to leak. I remember looking up to heaven and thinking, "I didn't expect it to be easy, but enough, already!"

Simon Loasby's role of managing the department's daily needs was being stretched to breaking point, in addition to which, quite naturally, he wanted to have some direct input via a BY713 proposal. With having to supervise work on-site and off, too much was expected of too few people.

This was a very frustrating time, and VW was watching how we operated. The irony was that while Engineering was absorbed with restructuring itself, the pending use of VW platforms would, arguably, reduce that department's workload, whilst increasing dependence on aesthetics to communicate Bentley's unique selling points. As a result, Styling was positioned more centre stage at Crewe.

Good work was done on interiors by Robin Page and Henric Nordin, and both showed signs of appreciating the scope that this area offered. Rather than sequential functions on a computer display, we planned a rather quaint rotating device with sat nav on one side, clock on the other, and so on: great fun, and certainly better than the 'pop-up toaster' we'd been forced into on the facia top roll. We also used Jonathan Gould for this – another Blackpool styling veteran.

In February we heard that VW was to show a mid-engined Bentley proposal at Geneva. As this was a personal dream project, my feelings were mixed. I had a conversation with Richard Charlesworth, the Company's PR man, regarding my attending. We decided it best to avoid going because if the VW Bentley mid-engined concept was at Geneva, I'd either have to avoid any comment or pretend some involvement.

Dr Robert Buechelhofer, VW's Sales and Marketing Director, visited to explain the company's perception of Bentley representing 'masculine' machines (it would only have confused him to point out many Bentleys were sold as 'stealth' Rolls-Royces).

In February 1999, the engineering team responsible for F2 P2000 declared independence by informing me it would arrange its own board viewings. However, the team very soon gratefully returned to the monthly Styling viewings.

BY713 'MSB' goes full-size

During January 1999, Ken Scott was in possession of the latest VW platform that BY713 would probably be shaped around. The situation was still fluid, however, with issues about wheelbase, four- or five-seater, two- or four-door, and whether to accommodate an opening roof, etc, apparently irresolvable. With the Product Plan and packaging of BY713 still not established, Styling carried on developing several concept themes.

Following December's PSK 'rough-cut' theme selection, our plan of attack was to create three in-house clays: Darren Day and Simon Loasby would do a two-door notchback and fastback, and Crispin Marshfield would tackle a four-door saloon. The platform used looked very low with a long wheelbase. VW platforms of this class had long front overhangs and short tails – the opposite of traditional Bentleys – and would need careful consideration.

Bali themes were my obvious starting point, with four

headlamps and a sloping front. A recognizably Bentley radiator shell would also slope. The side sculpting would have some reference to the front and rear 'classic' wings seen on Bali.

After a few weeks we were almost into a re-run of Bali issues concerning rear headroom, further complicated by the long nose increasing overall length. We had a large VW saloon package which might or might not carry the whole Bentley family. Styling again had to step into the minefield before the powers-that-be could establish the Product Plan. This was usually done with the help of packaging engineers acting as bomb disposal experts, but Crewe's Styling had to negotiate the mines alone, without losing too many limbs in the process.

By the end of February the Product Plan and associated family tree of cars proposed in it remained disorganised. When the VW takeover dust began to settle, Brand felt able to continue contributing to the Product Plan. BY713 might now be the P2000's replacement, with BY711 a Mercedes S Class-killer. Altogether, a family of four cars with various wheelbases was proposed, based on BY713 and BY711 and a smaller coupé. Essentially, Brand wanted larger cars, citing increased Maybach production and the belief that the BMW Rolls-Royce would be ten inches (254mm) longer than P3000 as the reasons for this. It was all too clever for me, as the two-door Medium-Sized (Priced) Bentley appeared to be the obvious route: a new saloon smaller than P2000 was possible, but extremely challenging. The Company had a good chance of trebling production with just an MSB two-door.

A month later we had the three clays in full-size, overloading the exhausted old Studio. Darren's clay had to be worked on at Futura in the Midlands, with Richard Stevens helping on one side. Simon's had to be copy-milled in Paris, with Crispin's the only clay staying at Crewe.

Hartmut Warkuss visited to view the new Corniche, P3000 Limousine, and see what his man, Crispin, was up to. We agreed that Heurliez's rear end theme should influence Crispin's clay. Understandably, the head of VW Styling gave Crispin his 'builds,' but I was beginning to wonder who was responsible for this particular clay, as it wasn't clear whether or not Crispin was working for me.

The following day VW Design's Her Knapp and Karl Taylor visited, also to see Crispin's clay, which clashed with my plans to visit Futura in Birmingham, DRA in Warwickshire, and TWR in Oxfordshire. As these were senior VW people, Futura and DRA were cancelled, but with two exteriors and an interior at TWR, I had no choice but to go there. I waited until the visitors arrived mid-morning, greeted them, and then made my excuses. Both men spoke excellent English, but were from a different world encompassing limitless resources. It simply wasn't possible to deliver the design properties and solutions that VW wanted, whilst simultaneously entertaining VW designers at the drop of a hat. However senior Knapp and Taylor were, they were simply curious to experience this novel outpost that was Crewe. I'd arranged for them to be shown around by Crispin, but they probably considered this a slight.

Despite language difficulties, Dr Warkus seemed a typical experienced stylist. However, as we discussed the clay, a profound difference in our approaches became apparent. The Germans greatly valued giving their cars a solid and substantial look, which is understandable with small cars, but this objective applied right through the range. In stark contrast, our aim was to give the impression of less weight, a variance borne out by Tony Gott's comment that Crispin's car "looked massive." I told Tony that German styling was not subtle enough at our size, but that it would be best if VW figured this out for itself. Tony thought I should have greater influence, so we took Crispin's clay outside on a Sunday morning to view, and I suggested fourteen basic 'builds.'

Robin Page and Henric Nordin continued exploratory work on interiors, particularly fascias based on the VW platform. As always, this was not the easiest area of a gentleman's motor car to get right.

TWR's professional work copying the Corniche replacement on a different platform led to me working with that concern on the P2000 F2 proposal. We completely remodelled the front end with four separate headlamps incorporating the deleted side lamp functions; new front and rear aprons; four exhaust pipes; new alloy wheels, and so on. TWR also had the capacity to work on the full-size clay of Simon Loasby's BY713.

On Sunday March 14, 1999, we had an outside viewing as the factory would be reasonably quiet. There was good BY713 theme progress, although engineering packaging still wasn't settled. Darren's and Crispin's clays were compared alongside a P2000 and a Mercedes S Class (Simon's clay was still being machined in Paris). Robin and Henrik presented interior properties.

At least the board had the opportunity to weigh-up theme direction, even if it hadn't yet chiselled the Product Plan in stone. Talking to Ian McKay about aesthetics, I repeated my opinion that, while most manufacturers try to make their small- and medium-sized cars appear more substantial, we were trying to make heavier cars look lighter.

End of play – I only asked for an office!

The following day an issue entirely unrelated to my styling ability and/or usefulness to the Company signalled the beginning of the end.

Styling now formally owned the Car Bond building in the north/east corner of the site, with the newly-purchased adjacent land for outside viewings. Building work was progressing and, although my office and small studio were still in the old Main Avenue bungalow, generally, other department members worked in the existing clay/viewing workshop in Third Avenue.

Styling studio layouts tend to follow much the same trend, with the clay workshop/viewing area and styling desks in a large, open-plan area, usually with a long, metal surface plate (which can accommodate several clays) running down the middle. Offices and conference rooms are usually grouped at one end.

The new facility represented Styling's 'coming of age' at Crewe, but an obvious omission was an office for the Chief Stylist. It transpired that it was now Company policy (or Engineering policy) not to have individual offices. My reasoning was that, considering the new area was a direct result of the proven effectiveness of previous premises, it seemed only sensible that I should have an office: after all, this open-plan area was essentially a workshop, and not office accommodation. Having exhausted all the usual channels, I made an appointment to see new MD Tony Gott.

At a meeting on Monday, March 15, 1999, I was told by Tony that my views about the lack of an office were academic, as a new VW director would be arriving to take over the Department. Apparently, I hadn't made enough effort to get to know the VW people, and Tony also found my general approach too intellectual. The die was apparently cast, even before my opinion was asked, or being advised to change my approach. It wasn't clear from which side of the channel the decision had come.

It had been obvious that the Crewe site, as structured, couldn't interface with VW. Not, I hasten to add, from the shopfloor or Production but from Engineering. At the time of my meeting with Tony, Styling had been pressing ahead with numerous projects and proposals, but without benefit of a complete Product Plan or platform/package. Indeed, we had relentlessly demonstrated packaging and product issues, to which Engineering had no resolutions, to the board. It was engineering design, and especially packaging, that Crewe needed to sort out. There was plenty of proven talent, not least of which was Peter Hill's terrific P250 and George Ray's plywood packaging mock-ups, but there was no overall car design structure to refer to. The independent project team cult simply wasn't working.

As for the Styling Department at Crewe, the sensible move would have been to bring over an experienced VW liaison engineer who understood our circumstances. After working with me for a couple of days, he would have been in a position to assess the true situation at Crewe.

The final score

In the nine months we'd been owned by VW, Styling had been engaged on the following projects –
- Completing the project Bali clay
- MSB quarter scales and full size clays
- P2000 F1
- P2000 F2
- P92 Siam (Corniche) plus Bentley variant
- Long-wheelbase P2000/P3000
- Interiors for all projects
- Establishing new Styling facility
- Model year changes, plus 'hygiene'
- Face-lifted Continental R
- Visiting and receiving VW and swapping stylist
- Colour and trim
- MPW special customer work
- Accommodating Brand requirements
- Changing from Marketing to Engineering ownership
- Computer-designed futuristic Rolls-Royce (Endeavour) + animated film
- Visiting Ital Design and Lamborghini to advise on a Bugatti and the Diablo replacement

Styling Department head count –
Graham Hull
Darren Day
Richard Stevens/Crispin Marshfield
Simon Loasby
Robin Page
Henrik Nordin
Caroline Walley (secretary)
(Steven Piantoni, pending Coventry course)

Apart from on-site work I was co-coordinating and working with six off-site studios – Futura, TWR, MGA, OMNI, DRA, and Heurliez

Comments that not enough effort was made to interface with VW were off-target; given the colossal head count mismatch, I'd done all the travelling possible. Hartmut Warkuss and his top people had been shown everything, and additionally, I facilitated and contributed towards a 'British' VW interior exercise from one of our consultants. Hartmut had generated a Bentley saloon and mid-engine sports car replicas with no reference to the marque's Chief Stylist, or invitation to him to contribute. I wasn't complaining, but to blame me was, I felt, a bit rich.

Regardless of whether the new appointment was home-grown or superimposed, filling the position of Design Director (Styling/Design) from VW's ranks made this 'cuckoo in Crewe's nest' the responsibility of VW, ahead of an eventual new Engineering structure. On a personal level spontaneous combustion was not a characteristic of mine: I would gain nothing from walking away, and could learn a lot by staying, however uncomfortable that might be.

"Bentley men are mountaineers, Rolls-Royce men own the mountains." – 1990s Crewe comment

BACK INTO THE RANKS
TWO CULTURES HARMONISE – AND A NICE FINAL NOTE

Informed that someone else would be taking over the Styling Department, my thoughts were mixed: frustrated by this abrupt turn of events, but also curious to know how VW would tackle aesthetics at the top of the luxury car market. David Chammings' parting words came back to me across the years, "You have to be a stoic to work here," and my own problems were put into perspective by the death of Frank Hart whilst driving home from work (Frank was a Purchase Department mainstay I'd worked with).

Of course, a new styling director would have several advantages. As a VW implant, the Crewe board would be bound to give him carte blanch regarding recruitment, etc, and he would also inherit our brand new studio. During nine months of ownership, VW would have a good idea of Engineering's strengths and weaknesses, and appeared to have accepted my marque visual cues philosophy as illustrated in the Rolls-Royce and Bentley Design Strategy Papers. We had also explored several promising themes for the Medium-Sized Bentley (MSB BY713), pending platform clarification, and progressive work had been done on interiors.

The day after the bombshell Tony Gott phoned to say the new man was with him, and I couldn't resist asking, "Dr Piech?" It was, of course, Dirk van Braeckel, and Tony was checking that if he invited me to his office I wasn't going to be "negative." My first impressions of Dirk – Belgian, Ford-sponsored at the Royal College of Art, ex-Audi and Skoda – were a shaved head, embarrassed smile, and very large feet. We had a chat in Tony's office, with Ian McKay also present. Ian explained Brand's viewpoint, which was absolutely fascinating, and I explained our Design Strategy. Dirk said he liked what we had been doing (later confessing he wasn't aware that the Company had a Styling Department!).

Afterwards it was business as usual. Dirk needed about three months to extricate himself from Skoda and find accommodation for his wife and daughter in the UK. I sent a large reference book covering the two marques to him in Prague.

As Simon Loasby was managing administration, I explained that he would soon have a new boss who knew the VW structure and, in Tony Gott's words, "how to get items through their PSK viewings." Simon, Darren Day and Crispin Marshfield could continue working on the BY713 exterior proposals and Robin Page and Henric Nordin on interiors. As MPW tended to monopolize Experimental Trim resources, we used Anderson & Ryan, a very experienced, Midlands-based trim company, to work to our drawings. I would continue working as Chief Stylist to cover all of the engineering teams we were involved with –

- BY713 (MSB)
- Bentley P2000 F1 & F2
- Rolls-Royce, including P3000 Limousine
- Continental R face-lift
- Other daily requirements
- Viewings

There was little time to brood. I told Tony that he

could expect Styling to more than double its head count but, as it happened, this estimation turned out to be on the cautious side.

We brought F2, with its new four-headlamp system, from TWR for a board viewing. As the new studio and outdoor viewing area wasn't quite finished, we had to go up to the 'badlands' at the top of the factory. The board, which rarely ventured up there, had to cram into a damp Portakabin for the Styling briefing, sitting on old, odd chairs. They probably thought I wanted to make them as uncomfortable as possible out of spite.

Brand asked for help in illustrating its strategy to VW, and, again, it was simple to show the face of Bentley as four large round headlamps, matrix grille, and large air intake, as demonstrated by F2 and Bali. At the end of March 1999, Tony formally announced Dirk's appointment, with some interesting provisos –
• Styling usually reported to Wolfsburg but Tony wanted Dirk to report to him
• Dirk would not be a main board director
• The Bali clay was not what VW usually saw, only finished exterior/interior replicas
• Tony added that all was not well with Crewe Engineering

A gradual handover
The transition period seemed to take a long time. Dirk came to Crewe whenever possible, and I took him to our off-site projects and explained ongoing issues. Although non-committal about our exterior work, interior projects obviously impressed him, especially the 'jewellery,' like our latest knurled surfaces for finger contact with controls such as some knobs, switches, and parts of handles. This was no surprise as stylists rarely praise each other's exterior work, although do appreciate that interiors are complex.

F1 and F2 P2000 upgrades, based on the born-again Crewe V8, had my full attention, as these were committed to production. A classic disagreement occurred over clearance gaps around exhaust pipes and composite body panels: Styling wanted the smallest cut-outs possible, whilst engineers were adamant that these would constitute a risk of the pipes touching the body. After much time and expenditure of verbal energy, it was realized that the exhaust pipes would hit a chassis cross-member before it got anywhere near Styling's 'tight' apertures. It was a pleasure to introduce body engineers to their chassis engineering colleagues. In truth, hot exhaust systems have a mind of their own, so give the boys a break.

VW Chief Engineer Dr Ulrich Hackenberg began

to strengthen Design Engineering, appointing ex-Rover packaging man Jim Shaw as head of a newly-formed design feasibility team. This brought 'neutral corner' engineering feasibility directly into Styling, and Jim into our new studio. Hooray! At an open meeting with my team in mid-May 1999, Dr Hackenberg asked me what my career had covered (Dirk wasn't present). The question threw me a bit, but did drive home the fact that Crewe Styling was so low profile that a senior man like Ulrich knew nothing about us (admittedly, all of the Blackpool cars were below the radar).

The three BY713 full-size clays were taken to the April PSK viewing at Wolfsburg. As is usually the case, some aspects were liked more than others, and generally the flusher, more integrated radiator shells were preferred. These Styling clay mock-ups from Crewe immediately helped clarify how best to use a VW platform for Bentley. The still-fluid Product Plan was now to recognise BY713 (MSB) as a two-door fastback on a shortened platform, and a four-door saloon BY711 to use a longer version of the platform. Our work also showed that the two different vehicles could share front ends; this also became a PSK decree. The interiors were well received, and it was heartening to hear Dr Piech praising simple controls for radios, and the knurled contact areas, both of which would have gladdened the heart of my ergonomics tutor at Loughborough University.

Over the previous months Styling had created quite a lot of drawings, full-size clays, interiors and scale models, and Tony requested that everything be shown to the workforce, thereby christening the outside viewing area.

During this period Dirk was visiting about once a week, while I kept things moving forward. One area I was more than pleased for Dirk to address was budgets, as these were integrated into Engineering projects, leaving Styling disadvantaged as to what needed doing, by whom and where. If Wolfsburg always expected replica quality Styling exteriors and interiors, this would entail significant spend. Styling's new head count budget was also going to upset the Crewe mindset.

When on-site, Dirk spent a lot of time on the phone trying to persuade a couple of specialists from VW's design studios to come and join us, his preference appearing to be an experienced exterior stylist to contribute to the BY713 and BY711, and a chief modeller or 'gang boss.' The latter, crucial position is unique to the motor industry, involved with everything to do with mock-ups, personnel, progress, transport and storage, etc. There was going to be a huge issue with salaries and housing allowances that would tempt people to the Cheshire Plains. Previous recruitment drives had resulted in those doing the interviewing realising that interviewees were being offered higher salaries than themselves, prompting at least one excellent senior engineer to take early retirement.

As my position was still officially Chief Stylist, I asked Dirk for clarification regarding BY713. Dirk said he would directly supervise the exterior whilst I carried on with the interior, and F1 and F2 exteriors and interiors. He was happy for me to continue organizing Crewe Styling viewings. F1 and F2 were the immediate hot potatoes, being the only vehicles definitely covered in the Product Plan, and required to hold the fort until BY713 and BY711 galloped to the rescue. F2's significant exterior and interior change made it the first car to be finalised in the new studio. Brand wanted to pick up again on Red (very traditional wood veneers) and Black (more modern interior materials – piano-black lacquered wood, engine-turned aluminium, and, perhaps, carbon-fibre – aggressive-looking alloy wheels and less chrome work externally) label philosophy. The differentiation appeared marginal, but I saw Red as the stealth Rolls-Royce and Black as the true Bentley bruiser.

The long process began on the F2 engine to educate Cosworth and Crewe engineers in the concept of aesthetic design for new castings, injection components, general plumbing, and covers.

That elusive Product Plan

By the middle of 1999, Crewe's Product Plan still hadn't gelled. At a meeting in the boardroom for all of the senior managers involved, chaired by Tony, I asked for clarification on notes I was taking, and the ensuing debate lasted over an hour, partially due to a surprising request to investigate VW's V16 engine in P2000, thus creating an F3.

Styling was now having to digest the following –
- F1 exterior/interior x 2 (Red & Black label) (L410 V8)
- F2 exterior/interior x 2 (Red & Black label) (L410 V8
- Need to work to process (ie agreed procedures)
- Empowerment was an act of faith, especially when it was financial

Perhaps the most interesting of these points was the fifth one – a Graham Morris adage – because a big difference between British and German meetings was that the latter wanted only to hear about problems: there's not a lot to be gained by hearing that things are okay, it's what's not okay that needs attention. Another of Tony's points was that truth could be a rarity at Crewe.

The following day I wrote a note to Dr Hackenberg regarding necessary Styling sequences, first showing it to Dirk who showed it to Tony in turn. Tony agreed things were wrong and had to change, but "... no need to send it to the good Doctor, though."

Meanwhile ...

Richard Hamblin of Omni Design told me he was working on one of nine clays that another company was considering, the sheer number of clays proving, yet again, how much effort went into styling. Additionally, if the resources were available, the time taken for theme selection could be reduced by having such a large choice of available single model clays, all with different features.

We were working on nine alloy wheels for model differentiation and options. Although not a fan of chrome wheels, chrome-plating and polishing had to be considered for both marques. (Our German supplier's chief engineer had raced a Steyr-Puch 650TR; I got on well with him as few Englishmen knew about this little Austrian rocket.) Unnervingly, after many successful designs, our supplier had a strong-looking five-spoker fail under static testing, though resolved the problem, luckily without changing the style.

A 19 inch wheel I worked on had a cosmetic 'bolted-rim.' It seemed reasonable to locate the valve in place of a bolt head, but this offended German laws of symmetry. I suggested having a valve in the tool kit which could replace a bolt when required; this slightly loopy idea was accepted. A side effect of larger wheels was that more of the brakes showed: when you find yourself styling grooves in brake discs you know aesthetics are gaining ground.

By mid-July 1999 Styling had moved into the new studio's office area, though I remained in my quaint bungalow until the new furniture arrived. There was still a 'no individual offices' policy which, no doubt, contributed to engineering efficiency.

We struggled to find representative cars to match Wolfsburg's viewing expectations. At Peter Forster's BMW Experimental Garage, hundreds of cars were used to test a single new component. The cars available to us were usually hulks abandoned by Development. The danger in presenting proposed exterior or interior changes on a non-representative vehicle was that this could spark erroneous investigations over the smallest detail. But each production unit was too valuable to give to Styling: I'm not sure if VW ever realized this.

The Brand department was somewhat diminished

when Graham Lendon became Marketing Operations Manager at Aston Martin, and another member joined KIA. In addition, some of the more experienced Blackpool engineers were slipping back to the Midlands. Against this trend, Steven Piantoni joined Styling from Coventry University and Richard Stevens re-joined us from his VW exchange.

Although VW appeared to have no objection to us working off-site, security was an issue, and Dr Hackenberg was keen to ensure we were protected. Everyone knew their job depended on total integrity, but it's a small world, and specialists are bound to jump ship occasionally. No doubt modellers who worked on Crewe product also worked on Goodwood's Rolls-Royces. People I worked with went on to Jaguar, Land-Rover and so on. Ironically, no car company wants to risk being too far out of mainstream appeal, so the fear of cross-fertilization is a bit of a false bogeyman.

No one, however, wants to be approached by the Security Chief clutching spy shots of your new front and rear lamps either. This happened to me once: thank goodness the pictures hadn't been taken in our studio. Perhaps the biggest risk is in technological areas, where supplier integrity is crucial.

As Dirk became full-time in the second half of 1999, Engineering decided that a low pressure turbo in the new Corniche would increase bhp from 300 to 325, but, guess what, it needed a bigger mouth to gulp in more air. We had a struggle persuading the team responsible that this modification had to be properly re-styled. This was beyond an eleventh hour mod, and at October's Styling viewing Tony Gott challenged this after sign-off request as no one had informed him of the requirement! It was obvious that this insular cellular team approach couldn't continue.

BY713 (Bentley Continental GT) emerges, and an historic desk is moved

Fifteen months had passed since VW had bought the Company, and Engineering finally understood the platform. The package chosen for the BY713 two-door fastback was a little more compact than previous proposals, and had the typical long nose, Audi-type overhang. The general theme of the front face had been established for some time; also bearing reference to classic Bentley wing styles.

Raul Pires, a pleasant young Brazilian, had eventually followed Dirk from Skoda, and had picked up on the growing trend of continuing the bonnet catwalks up the A posts – a bold solution to a notoriously difficult area.

Dirk, working with Raul, made rapid progress on the clay, and thus the Continental GT was established.

I carried on much as before. One sideline had echoes of my first Crewe project – Alex Moulton's knee pad – as Dr Piech wanted a rear bench seat in his Arnage.

Dirk must have mentioned to Christine Gaskell, Personnel Director, my apparent reticence to move from the bungalow into the new, rather crowded communal office, and I subsequently received a formal letter telling me to do so. As the smaller desk I was waiting for still hadn't arrived, my historic, tastefully distressed, ex-John Blatchley/Fritz Feller desk had to be squeezed in amongst the veneered chipboard modernity.

One of the joys of being in the small, open-plan office were the everyday conversations of those who drifted in to discuss this or that, or to practise their social skills on our long-suffering secretary, Caroline. Such set-ups tend to suit those who welcome filling their unused cranial capacity with outside stimulus, whereas I'd always needed every scrap of grey matter I could muster.

Maybe Dirk realised that forcing me to move had been rather heavy-handed, as he surprised me by asking my opinion about the BY713 and BY711 clays at a private, outside viewing session. BY713 was progressing well; it wasn't quite how I would have done it but, given the package, it was effective and would meet the demand for a smaller Bentley coupé. BY711 demonstrated how difficult three-box saloons are to resolve. A comfortable cabin demands length, with little left for bonnet and boot. Cars which manage to carry this off – most Jaguar saloons, the 2005 Mercedes E Class, and 2009 Passat – are to be applauded; the Seraph/Arnage isn't to be sneezed at, either. It wasn't relevant to stress my interest in rear three-quarter views as I'd already passed on Dr Piech's opinion that Bentleys were all about front end. We agreed BY711 had some way to go; I simply said that studying photos of painted Dynoc clays with real cars was my favourite trick. Dirk gave the modellers and stylists a pep talk about lack of progress.

Towards the end of September, Raul Pires, whose BY713 MSB coupé was entering its post-theme development stage, asked my opinion of it. This was awkward as I didn't want to be quoted behind Dirk's back, so I simply repeated my broken-record advice of "photograph it with other exotica such as Maserati." Working on clays daily, stylists can become a little subjective; seeing their work pictured in this way can allow them to consider it in a different light. I did query whether the height of the scuttle was package-driven, and drew attention to windscreen proportions and the rear three-quarter view. The main philosophy, I explained, was to see these cars 'in the round,' with only the radiator shell as a visual 'stopper.' Even to me I sounded like a benign uncle.

For years, Bentley had had an open goal with this type of vehicle, and the ball just needed a tap in. The Java concept car of 1994 had foretold the future, and as long as the shape didn't frighten the horses the coupé could treble production. There were exclusivity issues with such a production increase, but this was a very comfortable problem for the high table.

Engineering's new structure

Late in 1999, Dr Ulrich Hackenberg began to describe his proposed changes to Engineering, which featured concept teams, engineering teams and function-based organizations, as well as a large increase in staffing levels to process the new cars. Ken Scott continued to head the BY713/BY711 team, and was now using VW-speak such as Theme Selection, Styling Frozen and Data Control Model: all music to my ears as, previously, some engineering programmes had made no allowance for styling activity at all!

When the other shoe finally dropped, Dr Hackenberg's restructuring of Engineering was simple, with just four people reporting directly to him: Rob Oldaker (MPW), Jim Shaw (Concept Engineering), Brian Gush (Engineering Operations), and Dirk van Braeckel (Styling). Brian Gush had six vehicle managers, who made up the bulk of Engineering. This was the best deal in town for Styling as Concept Engineering's half dozen or so people were already embedded in our studio.

VW's Brian Gush was new to Crewe, sounded South African, and was restoring an early Cheshunt-built Lotus Élan. He'd stressed the need at meetings to report by exception: in other words, only those work issues that were a cause for concern. Over the years there had been many attempts to make meetings more productive, bringing in consultants to advise, and even industrial psychiatrists, although, in the macho environment that was the car industry, David Attenborough might have been a better bet for all the alpha males who worked within it!

By mid-2000, it was announced that Dr Hackenberg was returning full-time to Wolfsburg. Obviously a top man within VW, he had been sent to Crewe to restructure Engineering, but couldn't be spared full-time. It was intriguing watching VW engineers operate, because

German culture acknowledges their vital role, which attracts high-calibre people. Ulrich appeared without humour or, indeed, emotion, but being a motorcycle enthusiast this couldn't really have been the case. Sitting opposite him at a meeting he spent most of the time cleaning his füllfederhalter (fountain pen), making little comment, although by the end of the meeting everyone had been indexed in his personal filing system, no doubt.

After Ulrich departed, Brian Gush became acting Chief Engineer.

Feasibility/packaging

Witnessing the establishment of Jim Shaw's Concept Engineering team in our new studio, initially for the BY713 and BY711, cheered the soul. Apart from the creation of traditional, full-scale drawings, there were numerous CAD stations with experienced operators, which transformed the options open to Styling.

Previously, at the start of a project, metaphorically speaking, it was a case of jumping out of the aircraft in the hope that someone would skydive after you and clip on a feasibility 'parachute.' Now, apart from up-front packaging, electronic data capture techniques from clays ensured everyone was kept in the information loop. Of course, packaging clashes and debates still occurred, but these were much further upstream, and were more easily resolved. There were also real-time update links with central VW information.

Packaging/feasibility is at the heart of vehicle design. The specialists involved may feel a little undervalued as they appear to be just doing the will of the stylist, but it's a much closer co-operation than that, and they should be highly rated. At Rover, Jim Shaw had worked on radical replacements for the classic Mini, which were further-reaching than BMW's – admittedly successful – final choice. One team member had been involved with the legendary McLaren F1, and I welcomed his views on a private project I was considering.

The key to the future

Although producing amongst the most charismatic cars in the world, these were brought to life via an amorphous black plastic device, common to all manufacturers.

We developed the most exotic car key ever: a hide-covered clamshell body, from which the shaft emerged switchblade-like: some parts would even be gold-plated. Handed around at our large, seated Styling viewing, this superb creation was much admired. For the benefit of the minutes I ensured that our Marketing Director was aware of and bought into the gold-plating, which was just as well because after these were circulated, he changed his mind about the gold. Our Personnel Director who, unusually, hadn't been at the viewing, asked to discuss this with me: perhaps they thought, due to the circumstances of my reduced status, I'd become subversive. Most likely it was more a case of it being easier to point up lesser issues than address the bigger picture. This new feature became the first element in the fledgling five-year Product Plan. Never in the history of keys has so much been ...

A Bentley for Her Majesty

A surprise request was to supply Her Majesty the Queen with a Head of State car (Hoscar), the novel twist being that it was to be a Bentley rather than the previously ubiquitous Rolls-Royce. Whilst the superb Mulliner Park Ward royal cars were before my time, I'd studied them for subsequent Hoscars. These MPW vehicles were either hugely modified production cars or all-new.

Previous royal cars had been on a Phantom chassis, which automatically gave a high floor so that the crowds could see members of the Royal Family, and to enable royalty to get in and out without stooping or knocking off their hats. Crewe's PR maestro, Richard Charlesworth, now with MPW, was liaising with the palace to establish interior arrangements, etc. Due to his efforts, he was subsequently awarded the Royal Order of Queen Victoria's Garter, or some such.

Initially, I provided Crispin Marshfield and Richard Stevens with my thoughts, gleaned from previous very, very large cars. It was essential to avoid the 'Popemobile' type of mobile glasshouse, and Dirk, working with Crispin, came up with the eventual exterior.

Whenever this statuesque vehicle appears on television I get much simple pleasure from seeing the Hull/Maddocks/Hollings door handles.

Arnage's upward spiral

Engineering's Francis Ellison was leading the P2000 upgrades with the ever-helpful Tim Oakes getting everything made at MPW: a mock-up of this partially re-skinned, W16-powered F3 was under way in the studio. I avoided becoming involved and, thankfully, the project was aborted. VW was beginning to appreciate the British V8 engine, now revitalized with twin turbos.

Nomenclature is interesting to historians, but project codes often have a temporary life: there was F2-and-a-half,

all the way to F6, with some packages only enduring for a couple of board meetings. Model year programmes seemed to make more sense – 2000MY – and so on.

The interior of F2 P2000 was a tour de force. We offered new seats and trim in a quilted pattern used previously on one-offs only; tinted, engine-turned alloy panels, and knurled contact areas for finger grip (knurling had fascinated when, as a schoolboy, I watched my father demonstrate this metal-working technique). This interior was particularly well received at Wolfsburg's December PSK, but, still dealing with cellular teams of engineers at Crewe, old battles were re-enacted. "Why can't switches and suchlike be made of plated plastic?" Styling's answer, hoarse from repetition, "If it looks like metal, it *is* metal."

Apart from issues of influencing the under-bonnet appearance of the born-again Crewe V8, exterior modifications were not a walkover. Conflicting requirements concerning the front apron were eased by Dr Hackenberg allowing a 15 degree ramp angle rather than the existing 16 degree version.

After F3 was abandoned, for some reason F2 became F6 by the turn of the year. The Red and Black interiors were my main interest. Styling was still understaffed, and we were using Jonathan Gould, a veteran of Blackpool and Corniche projects, on the Black label seats. Jonathan was in tune with our approach (we both used Giugiaro's chirpy Daewoo Matiz as second cars, despite *Autocar* rolling one while reversing it).

The F6 exterior was the closest I came to openly disagreeing with Dirk. The front apron was at Styling release stage, but it just wasn't good enough, and whilst mainly philosophical about exterior work, Arnage was my car (Dirk was understandably closer to BY713 and BY711). Although I was expecting a bust-up, Dirk and Hackenberg accommodated my objections, and a better solution emerged. Hackenberg also supported my views on some contentious F6 seat feasibility issues.

It was heartening to hear Channel 4's *Driven* presenter describe the latest Arnage (F1 P2000) as the most charismatic car he'd ever driven.

Not forgetting Rolls-Royce

Even if only minding the Rolls-Royce shop, VW's professionalism was admirable, ensuring, as it did, that Seraph and Corniche benefited from ongoing developments. Considering the circumstances of the temporary custodianship, this attitude was exemplary.

By March 2000, over 136 new Corniches had been

continued page 158

Opposite: In best Company tradition every visual and tactile element of the vehicle is carefully considered: an objective that includes everything from engine bay to the reflection of the knurled grip under the door handle.

"The fastest lorries in the world"? Ettore Bugatti's 1920s quote about Bentleys shows how far the marque had progressed over the years. Whilst continuing to add dynamic attributes, Bentley shared the obsessive attention to detail and comfort enjoyed by its more famous Crewe stable-mate, Rolls-Royce. By the January 2002 introduction of the twin turbo, 6.75-litre V8 in the Arnage T, the marque was demonstrating perhaps the highest levels achieved to date by Crewe craftsmen and women.
This vehicle won 'the most beautiful luxury car' accolade, awarded by an international jury in 2002.

sold, which was 65 per cent of the annual target. This was cheering as I couldn't see Crewe models surviving the move to Goodwood. Total sales were up 41 per cent over the previous year, with 73 per cent of Arnage's 'conquest sales,' as were 61 per cent of Seraph's. Recent reintroduction of the L410 V8 in the Red label Bentley undoubtedly helped; there was also new confidence following the torrid ownership struggle over the two marques. It seemed that Corniche was outselling Seraph (250/159), again raising questions about engines as Seraph had BMW's V12 and Corniche Crewe's V8 (albeit lightly turbocharged). Understandably, BMW didn't want us to replace its V12 with Crewe's V8 in Seraph: candidly, the V12 felt good in the Rolls-Royce.

As well as usual 'hygiene' improvements it was decided to give Rolls-Royce larger wheels, such as the Bentleys were getting. Interestingly, Dr Piech wanted to retain the style but increase the diameter. This was one of my favourite wheels, featuring a large, stainless steel centre plate set into delicate cast spokes/vanes. Getting Dirk to okay modifications to the wheel I'd styled was a twist of the knife.

January 2001 saw me working with Tim Oakes at MPW on the long-stretch P3000 Seraph, which required a new infill panel, with glass between the doors, and also a small backlight option.

The devil's in the detail (again)

Engine-turned interior elements were a subject for debate. Dr Piech and Dr Winterkorn acknowledge their unique appearance, but whether this chimed with their picture of classic veneered interiors wasn't clear. American dealers tended not to order it so their customers never saw it to decide for themselves. It seemed an interesting option to me, and our idea of adding tinted lacquer on F6 looked better again. A retracting, winged B mascot to echo the 'disappearing' Spirit of Ecstasy was again worked on.

Top Gear magazine published a rare letter from me. In an excellent article on Bentley owners, the magazine had referred to the Arnage's "plastic' grille matrix," and I had to put it straight on this as the laser-cut stainless steel matrix cost a lot of time and money. Tony Gott seemed pleased with this little piece of PR as the magazine featured a photo as well as my response.

In early 2000 it seemed I could be free of Colour and Trim responsibility as Dirk's wife took this over. What was possibly the largest colour range in the automotive world had previously been handled on an ad hoc basis, and it was quite extraordinary that it had never been the

principle job for anyone! However, August saw me sucked back into Colour and Trim's whirlpool. Whilst Brand was happy to wax lyrical with value judgements, no one in the F6 team wanted to take on this perpetual orphan, and it was therefore once again necessary to act as bogey-man, reminding the team about swatch-packs for dealers and fresh paint colours for brochure shots, etc. Each isolated project team required the same learning curve, as it wasn't possible to put old heads on young shoulders: experience – an old-fashioned concept – really does count.

We at last saw some return on the much-modified F6 twin turbo engine bay. Cosworth was finally giving us what we wanted and the general picture was excellent. As usual, it was the art that concealed art, but it was satisfying as this demanded the best appearance Crewe (car) engine-room so far.

BY progress

The new Bentley BY713 two-door was now coded BY614, and the BY711 saloon was now BY611. VW's PSK January 2000 viewing had okayed the two-door, with 'builds,' for a fibreglass replica. These two new cars were exploiting VW's latest bumper technology, allowing a much more integrated style; even so, the four-door still looked bigger than Arnage which Dr Piech wished to stay at the top of the range. The front end shared by the two new cars was finalised, but, as ever, the rest of the saloon style was the challenge. Arnage styling minimised its size.

Early in December 2000, marketing chiefs worldwide descended unannounced on the studio to see BY611. Dirk wasn't there, so yours truly had to operate the new turntable for the benefit of this august body. BY611 – described as the fourth iteration by Marketing Director Adrian Hallmark (later of Jaguar) – shouldn't have been viewed, as work continued on the difficult rear quarter/rear door area. Unaccustomed to viewings, the visitors stood too close to the vehicle, with marketing people, characteristically gregarious, chatting in shoal-like formations. Avoiding making any aesthetic value judgements in Dirk's absence, I restricted myself to suggesting studying photos of the model alongside a Mercedes S Class for comparison. Marketing said it could sell the car: fair enough!

Work continued on the BY611 clay through February 2001. As a bystander, development of what became the Flying Spur fascinated me. Anyone who imagines that styling is the result of artistic whim quickly dashed off has no idea: it can be hard work, particularly with a demanding package and a unique marque to project.

The end game

In October 2000 my father had passed away. Starting out as an engineering apprentice at Handley Page (the UK's first publicly traded aircraft manufacturing company), he'd always been quietly pleased by my working at Rolls-Royce and Bentley. Despite what some might regard as a change in status from 'hero to zero,' I hadn't wanted to throw in the towel during my father's fight with cancer. When my sister had died, my parents joined me from London, so I now had the option of persevering at Bentley, and probably soon having to put my mother into a care home, or caring for her full-time myself. The decision wasn't as hard as it might have been had I still been in charge of Crewe Styling. My father remains my template. During service in the Royal Army Medical Corps at the Battle of Arnhem, he had probably helped almost as many wounded German soldiers as British ones. He always said that Germans were very efficient, but had a terrible sense of humour: not a bad summary.

When originally informed in March 1999 that a director was being bought in to take over my position I went to see Christine Gaskell, Personnel Director. Although still officially Chief Stylist, I wanted to ensure some redundancy compensation was fenced off for me, should the situation prove untenable. Tony, Dirk and Christine didn't appear hellbent on driving me out, but the two years I carried on afterward doing my best for the Company was not a bad effort, under the circumstances.

Tony Gott later mentioned that although VW thought Rolls-Royce and Bentley styling had been good, world-class status was required; hence Dirk. I wasn't sure whether this comment was meant to mollify or insult me. I'd had a couple of chats with Dirk without problems, but no one in his shoes would want a predecessor peering over their shoulder; once I'd departed, he would be able to restructure the department. Robin Page was just about ready to take on the position of Interiors Manager, which would have been an obvious alternative role for me. Dirk expressed his frustration that not a single Styling project had had support from Engineering from the start, a situation that couldn't be changed overnight, even with the help of our new Chief Engineer, Hans-Joachim Rothenpieler.

By remaining with the Company until 2001 I ensured that Arnage F6 (Arnage T of 2002) was completed – and a career spanning 30 years (1971-2001) was pretty reasonable. As it was unlikely that anyone else would do it, I tidied up the old studio drawing store, and put a large collection of photographs into Barry Greenwood's archive. Ron Maddocks' 1970s, eighth-scale model of Mulsanne, created in lunch breaks, was rescued, and presented to him at his superbly converted Cheshire water mill home.

On my last day, Ian Rimmer, author of a very worthy book on Crewe Experimental Cars, popped in to have a chat, and then an old college chum phoned: an interesting character, who began his career at Lotus, and had also been road manager for a 1960s group which had had a number one hit. Now living in an Austrian Schloss, and running an industrial design company, he invited me to visit and represent Bentley at a function.

After handing in the keys to my Audi A6 Avant, on my last official day I drove out of the gates in our Daewoo Matiz: a small, red car with 800cc and three cylinders. My thoughts drifted back 30 years, when I'd driven in through these gates in a Steyr-Puch 650TR: a small, red car with 650cc and two cylinders ...

Postscript

I was back in the studio the following week for a formal presentation. The team laid on a buffet and I was presented with an attractive, veneered object d'art, with a descriptive plaque and silver inlays of Seraph on one side and Arnage on the other: it was certainly superior to the Rolls-Royce ashtray I'd been given at the 25th Anniversary.

It took *Autocar* a fortnight to discover that I'd 'left the building,' and it phoned to suggest I draw the new Bentleys for the magazine 'for a small consideration.' This no doubt thoughtful offer was declined, although I did stay in touch with Chief Editor Steve Cropley, who had printed nice words about Seraph/Arnage.

A few months later Arnage T was launched; Julian Hadrill of MPW kindly obtained a brochure for my collection. The vehicle won an award from an international design jury for being the most beautiful luxury car: not a bad note to go out on.

VW enabling Bentley to return and win at Le Mans in 2003 was a memorable moment. Previously, just having a 'jolly-good' but inevitably under-funded try wasn't even worth contemplating: imagine the ignominy of the Bentleys retiring in the early hours of Sunday morning with full ashtrays ...

REFLECTIONS
1971-2001

The Company

The last thirty years of the 20th century witnessed great changes in the UK, and R-RMC echoed the transitions that took place: cut a slice through the Company and count the growth rings of socioeconomic and industrial change during that time. Like any commercial enterprise, Rolls-Royce operated behind a professional facade of confident success, but, like any celebrity, even when on the red carpet the possibility of having to be rushed to a rehab clinic is very real. The Company, to insiders, often seemed a mass of contradictions, conundrums and complexities, but despite all its ups and downs, R-RMC was a true star, rising to the occasion and delivering the goods.

Maintaining 'Best Car in the World' status required ever-increasing funding, especially for Research & Development and tooling. Could Crewe output even support the factory, let alone allow investment for the future? The motor cars were truly exceptional, partly due to the many man-hours invested in each one. Being forced to stand alone in 1971, Rolls-Royce Motor Cars quickly had to find a benefactor, and did so in the shape of Vickers. Under the aegis of Vickers, the Company appeared to be plugged into the financial mains, although there were still those who questioned which way the current might be flowing.

In 1971, SY, the Rolls-Royce Silver Shadow, still reigned: its monocoque body with subframes was a radical departure from chassis cars, and it was probably still the best car in the world; barely, if at all, suffering any depreciation. Crewe appeared to have found the perfect vehicle to carry that iconic radiator shell and mascot.

SY's styling was super-conservative compared to its more glamorous sibling, MPW's two-door (Corniche from 1971). The decision to retain SY's well-proven platform (with some upgrades)and essentially just re-skin it was logical. 'Never change a winning team,' especially when resources are limited. SY never looked quite commanding enough in the key market of America, and by the late 1970s, lacking Corniche's charisma, appeared dated. At the time, a carry-over or shared platform wasn't such a topic of conversation, but Pininfarina's Camargue of 1975 had also given rise to a 'new' car with a change of clothes for SY, prompting the use of the same tactic for the new saloon. Thus, the Silver Spirit – SZ – began its 18-year life. The new style wasn't short on presence, and featured state-of-the-art front and rear lamps.

The launch of SZ triggered one of those things that can make life so interesting; in this case, the re-birth of Bentley. Despite almost no commercial activity from Crewe's second marque, Styling blew on Bentley's embers and got them glowing. MD David Plastow wasn't averse to a Bentley revival, and Styling had thought of a name and modelled a radiator shell. Thus, when SZ was launched, a couple of Bentley Mulsannes were present in the background: Rolls-Royces sans that radiator.

Returning from the launch Fritz Feller said that the Bentleys got a lot of attention, and it's hard to imagine any other marque revival being treated in such a fashion: no committees, and no focus groups or mission statements, etc, just what amounted to a nod. Coincidentally, the turbocharger was developed and put into the Mulsanne. Although painting the radiator shell was agreed, Styling couldn't get any traction for alloy wheels, body-coloured air dams, and so on. The idea of the shared body carrying numerous marque differentiation features took a while to get established. Peter Ward, first as Marketing Director and then MD, dealt with Company preconceptions, and freed-up purse strings, allowing Rolls-Royce and Bentley to be separate entities. The rejuvenated marque was at last allowed to share centre stage with Rolls-Royce.

It's doubtful the Company could have survived with Spirit/Spur alone, as there was a new sensitivity about sitting behind that Parthenon radiator shell. Heroically, Bentley rode to the rescue as a stealth Rolls-Royce, in true gentleman's sporting carriage style. Styling had considered a sporting Rolls-Royce, but with a frisky Bentley in the stable, this wasn't necessary. So if a Rolls-Royce bodyshell made a credible Bentley, a dedicated coupé style had to be very desirable indeed. Styling suggested hijacking a Corniche replacement project to create this coupé, and the resultant Bentley Continental R was a triumphant example of getting the best out of off-site and home-grown talent. If the reborn Bentley gave the Company a much-needed tonic, Continental R was a potent chaser, which sparked the extraordinary 1990s period of specially-commissioned projects which enabled the two marques to survive long enough to launch a new production saloon, refurbish the factory, and attract two wealthy suitors.

This achievement, however, was a close run thing, as the new Rolls-Royce Silver Seraph and Bentley Arnage had to use engines from another manufacturer , and, although excellent, BMW's V12 and V8 seemed to represent a big compromise. Still, enough had been done to prove that both marques remained viable for the 21st century and worthy of VW's and BMW's significant commitment.

Some historians suggest that having led the world into the Industrial Revolution, the British lost the will to remain at the forefront. It's not as simple as that, but the fact remains that the British couldn't or wouldn't finance companies that other countries fought over. One can do worse than quote Sir Winston Churchill in this respect: "In Britain, finance is too proud, industry too humble."

The people

Designers are usually focused on the end result, and are not naturally 'people' people – even if that's who they are designing for. Whilst the creative drive carried me through thick and thin, it was impossible to ignore the human aspect when working at R-RMC.

The whole enterprise had been conceived by two exceptional people – Rolls and Royce – and this melding of rare spirits then absorbed another: Bentley. The customers buying these motor cars were nothing if not extraordinary, but as for the people creating them, well, the whole of life was there. R-RMC employees viewed the Company's product, people and location in different ways. The factory was a world all of its own, with many layers and sub-divisions – some subtle; some not. Factory life is becoming less and less the norm in the UK, but by any standards the Crewe Rolls-Royce/Bentley site was unique; frankly, I doubt we'll ever see its like again.

Stylists are often accused of living in ivory towers, and at Crewe, it was necessary to understand how the cars were built, which meant that Styling bumped up against more facets of factory culture than most. Amongst personnel there was a great divide between hourly-paid workers and staff. Styling workers were staff, and however much the gap with shop floor 'clockers-on' was bridged during a working day, at the end of it you crossed back to your side. Until MD Dick Perry introduced an all-in-one restaurant, segregated dining rooms added insult to injury.

Before the factory was converted to open-plan in the 1990s, there existed a veritable rabbit warren of separate enclosures and mini kingdoms, which tended to encourage a very insular atmosphere bordering on tribalism, each area with its own mindset and perception – inevitable with such a multitude of skill sets. Paint Shop operatives were completely different to those in, say, Road Test; the special talents of those in the Wood Shop were a world apart from those on the Production Line. The superb Trim Shop was unique in that many of its workers were female, and the extensive Machine Shop – which used to process most chassis-related parts and military and aero engines – was really a factory within a factory.

Some employees could relate more directly to the product than others, and even with so much wonderful craftsmanship, the few individuals capable of making the Rolls-Royce radiator shell knew that what they produced was the crowning glory. The site's skills and abilities made a factory tour a prime sales aid; having conducted a few, the sheer quality and effort going into each vehicle affected me every time, so must really have impressed perspective customers. Operatives on the tour route became star turns, and should have held Equity cards, as some of the audience probably did (it was quite usual to see celebrities and film crews on-site, and tourists posing in front of the factory for snapshots). Despite this showbiz element, it was still a factory, and the home-time stampede was a daily phenomenon. The klaxon sounded as I was showing around a VW visitor one day, and I ushered him into a doorway as the frontrunners thundered by.

"Why are they all running?" he apprehensively enquired, fearing a fire or bomb threat.

"They want to get to the car park first." I replied.

"But if they all run they'll all get there at the same time anyway." he said. There's no answer to that kind of logic.

En masse, the Crewe workforce could seem as semi-disgruntled, cross-threaded and disinterested as anybody working for a living. Mike Dunn once commented that if a flying saucer was to land in the factory yard, no one would bother to go and look at it, or a few might possibly drift over during a tea break. Despite an air of seen-it-all nonchalance, working at 'Royce's' instilled a lot of pride, and ranks could close if required.

With a fluctuating local workforce of several thousand, there were inevitably many family and friends networks. Every close and distant link was there, plus numerous social relationships. Not what you knew, but who you knew, was never truer than at R-RMC. Someone I knew was racing a 1930s Aero Morgan and needed a pair of front stub axles. A colleague gave me a name of one of the men on the shop floor and, before I knew it, the metal store had cut off two lengths of EN19 steel bar and, at the 'shadowlands' top of the factory, adjacent to West Street, machined the axles on a skunk-works lathe. No money changed hands. Computer-controlled stock inventories and over-zealous managers at the top of the factory made things like this a little more difficult. Of course, in the local area, shop floor skills were fair game: a Pininfarina A40 I was using got a Rolls-Royce paint job at a very reasonable price.

Security is tight at any factory, and was particularly so at the Pym's Lane site. Actually, the only time I was ever challenged was when I rushed out the gate clutching a Rolls-Royce radiator shell complete with mascot! Luckily, by this time, the Guardians of the Gate had come to understand Styling's sometimes eccentric ways and, in any case, my colleague, Martin Bourne, knew everyone and probably told them I was alright. A 'special' that was being built at my father's school acquired a pair of Corniche headlamps, completely above board as items surplus to requirements could be purchased or covered by a 'scrap' note. As I say, it wasn't *what* you knew ...

Being so absorbed in the world of styling, some of the factory's 'people' issues passed unnoticed. Apart from the ongoing works/staff divide, the site, like any, was riddled with pay disputes, which could cause fuses to blow if it was discovered that one worker was higher paid than another.

Recession gave rise to reduced working days, lay-offs, redundancy and staff capping; good times caused problems over contract workers and head-hunted recruits offered the top end of a salary band. Whenever these bewildering issues affected me I thanked God that my motivation was the urge to create rather than simply make money. As Fritz Feller so sagely commented, "Creativity is its own reward." (ie don't expect a pay rise any time soon!).

Styling experienced salary issues but escaped most of the other factors affecting the workforce, such as countless and constant variations on new work practices and efficiency drives.

Life is about change, and Crewe has seen its share. In 1971 the shop floor was still recognizable as how it had looked in photographs taken in circa 1900 , although, to me, the precious work-in-progress lying or stacked around with no apparent home was always surprising. By the new millennium the site and its people were as well organised and efficient as any modern workplace.

The motor cars

Regardless of the environment that they were built in, history will judge the Company by its product: the cars. It's impossible to be neutral about a Rolls-Royce or Bentley. How many other man-made objects do you know of that have become the template against which all else is compared or likened to? 'The Roll-Royce of ...' has become an advertising cliché used for anything from razors to lawn mowers. This worldwide recognition is the result of the genuine engineering excellence used in the cars' creation.

The prospect of driving one of these very large, imposing horseless carriages could intimidate, and my first drive wasn't terribly reassuring: 6.75 litres under my right foot, two-and-a-quarter tons (2286kg) under my backside, and new to automatics and column gear-changes. In addition, having Jim Farmer (Farmer Jim), the Company Security Chief/Driving Instructor beside me shredded what little nerve I might have mustered (Jim had all the charm and easy manner of a Regimental Sergeant Major). The test vehicle was an early SY which – apologies to the Rolls-Royce Enthusiasts Club – didn't fill me with confidence. Jim was obviously not too confident about my driving ability either, barking "Brake ... BRAKE!" as we approached bends.

Having driven Austin A30s and Riley 1.5s, I was used to spindly butyrate (shiny, black plastic) steering wheels, roll and understeer, but the momentum of the SY's weight, once in motion, was a new thrill. It is a very easy car to drive gently, but it's necessary to remember your responsibilities at speed. Having driven a Silver Cloud, including on motorways, it soon becomes apparent that, if treated with a light touch and due reverence, they are a joy. So it was me at fault and not the car.

The Rolls-Royce's and Bentley's very soft ride and handling characteristics were a result of the important American market. Development engineers such as Peter Hill and Phil Harding could have dialled in firmer suspension, but were not let off the leash until Mike Dunn's 1980s Bentley work. Driving the Turbo R and later developments was a revelation. Genuine performance cars, they could still be pussy cats when required.

Constant refinement and development created a driving experience quite unlike any other. It wasn't simply a case of being cocooned from the world, because a Corniche with the hood down was a delight, too. Even though Germany and Japan produced very fine luxury automobiles, in my opinion, these lacked character. A car should feel like it was built *by* people *for* people, and the Crewe product conveyed that like no other car could. Hopefully, this will long continue to be the case at Crewe and Goodwood.

Styling

The best chassis in the world can't have a shed for a body, nor kitchen chairs for seats. As well as engineering excellence, Rolls-Royce motor cars gained a reputation for elegant bodies, superb paint, flawless chrome, perfect door shuts, interiors featuring the best hide, beautiful veneers and overall attention to detail. The Company also set the absolute industry standard for bespoke customer choice.

The automotive world gradually adopted the Company's technological aspects, and soon the market began to take for granted such things as powered seats and windows. As these became more commonplace, vehicle appearance (size, implied status, and aesthetics) took on more responsibility for product appeal. Whilst the powers-that-be were aware of the changes that were occurring, their reaction to it was questionable. When I visited GM's Cadillac studios, everyone lined up, as if for an inspection, declaring, "We design the cars for your chauffeurs."

In fact, R-RMC Styling facilities weren't in the same league as those at GM; although Crewe was making only a handful of cars compared to Michigan, it did employ large teams of engineers, draughtsman and marketeers. SZ styling was achieved with a level of resource similar to that of its predecessor. Indeed, SY's John Blatchley – a very experienced stylist – was replaced by engine designer Fritz Feller who, for all his qualities, had no experience in styling. In the event, SZ achieved a very long run and also doubled as a Bentley. I'm truly grateful for my involvement although, in retrospect, the approach was rather laissez faire. Following the R-Type Continental, Silver Cloud, SY and Corniche, the board seemed to assume – in that very British way – that a rabbit would always be pulled out of Styling's rather modest hat.

If Pininfarina's Camargue had been a stunner, Crewe Styling Department might have disappeared altogether. As it was David Plastow allowed Fritz Feller's little team to be the sole source of aesthetic creativity for the 1970s work that led to SZ. Industry norm clay modelling wasn't seriously considered, as previous styles had been carved in wood or Epowood. Even after we'd convinced people we needed to use clay for the 1980s SX, we still weren't allowed to have modellers on-site, as the Crewe board simply was not prepared to tackle this thorny industrial relations issue.

After SX, the new Head of Styling – yours truly – was struggling to feed the new and voracious Bentley furnace. Crewe's first product planning director turned to consultants for P90, the Bentley two-door coupé proposal, who worked off-site using clay modelling. After a Geneva showing the coupé was shelved; so, too, a later Corniche proposal from the same source. At this point the board instructed me to work with the consultants; the resulting, more successful, Corniche proposal morphing into the Continental R.

Styling might sometimes have been tempted to employ consultants with little briefing, input, or expectation of success. For instance, Engineering's post-SZ plans for a smaller, radically weight-saving saloon seriously compromised the vehicle's proportions and 'presence,' but Fritz asked Tom Karen of Ogle Design and Giugiaro of Ital Design (by 2010, the VW group was a majority shareholder in Ital) to show us renderings of such a Rolls-Royce model. Both proposals were world-class, and Ital's was scale modelled.

At the presentaton to the board Fritz was poker-faced. Given his opposition to such a down-sizing, the

Machiavellian glint in his eye was no surprise. In any case, it was immediately obvious that Engineering's approach wasn't on. Styling had made its point without the need to throw chairs around. (Montaged photos and full-size comparison drawings were often used subsequently to guide the board before expending precious resources.)

Styling could never have dealt with, on-site, all of the work required by both marques. Indeed, with the special commissions in the 1990s, it's doubtful whether any company in the world could provide the additional resources required. We were using the cream of the world's consultancies and workshops to create a GM-type network of studios; when necessary bringing in people to work alongside us at Crewe.

Given that the projects concerned had very demanding standards, it was probably a matter of luck that we didn't fall out with any of the many people involved. Because the required quality was so high, I may have given the impression of never being satisfied, or of trying to achieve the unachievable. An advantage of such prestigious projects is that most people identify with striving for perfection, and this was very much a traditional Crewe shop floor characteristic, because I never saw any evidence of complacency there: quite the opposite, in fact.

Although chief stylists are usually promoted from within the ranks, this can lead to a rather perverse situation. A successful stylist possesses and uses hands-on talent, and to suddenly be told that, in the top job, he must now work through others (and do the administration!) takes some getting used to. A good analogy is that of a violinist or pianist having to put down his instrument, pick up the baton, and tell the orchestra which notes to play (and count the door takings). This is not always easy to do, day-in, day-out, with an in-house team (though somewhat easier working off-site). Hopefully, my efforts in this respect were more Halle Orchestra than Spike Jones ...

Throughout the 1980s and 1990s, Crewe Styling was faced with unique issues concerning mainstream production saloon cars. Our Design Strategy document emphasized the dichotomy between Rolls-Royce and Bentley, although both marques had to provide the ultimate in luxury motoring whilst projecting different personas, but in the end, one four-door bodyshell had to serve both camps. The interiors were relatively easy, but exterior body language was a greater challenge altogether.

There was a conflicting dictate: "Get the Rolls-Royce right, but remember it's the Bentley that's going to sell more." Whether anyone could have done better than Seraph/Arnage will never be known because, afterward, the marques attracted enough funds to go their separate ways.

Styling never rested easily within Marketing or Engineering, but it couldn't stand alone without the latter's resource. As motor cars became more sophisticated, Engineering had its hands full keeping up with developments, whilst Marketing was kept busy with a faltering main brand and a runaway success secondary brand. Styling's survival was a credit to British pragmatism and compromise. During the manic 1990s, the department was almost a free agent relative to Company structure, and whilst reporting to Marketing, it was using Engineering budgets. Due to my relatively minor position I could avoid most top-end politics, although still run monthly viewings for the MD and the board.

Our tiny team maintained and increased the potency of Crewe interiors. Instead of imposing arbitrary styles, our proximity to our craftsmen and engineers ensured timeless qualities shone through: at the turn of the century the highest possible standards to date were achieved.

If Crewe Styling had only concentrated on interiors it would have been enough; that it was also able to work exteriors on-site flew in the face of convention. Whilst industry norm techniques were resisted on-site until the 1990s, it wasn't all bad news. After the Camargue of 1975, no Rolls-Royce or Bentley resulted from stand-alone consultancy work, as we used off-site resources as additional studios. Styling staff saw how the cream of consultants and top companies such as BMW operated and worked with them, and in addition this prevented young Crewe stylists from becoming institutionalised in the slightly in-bred home environment. It also kept everyone up to speed with latest techniques, computers, and packaging, etc.

The greatest motivation for any designer is to see their product in the marketplace, as this reflects the fact that they have had the rare privilege of influencing man's progress in the world. As the saying goes: you need money to survive but fulfilment to thrive. Although the situation in the Rolls-Royce and Bentley Styling Department was not always ideal, the opportunity to shape these fantastic motor cars was an extraordinary and unparalleled privilege.

"The quality remains long after the price has been forgotten." – Sir Henry Royce

60TH ANNIVERSARY OF CAR PRODUCTION AT CREWE

It was with surprise and delight that I received an invitation to the 60th anniversay celebrations on September 16, 2006, signed by Dr Franz-Josef Paefgen, Chairman and Chief Executive of Bentley Motors.

A marquee had been set up beside the Legends Health and Leisure Centre in Sunnybank Road, adjacent to the Bentley factory, and an excellent lunch with string quartet accompaniment laid on. Many fine examples of Rolls-Royce and Bentley motor cars from over the years were on display with their very enthusiastic owners. Several of the previous managing directors were present, and I spoke to Sir David Plastow, George Fenn and Graham Morris. It was pleasant to talk to some of my once immediate bosses, including Dereck Best and Ian McKay, and Ken Lee, an ex-chief engineer, enthused about a unique experimental Company car he was rebuilding.

The ever-ebullient Richard Charlesworth gave a conducted tour of the factory to see the latest Bentleys being built in the immaculate production facilities, and it was nice to come across the large sepia painting I'd done of a Cricklewood Bentley at Brooklands, still on display (this had also featured at the Arnage launch at Le Mans).

Strolling back from the factory tour to the Health and Leisure Centre for lunch, I chatted to Mike Dunn. It always seemed regrettable that Marketing in full flood in the early 1990s had apparently made matters unworkable for a board member of Engineering. Mike had the level of professionalism later seen in the VW approach, and, twenty years on, I could sympathize with his having to get a handle on the 'unique' styling resource in 1984: as Feller departed, yours truly was struggling to fit the oars into the rowlocks before being swept over the weir.

At lunch I was sitting between David Roscoe, ex-Crewe PR guru, and Dr Ulrich Eichhorn, member of the board (Engineering). David was great fun to talk to and we discovered a shared interest in model aircraft. Dr Eichhorn described repairing sills on a rare Fiat Spyder. When asked if he'd seen much of the UK, the latter shook his head: he'd had to engineer two convertibles that year, which had taken up much of his time – a salutary reminder of the pressures of the motor industry.

At the end of the meal, Dr Paefgen addressed the gathering. It was an extraordinary moment: the representative of VW talking to this group of chief executives, directors and managers, who had kept the flame burning for so many years, and Dr Paefgen admitted that this was the most difficult speech he'd ever had to make. Sir David Plastow, in turn, stood for his speech, his words measured but as generous as you might expect. There were many wry smiles around the tables as Sir David mentioned the 500 million pounds that VW had rapidly invested, which any MD would have given their right arm to have had. It wasn't lost on the new owners that those present were some of the individuals who'd breathed life into the almost extinct marque that VW was now developing so effectively.

Dr Hackenberg, the first chief engineer to arrive from VW, came up to me for a chat about interiors.

Graham Morris joined us, and I reminded him of his classic joke about a frustrated gorilla ...

Whilst saying goodbye to Tom Neville, a former finance director, Doug Dickson came to shake hands. Doug – a director of manufacturing at VW Bentley – always made pertinent comments at Styling viewings.

It doesn't pay to get too sentimental about any profit-making organisation, of course, but for a couple of hours that September afternoon, it seemed as if the Company's strivings over the years had risen above the purely commercial.

Left and below: Following the author's Crewe years, the dichotomy span of marques is considered. Regardless of power source or autonomous systems, the core DNA will remain.

APPENDIX
SEQUENCE OF STYLING DEVELOPMENT FOR THE EXTERIORS OF THREE MOTOR CARS

The process described concerns three vehicles commissioned by individuals, but the technique of developing full-size clay mock-ups is similar throughout the automotive industry. This work follows board and customer style selection from renderings.

The vehicles in question –

- P240: a modern interpretation of the Rolls-Royce Silver Cloud
- P250: a Bentley 'Grand Prix' sports car
- P560: a Bentley 'Highlander' four-door coupé

Full-size clay work begins with getting basic proportions right and then developing details. The clay can be temporarily dressed with reflective painted film and graphics to aid assessment: a process that is repeated numerous times until the best possible result is achieved.

As Chief Stylist, my role in these particular projects was to help ensure that the Company's aspirations were met in several areas –

- Requirement for Rolls-Royce and Bentley aesthetics, marque values and differentiation be incorporated
- Maintain a uniform level of value judgements across separate self-contained projects
- Ensure clients received the necessary degree of exclusivity
- Control interpretation of original vehicle renderings
- Ensure chief executive and Crewe board members were involved in ongoing developments and approval

Each project would have one or two key stylists progressing the work through daily procedures and activities. The following are dated logs of my instructions. Interior styling development follows a very similar approach, but is more complicated to describe in detail.

P240 Rolls-Royce 'Cloudesque' – 3D styling development

18.1.94
- 2D quarter-scale theme tried on SZ Spur and SZ Touring Limousine packages
- Original Silver Cloud had relatively small, narrow cabin in relation to the rest of the vehicle
- Consider implications of division for 'replica'
- Split quarter-scale: one side based on SZ hard points, the other side doing whatever is required to achieve preferred proportions

21.1.94
- Basic proportions being considered
  a Windscreen needs to be more vertical
  b Front wings need to be more rounded

24.1.94
- It has become apparent that the challenge of the project is to incorporate a more generous cabin space within the Cloud's aesthetic image
  a Emphasise rear wheelarch
  b Must attempt to achieve original Cloud's

relationship between radiator shell and front wings

c Need to achieve 'hatch' side doors by having land between door shuts

14.3.94

- Two weeks' work into final quarter-scale model phase
  a Lower front wing a lot
  b Crown bonnet more
  c Move outer corner of D post forward
  d Move front of D post forward
  e Move whole rear mudguard forward to relate to rear door shut as Cloud
  f Try to reduce side DLO (daylight opening)
  g Keep comparing to original Cloud quarter-scale model

21.3.94

- General engineering feasibility being considered
  a Need to check under-bumper air intake requirements for SZ turbocharged engine

22.3.94

- A week to go before viewing of fully-dressed, quarter-scale model
- Full-size clay being roughed in for three-quarter front and rear viewing of proportions
  a Quarter-scale radiator looks too wide and front wings too bulbous, but little achieved in modifying before going full-size: ie wait to see full-size picture

29.3.94

- Very nicely finished quarter-scale model – bright bumpers, lights, etc
  a Full-size sketch model looking a little Jaguar Mk9
  b Cabin proportions are dominating the Cloudesque wings. The Cloud features are being 'cartooned' too much to compensate for the large cabin Consider shortening the wheelbase (currently SZ Touring Limousine)
  c Double-check on shoulder and head clearance
  d Need to see effect of large, separate Cloud-type bumpers that will help counterbalance cabin mass

11.4.94

- Viewing of early full-size clay; proportions generally accepted; wheelbase dimension accepted
  a Radiator shell and front wings need work. Front wings to be lowered 25mm, R-R shell narrowed

15.4.94

- Lowering the front wings and narrowing the radiator shell has improved proportions: wings look longer and stronger
  a Critical that classic Cloud rear window is achieved: start with window/surround and blend roof into it
  b Classic Cloud boot needs more centre line shape; this also has to blend better into rear window surround
  c With boot established, balance rear wings against it – probably raising rear lamps
  d Push in trailing edge of rear wings in plan; leave tyre cover as is (this allows narrower rear bumper)
  e Side glass DLO needs aspect ratio nearer to Cloud: ie pull front edge of D post forward about 25mm Keep rear occupant line of sight as Touring Limousine
  f Move rear wings forward more until door shut can cut through with a fuller section
  g Cantrail section looks weak against roof bulge; therefore, raise door aperture and cantrail with it (this also improves side glass proportions)
  h Windscreen looks shallow on centre line and scuttle too high. Pull down centre line of scuttle and windscreen with it
  i Tyre section can be increased to help overall diameter
  j Trailing edge of roof will need balancing against backlight
  k At this stage entire car needs various adjustments, so avoid detail work because it can fall foul of larger movements
  l Main line through car side needs work to achieve Cloud posture

22.4.94

- Adjustments continue to balance cabin mass against wings
  a Correct headlamp angle to radiator shell
  b Make A post more vertical: ie move base rearward; consider moving whole screen rearward
  c Tuck under front apron outer corner
  d Push in front area above kickstrip and fade out to rear
  e Raise whole top of cantrail, but more over rear door; get more arc onto top of door frames
  f Drop rear door frame trailing corner
  g Let cantrail carry on dropping across rear quarter
  h More curvature required on lower rear quarter
  i Pull rear of rear wing forward
  j Get more Cloud intersection at base of rear quarter

k Push in side of rear wing to create eyebrow
l Enlarge backlight top and bottom 25mm
m Pad trailing edge of roof on centre line
n Soften roof trailing edge
o Mock-up rear lamps in position to check whole rear length

9.5.94

- Two days before presentation painting of full-size clay
  a Tuck under front apron lower edge
  b Soften out rear of bonnet considerably, and blend into base of screen better
  c Adjust rear door radius to allow door shut to go back onto wing bulge more
  d Coax scimitar-shaped brightwork forward a little
  e Soften rear roof outer corners
  f Push down trailing edge of boot considerably
  g Lower rear cantrail trailing edge
  h Lower rear wing trailing edge
  i Improve headlamp fillet radius condition
  j More spherical corners on boot outers
  k Tuck under rear lower wing
  l Fill in small depression on lower rear door

27.5.94

- Viewing of fully-dressed P240 clay
- Cloudesque-style seen as successful: however, despite earlier efforts, vehicle still appeared high at scuttle
  a Drop trailing edge of bonnet by 12-15mm on centre line
  b Refine all surfaces at base of rear quarte
  c Improve feature lines on top of rear wings to smooth 'balloon' on top
  d Increase size of rear lamps: ie as Cloud but on big, bright plinth
  e Check inner height of doorstep
  f Try Corniche door handles
  g Deepen water gutter on roof if necessary: ie test with water
  h Check position of division (rear seats to be adjustable) to BC posts

16.6.94

- Final check on clay
- Lowering rear of bonnet has done the trick
- Final position of door-shut does coincide with feature, causing a little shut gapping but it's better than the original Cloud in this respect

- Due to need to achieve a better step-in condition outer door shut has been lowered 23mm; this tends to help door to car ratio

P250 Bentley 'Grand Prix' sportscar – 4-wheel-drive – 3D styling development

6.5.94

- At this date basic quarter-scale model for aerodynamic studies has been tested in the wind-tunnel
- Styling theme being blocked in on full-size clay

9.5.94

- So great is the enthusiasm for such an exciting vehicle that the clay is threatening to be a very loose interpretation of the approved theme
  a It is necessary to impose the discipline of the approved 2D renderings onto the clay
  b Renderings don't imply the 'Austin Healey'-type wing shapes emerging on the clay; therefore, lower front and rear wings
  c Renderings clearly show a definite waist line shoulder or step running through the car
  d Extend rear end overhang at least 50mm
  e Make back end of car more vertical
  f Depending on package constraints, lower front of bonnet or raise scuttle to avoid appearance of car breaking in two
  g Windscreen flows into roof with no feature: need to create a header as rendering indicates
  h Block in bumper mass at this stage
  i Enlarge front air intakes
  j Put largest wheels and tyres onto model; open up wheel cut-outs; apply eyebrows to eat into wing mass
  k Sill needs to look more integrated
  l Confirm all packaging hard points
  m Track pulled out 25mm each side

20.5.94

  a At this date full-size clay is still struggling to echo ethos of original styling renderings
  b Currently, the front and rear three-quarter views are communicating too much Mazda RX7, and the side view Saab Sonnet
  c Rear wing is still far too humped; rendering indicates something more sophisticated than typical wedge
  d Sill is too heavy
  e Base of A post doesn't allow shoulder to run through car; need to achieve 'turret' look: ie cabin inboard

f Scuttle is about as high as it can go due to shallow line of sight for driver

g Bonnet front can be dropped lower if radiator matrix can get past steering rack

h Header tank lacks Bentley definition

i Front wings still need to be lower

j Tyre profile looks too low against mass of front and rear wings

k Wind-tunnel tests proved requirement for front air dam: need to confirm ramp angle is viable

l Due to concept's great width to length ratio, it lends itself to the soft, cornered 'in the round' look

m Need to turn full-size clay 90 degrees in studio to properly view the front and rear plan taper, which is currently much too violent. Catwalks off back of radiator header tank need adjusting

27.5.94

a Bonnet to be lower over wheel centre line

b More definition required on top of windscreen header

c Rear wing crown to be lower over wheel centre line

d Whole waist line of car needs easing down

e Eyebrows to be softened

f Rear wheel track to be increased

g Catwalks off radiator header tank need refining

h Large side vent to be adjusted with clamshell bonnet line

10.6.94

• Previous modifications all successful, particularly lowering wing core line. The lowered wings have improved proportions of wheels to body, and helped feature the character of the separate bonnet form

a Front end needs to be more like rendering: ie radiator shell can lift with bonnet, if necessary

b Bumper line lowered 10mm through vehicle front to rear

c Windscreen/side glass DLO and windscreen aperture all need proportional adjustment. Start off with required DLO shape at side and adjust other elements to fit around it

d Rear wing haunch too sharp on top – needs to be softer, like Mazda RX7

e In rear view the backlight is too big: push in top corners and round off

f Fill in MGB-type return on top of rear wings

g At this date clay is entirely missing the rear bumper diffuser which is a major element. The inner angles

of this diffuser can throw attention onto the wheels

h Wheels need widest possible tread footprint for the tyres

i When more of rear view background is established, rear lamps may need adjusting

4.7.94

• All previous modifications successful

• Rearward engine bias has caused difficulties at windscreen base for wiper, although windscreen style has not got excessive plan shape. Wiper condition can probably be rectified by using Jaguar parts

a More angle required on Bentley radiator shell

b Too much plan curvature on bumper to body intersection

c Delete delicate lower feature line of bumpers

d Entire diffuser under rear bumper to be natural black carbon fibre

e Soften all diffuser radius and recess more centre blade/ strut

f May need client feedback on large side wing vents

8.7.94

• Target date for sign-off viewing

a Reduce and blend in better at rear of front eyebrow

b Increase fillet radius in section by door shut

c Crank forward door shut to meet glass guide

d Blend edge of backlight better into body

e Reduce and blend in better at rear of rear eyebrow

f Front wing vent to be coarser pitch, and lower

g Rear wing to be eased down to reduce pinched wing peak condition

h Lower top of main air intake by rolling a larger radius under bumper edge

i Raise lower line of main air intake by 8mm; step carbon fibre back as rendering Reduce length of grille bars and increase fillet rads

j Smooth away S-bend on top of front bumper elevation

k Refine surfacing immediately inboard of headlamps

l Rear lamp lenses to be unbroken red

m Unique radiator grille matrix works well but holes to be larger

n Bentley radiator shell to have increased plan angle

o Rear wheels are 10-12mm too far outboard according to engineering feasibility

29-7-94

• Since 'sign-off' viewing all adjustments completed

- Also greater understanding of wheel envelope feasibility has led to eyebrows needing to be extended an extra 25mm. This causes some extension of eyebrow section onto rear bumper
  a Final aesthetic modification is to increase all internal radius on the three front air intakes

P560 'Highlander' – 4-door Coupé – 3D styling development

24-4-96

- General 2D styling theme established as 4-door coupé image

2 5 96

- First viewing of blocked in full-size clay
  a Even 19 inch wheels look small in proportion
  b Entire waist of car needs dropping to allow wheels more visual impact
  c More shape/section needed on header tank
  d Rear decking/spoiler needs pulling down
  e Look at ways of pulling down top of all DLO (daylight opening)

17 5 96

- All of last viewing instructions have worked: ie mainly aimed at lowering waist line and DLO
  a Rear header needs smoothing out
  b More feed-in required on front header: ie clay has 'table top' roof
  c Rear decking needs lowering more
  d Pad out car sides; door sections at BC posts too concave
  e Lower the styling feature line/angle that runs above wheelarches
  f Make whole front more like rendering: ie reduce exaggerated chin/apron and bulbous header
  g Make backlight bigger
  h Sill needs to be fuller

23-5-96

- Proportions still being worked and details being added
  a Flatten fairing angle above front bumper
  b More forehead on Bentley header tank; widen grille
  c Windscreen must look wider – probably the bright glazing strip has to go right outboard and forward of the glass plane
  d Much more section/shape required in all features of front apron

e Bright feature line on bumpers to be lower and in a deeper trough with more section on brightwork
f Louvres on bonnet top à la Morgan, linked to more pull-down on header tank
g More extreme bonnet shut condition adjacent to radiator shell as rendering
h Whole waist chamfer feature to be pulled down further still
i Increase light catchers at top of eyebrow to make wheels look bigger
j Bigger, more pronounced front wing side vents
k Big fillet radius at base of A post must be reduced, and wing crown strengthened: ie it appears concave
l Front door, front shut to be moved forward 25mm
m Make door frame pressing much wider, and take further onto roof, probably including all of A post up to glazing
n BC post to be narrower, sub-divided or grey paint, etc
o Rear header still appears to have a lump in it
p The side lines of the boot/spoiler mustn't get too close to the rear door shut
q All rear decking to be dropped approx 25mm
r Rear bumper to body joint to be dropped down
s Exhaust cut-outs to be opened out and raised in rear apron
t Use light catcher 'blip' under rear bumper section
u Light catcher on sill and bumper to be much stronger
v Rear number plate aperture to be wider and lower; top brightwork to have more shape
w Backlight sides to be more formal – pull out top and bottom in end elevation
x Make sure 19 inch wheels are fitted during clay work Check envelopes
y Rear panel is too flat
z Bright trim on rear doors has to carry on through from bumpers: could try just highlight ledge

7 6 96

- At this stage efforts are being made to combine two separate alloy wheel styles for the 19 inch P550 and P560, relying on different hub caps: compromise not helping the aesthetic of making the wheel look as big as possible

19 6 96

- Sign-off viewing event with two weeks of adjustments possible before 5 July digitizing a Bentley header tank to have fuller forehead

b Convert bonnet to conventional shut line

c Top of Bentley radiator aperture to be lowered 10mm

d Bottom of headlamps to be raised 10mm

e Bumper fairings to be reduced, thus visually lifting headlamps

f Highlights at bottom of radiator shell and lower air intake need to be stronger: ie increase section

g Car looks narrow across windscreen: push brightwork further onto paint and conceal true. A post inner flange condition. Brightwork to disappear below scuttle, not run across bonnet

h Wing side vents to be lifted 10mm, and reduce air exit image: ie less see-through

i Front wing lower light catcher to be stronger, like rear one

j Local glitch on rear door waist feature: smooth it and emphasise waist dip

k Add a small overhang lip on boot spoiler

l Put CHMSL (centrally high-mounted stop lamp) into back glass as small and low as possible: ie remove from boot lid

m Move boot badge as high as possible on number plate brightwork

n Pull down bottom of number plate aperture

o Flatten angle on rear bumper fairing

p Bonnet louvres need to be more Morganesque

q Back glass to be pulled out 10mm a side at top

r Rear eyebrow is shapeless and biased rearward: make section more like front

s Rear lamps to have 'secret til lit' reverse on one side of car and high intensity fog on the other

Builds on alloy wheel clay at this date –

t Hub recess needs to be deeper

u Spoke base needs to be wider

v Spoke 'finger' needs to be stronger/fatter

w Push down main spoke more at rim

x Delete outer rim bead section (hidden balance weights)

4 7 96

- All previously requested modifications incorporated in clay; overall effect is true to original intent
- Some items still need attention –

  a As the trailing edge of the rear quarter meets the front end of the boot lid edge the junction is too concave. Re-surfacing is necessary to avoid BIW (body-in-white) problem

  b Top of number plate brightwork to be tucked up closer to boot spoiler undercut

  c Badge plinth above number plate to be squarer

  d Top of number plate brightwork to be hollow ground

  e Trailing boot edge spoiler overhang to be pulled rearward slightly on centre line

  f Client prefers recessed bonnet louvres

  g Front wing louvres module needs to be raised slightly; top line to be slightly curved

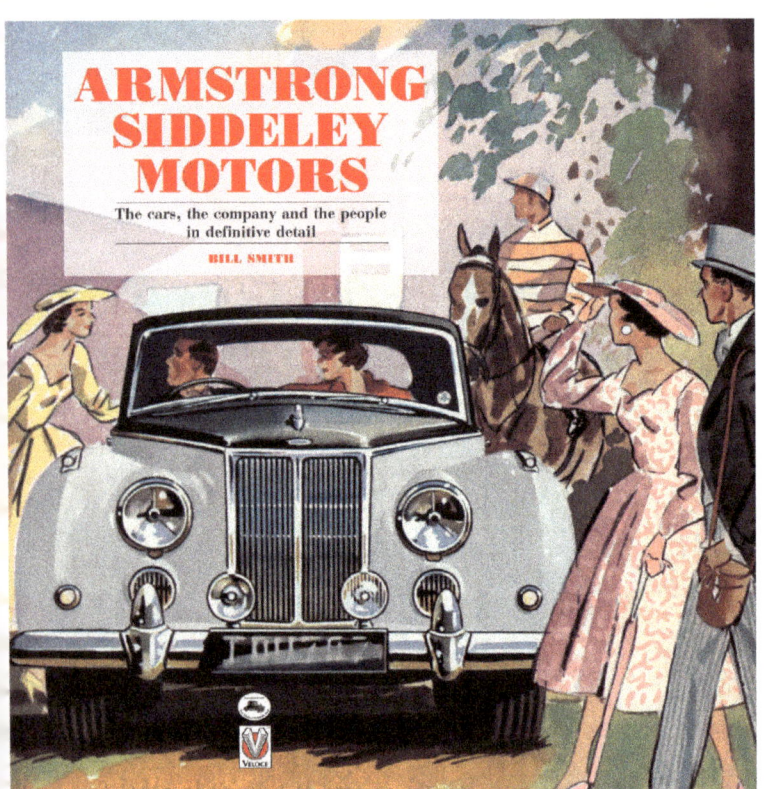

Hardback • 25x25cm • 496 pages
• 365 photos & illustrations
• ISBN: 978-1-904788-36-2

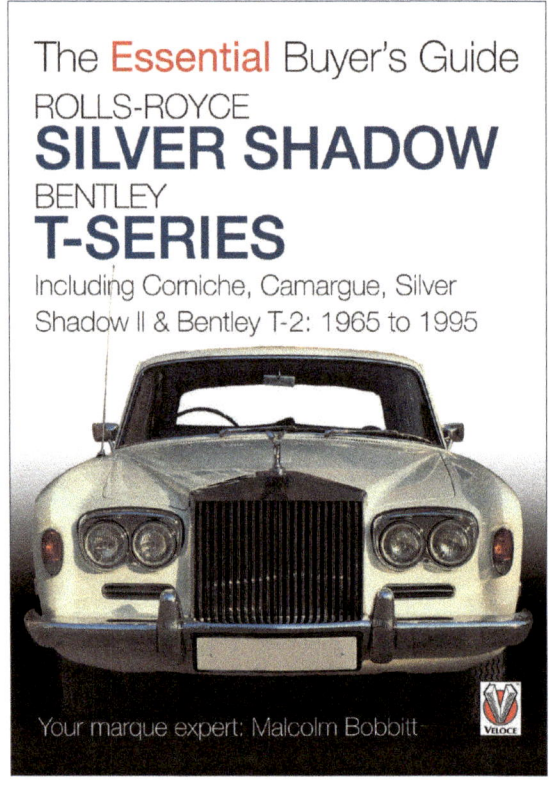

Paperback • 19.5x13.9cm • 64 pages • c100 colour photos • ISBN: 978-1-787113-40-4

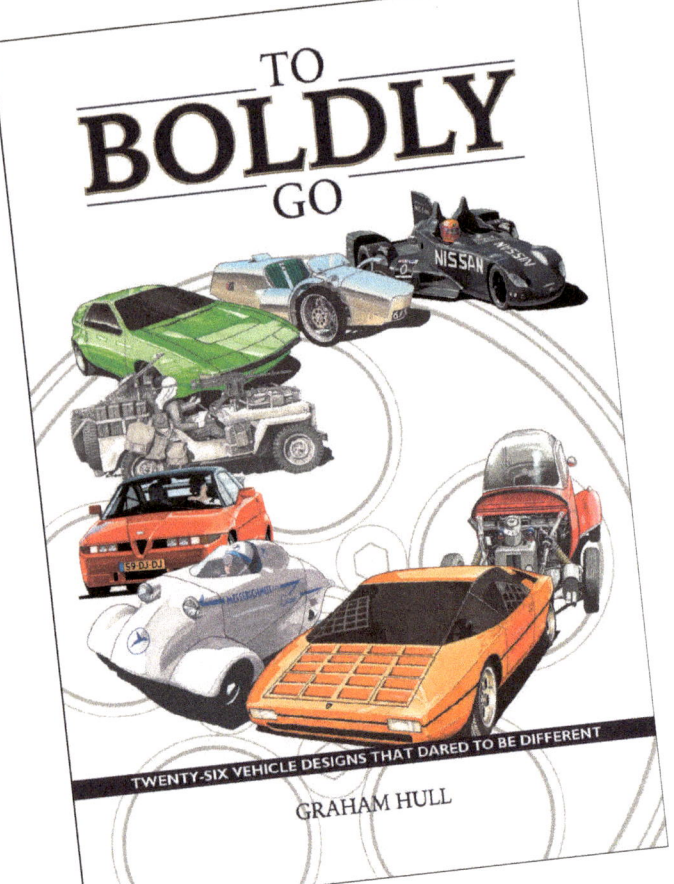

Hardback • 15.2x22.5cm • 160 pages
• 80 colour/b&w photos
• ISBN: 978-1-78711-002-1

INDEX